WICCA

MAGICKAL BEGINNINGS

ACKNOWLEDGEMENTS

This book is dedicated to Aeron,
a great bear who walks amongst mankind now.

We would like to take this opportunity to thank the following people for their contributions to this work, whether directly or indirectly: Emily Ounsted, Emily Parslow, Francesca Vaughan, Fred Lamond, Galatea, Harry Barron, Helene Hodge, Hilda Starling, Jim & Lisa Bennett, John Canard, Kay Gillard, Lezley Butler, Magin Rose, Maxine Sanders, Mea N., Mogg & Kim Morgan, Pete Nash, Philip Heselton, Professor Ronald Hutton, Stephen Blake, Stephen Skinner, Sue Bowman and Tam Campbell. Finally, our thanks also to all our students, both past and present, as well as all the beautiful members of the StarStone Network, whom we have learned from and with.

"Remember all ye that existence is pure joy, the joy of the silver stars: that all the sorrows are but as shadows; they pass and they are done, but there is that which remains ..."

ABOUT THE AUTHORS

Sorita d'Este and David Rankine are students and practitioners of the Western Esoteric Tradition who live and work somewhere near the borders of Wales and England (UK). Upon their first meeting in Atlantis Bookshop they had a long debate about incenses and when they finally *'got it together'* more than a year later they still found themselves debating some intricate matter related to something magickal, political, historical or religious and happily are still continuing their debate to this day. In late 2000 they founded their first Wiccan training circle together in Chiswick (West London), this group would develop into what is today the StarStone Network, a network of covens (Alexandrian lineaged) and groups focused on creating a community of peers.

You are welcome to write to the authors:

Sorita d'Este & David Rankine

c/o BM Avalonia, London, WC1N 3XX, United Kingdom

For more information on their work see: www.avalonia.co.uk

WICCA

MAGICKAL BEGINNINGS

*A Study of the Possible Origins of the Rituals and Practices Found in
this Modern Tradition of Pagan Witchcraft and Magick*

Sorita d'Este & David Rankine

Published by Avalonia

BM Avalonia
London
WC1N 3XX
England, UK

www.avaloniabooks.co.uk

WICCA: MAGICKAL BEGINNINGS

ISBN (10)   1-905297-15-7
ISBN (13)   978-1-905297-15-3

Second Edition 2008, Second Printing June 2008

Design by Satori, Illustrations (unless otherwise stated) by Jack D.
Copyright © Sorita and David Rankine

OTHER BOOKS BY THESE AUTHORS

Sorita d'Este and David Rankine are also the authors, or co-authors of, the following works:

Books by Sorita d'Este & David Rankine

Circle of Fire, 2005 & 2008
The Guises of the Morrigan, 2005
Avalonia's Book of Chakras, 2006
The Isles of the Many Gods, 2007
Practical Planetary Magick, 2007
Practical Elemental Magick, 2008
Wicca : Magickal Beginnings, 2008

Books by, or edited by, Sorita d'Este

Artemis, Virgin Goddess of the Sun & Moon, 2005
Hekate, Keys to the Crossroads (Edited by Sorita d'Este), 2006
Horns of Power (Edited by Sorita d'Este), 2008
Towards the Wiccan Circle (Edited by Sorita d'Este), 2008

Books by David Rankine

Heka : The Practices of Ancient Egyptian Ritual & Magic, 2006
Climbing the Tree of Life, 2005
Becoming Magick, 2004
Crystals Healing & Folklore, 2002
Magick Without Peers, 1997 (co-authored with Ariadne Rainbird)

Sourceworks of Ceremonial Magic - Stephen Skinner & David Rankine

Volume I – The Practical Angel Magic of Dr John Dee's Enochian Tables, 2004
Volume II – The Keys to the Gateway of Magic, 2005
Volume III – The Goetia of Dr Rudd, 2007
Volume IV – The Veritable Key of Solomon, 2008

CONTENTS

PREFACE

All books have a moment of conception, and this book was born out of a discussion on the origins of the Wiccan Tradition as known today, with some of our students in late 2001. Whilst debating the possible starting point of this magickal tradition, we realised that all the evidence being presented was focused on the people who were the early public face of the tradition and their contemporaries. Yet this is a tradition which is also called a *'Craft'* and which is an experiential tradition where personal experience is paramount for the understanding of the practices and beliefs. So why were we debating the origins of the tradition in terms of who said or did what?

Has Wiccan history tied itself into knots of personalities in an effort to conceal its true origins? Was there something we were missing? Why was it that whilst some people claimed that the tradition was the continuation of a very ancient Pagan religion, others stated that it was created (or compiled) in the 1950's or 1940's in England? Why was it that Gerald Gardner was greatly respected as the *'Father'* of the modern movement and simultaneously viewed as a charlatan? Could it be that in an effort to cover up the ludicrous and unsubstantiated claims that the tradition originated in the Stone Age (or thereabouts) the pendulum has swung too far in the other direction and got stuck? We agree that an academically sound historical foundation will provide more credibility to a tradition and its practitioners, but did that come at a price? What was being sacrificed in order to lend credibility to the tradition? What really made Wicca, Wicca?

Having asked ourselves all these questions again and again over the years, sometimes obtaining different answers to the same questions based on changes in our perspective, we found that ultimately Wicca remained a mystery tradition at its heart. The practices and beliefs could only be fully understood through direct experience thereof and it was through this that the tradition could be best defined, not through the endless debates about lineages, initiations and personalities!

We set about systematically researching the origins of the practices and beliefs which were passed to us through our initiators and colleagues. Our preconceptions were constantly challenged as we explored the origins of the practices and beliefs from different angles in an effort to find possible solutions to the question of when and where the tradition may have originated. We separated the rituals into their component parts, then looked at each individually and even divided them up into smaller parts, before finally putting it all back together creating a colourful mosaic with our findings.

Faced with several possible interpretations based on the evidence we correlated, it became clear that although it remained possible that Gerald Gardner may have created the tradition, it was certainly not that plausible in comparison to some of the other conclusions that we reached. In fact, at this stage of our research we feel that it is most likely that Gardner was not that much of a charlatan after all, but that his accounts of initiation into an existing tradition, upon which he later expanded, were truthful. When stripped right back, without the many additions and evolutions it has undergone since the 1950's, Gerald Gardner's 'Witch Cult' appears to predate him by at least some years.

Of course we realise that for some this would be a controversial conclusion, and as such we present the practice-based evidence in this volume in a way which allows for individual interpretation. We also focused on the component parts which were common to all the traditions, both esoteric and exoteric, that we have personal knowledge of. This means that whilst we touch on the subject of deity, it is important for the reader to understand that theological debate is not within the scope of the work presented here. The individual beliefs in the Goddess and God vary, in some instances significantly so, between traditions in existence today. Additionally, we have not included evidence or debate on the inclusion of many of the folk practices which are found in some Wiccan groups today, such as May pole dancing at Beltane or making Brighid crosses for Imbolc. These practices were well known throughout the nineteenth and early twentieth centuries as the countless books and magazine articles published in those eras attest to. As such their inclusion might be incidental. Moreover, they are not considered relevant by all of the traditions and as such, though of extreme importance to some, are not even considered by others.

Whilst some of the material here will undoubtedly be of interest to those with a casual interest in this modern tradition of witchcraft, the bulk of it is aimed at people who are practitioners and who, like us, want to develop a deeper understanding of the origins of their practices and beliefs. Through an honest understanding of our history, we are after all better able to build on its foundations and take it forward in and with the light of truth.

Sorita d'Este and David Rankine
April 2008

BEGINNINGS

CHAPTER 1

EMERGENCE

Wicca has had a huge impact on the modern revival of interest in esoteric spirituality in the Western world. It first emerged to public attention in the 1950's, primarily through the work of Gerald Brosseau Gardner and a subsequent succession of people associated with him. During the transitional period of the 1950s, between the austerity of post-war Britain and the swinging sixties, Wicca quickly gained media attention as something mysterious and beyond the norm.

It would be very naive to believe that all the practices and beliefs of the tradition sprang fully formed into being from nowhere and that it was completely unknown or thought of prior to Gerald Gardner. Undoubtedly the publication of his factional novel *High Magic's Aid* in 1949, and subsequent writings, teachings and media exposure inspired and fuelled the interest of many people to explore what Gardner referred to as '*the witch cult*'. It would however probably be more accurate to view Gardner's work as being the product of, or the continuation of, a growing spiritual and magickal current fuelled by a wealth of material published in numerous sources by a range of authors in the previous years, as well as the practices of a wide spectrum of esoteric groups and orders which flourished at the time and in the preceding decades.

The end of the nineteenth century and the first few decades of the twentieth century were to be particularly fruitful in the fields of anthropology and folklore research. In 1890 the folklorist J.G. Frazer published his classic work *The Golden Bough*, exploring the relationships between myth, religion and ritual in a global context by studying cultural behaviours and patterns from around the world. By 1936 the two volumes of the original work had expanded to thirteen.

Contemporary with Frazer was the American anthropologist Charles Godfrey Leland, who published a number of significant books. Amongst these was *Aradia Gospel of the Witches* in 1899, a polyglot text which would contribute to some of the most influential material in the Gardnerian *Book of Shadows*, specifically the *Charge of the Goddess*. There has been a great deal of dispute about the veracity of Leland's *Aradia*, but regardless of whether its authenticity can ever be proved or disproved, it was and still continues to be, albeit sometimes without due credit, a hugely influential text.

What is relevant, yet often ignored about the *Aradia* is that it continues a trail of many centuries of Italian texts referring to a witchcraft cult, real or possibly mythical, that worshipped the goddess Diana. For example, in 1749 Girolamo Tartarotti published a book called *Del Congresso Notturno Delle Lammie* (*"Of the Nocturnal Meeting of Spirits"*) which declared that *"The identity of the Dianic cult with modern witchcraft is demonstrated and proven"*. Prior to this in 1647 Peter Pipernus wrote *De Nuce Maga Beneventana & De Effectibus Magicis* (*"Six Books of Magic Effects and of the Witch Walnut Tree of Benevento"*). Earlier still in 1576 Bartolo Spina wrote of witches gathering at night to worship Diana in his work, *Quaestio de Strigus* (*"An Investigation of Witches"*). This trail of documentation, which only lightly scrapes at the surface of what is available from preceding centuries, does strongly suggest that the Leland material was indeed based on an existing tradition, rather than one fabricated out of thin air by Leland or his informant, the witch Maddalena.

Following on from Frazer's work, the Cambridge classical scholar and linguist Jane Ellen Harrison published several important works focusing on myth and ritual, specifically in the context of ancient Greece. The most significant of these were probably *Prolegomena to the Study of Greek Religion* in 1903 and *Ancient Art & Ritual* in 1912. Harrison was to bring the use of archaeological discoveries and contemporary mythology together in a way which laid the groundwork for subsequent scholars, providing the foundations which would be built upon by such major figures as Karl Kerenyi and Walter Buckert.

Amongst the most challenging works published during this era in regards to anthropology and pagan religious history were probably those of the respected Egyptologist, Margaret Murray. In 1921 Murray published *The Witch Cult in Western Europe*, postulating the survival of a pre-Christian pagan horned god cult into the Middle Ages. She expanded further on this theme in 1933 with her work, *The God of the Witches*. Whilst some scholars have repudiated Murray's work it is undisputable that her work was and continues to be of great importance through the ideas it expressed. She further provided the entry on *Witchcraft* for the respected and widely used *Encyclopaedia Britannica* in which she perpetuated her ideas and research, potentially influencing thousands of people in the first part of the twentieth century. Far from standing alone in her views, Murray continued the trends set by earlier luminaries like Frazer.

Another contemporary of Murray was the folklorist Jessie L. Weston, who published *From Ritual to Romance* in 1920. This work explored the magickal and mythical themes within the Arthurian cycle and emphasised the value of the Celtic hero cycle, whilst claiming ancient pre-Christian roots to the popular medieval romances. The Arthurian cycle would later become a significant theme in the modern pagan revival.

All of these works can be seen as being indicative of a popular perception of the survival of ancient pagan ideas transmitted through to the Middle Ages and beyond across Europe. These works, even in instances when they are not considered that influential on an individual basis, would as a whole provide the backdrop of mythical and magickal ideas which would find subsequent expressions in Gardner's published material in the 1950s, and by the authors and practitioners who followed him through to the present time.

Another source of materials which emerged in the late nineteenth and early twentieth centuries, were the translations of French magickal works into the English language. Works such as Samuel Liddell MacGregor Mathers' translation of the *Key of Solomon* in 1889, Grillot de Givry's *Witchcraft Magic and Alchemy* in 1931 and Jules Michelet's *La Sorcière* in 1939 would all prove influential. All these important works were previously only available in French and their availability in the English language greatly expanded the range of readily available source material for those interested in the occult arts.

It was not just in magick, folklore and anthropology that the rising tides of illumination sought expression. Another significant outlet for the outward radiation of the mysteries was the developing field of psychology. Sigmund Freud was not only the founder of psychoanalytical psychology, but also postulated that sexual desire was a prime motivation in human behaviour. Freud drew on ancient Greek mythology to name the incestual desire he called the *'Oedipus Complex'*. This mythic theme was further expressed in his idea of the twin poles of *'Eros and Thanatos'*, or sex and death, as the conflicting desires within each of us.

Carl Gustav Jung, a pupil of Freud, was to expand his work even further into the mythical and magickal realms. Jung concentrated on plumbing the depths of the unconscious mind, drawing on alchemy, mythology and religion in his attempts to explore the mysteries of the psyche through dreams and other expressions. Jung also explored and wrote prolifically on two concepts that have become well known in modern magick – synchronicity and archetypes.

Wilhelm Reich was to take Freud's ideas on sexuality significantly further and challenge the establishment on a whole range of ideas. When he wrote on character analysis and sexuality, Reich drew his ideas from a wide range of studies including anthropology, ethics, psychoanalysis and sociology and in the process synthesised challenging and often radical views. His ideas straddled the mundane and esoteric worlds and included pioneering work in areas such as orgone energy, sexuality and true independence for women.

Whilst the influence of magick on psychology is well documented, the influence of the newly developing field of psychology on the magickians of the early twentieth century is perhaps not so well known. Freud, Jung and Reich all postulated ideas which would influence the magickal writings and practices of major magickal figures of the early twentieth century. Such magickians as Aleister Crowley, Dion Fortune and Israel Regardie all acknowledged the influence of these psychologists in their writing. Examples of this influence can be found in the writings of Crowley in his notes on the *Goetia*, Fortune in her *The Secrets of Dr Taverner* and Regardie in *The Middle Pillar*. As all of these authors produced work which impacted on the development of the Wiccan tradition to a greater or lesser extent, this convergence of ancient magick and newborn psychology in the early twentieth century provided a strong and significant current of esoteric expression whose influence has perhaps not been sufficiently considered.

Aleister Crowley is arguably the single most influential figure in the development of modern magick, including that of the Wiccan tradition. The wealth of his magickal writings, spread over fifty years of intense study and practice, has contributed to Wicca in many ways. Not only was Crowley the single most significant and influential magickal practitioner of the first half of the twentieth century, but he also had connections to an astonishing range of other magickians, artists and talented individuals. Crowley documented his experiences in great detail and corresponded with many of his associates.

> *"...The time is just ripe for a natural religion. People like rites and ceremonies, and are tired of hypothetical gods. Insist on the real benefits of the Sun and the Moon, the Mother-Force and the Father-force and so on; and show that by celebrating these benefits worthily the worshippers unite themselves more fully with the current of life. Let the religion be a joy, with but a worthy and dignified sorrow in*

18

death itself; and treat death as an ordeal, an initiation. Do not gloss over facts, but transmute them in the athanor of your ecstasy. In short, be the founder of a new and greater Pagan cult in the beautiful land which you have made your home. As you go on, you can add new festivals of corn and wine, and all things noble and inspiring."

This quote from a letter written by Crowley to one of his magickal disciples Charles Stansfield Jones (Frater Achad) in 1914, and subsequently reproduced by John Symonds in his biography of Crowley *The Great Beast* in 1951, could be seen as unequivocally predicting and encouraging a tradition of magick which sounds extraordinarily like that which would manifest as *'Wicca'* in the years which followed.

Crowley would make other allusions of a similar nature in his writings. For example, in 1916 in his book *The Gospel According to Saint Bernard Shaw* he declared:

"For not only do I hold the cult of John Barleycorn to be the only true religion, but have established his worship anew; in the last three years branches of my organisation have sprung up all over the world to celebrate the ancient rite. So mote it be!"

From the date of this quote it would initially seem that Crowley was referring to the Ordo Templi Orientis (O.T.O.), the magickal order which he became the world head of in the 1920s. However the published material regarding the Ordo Templi Orientis contains no references or allusions to John Barleycorn. Also the phrase *"my organisation"* makes it clear that at this time he was not referring to the Ordo Templi Orientis; but that he was actually referring to the Astreum Argenteum (A.A.).

The Astreum Argenteum was established by Crowley to propagate the teachings of the law of Thelema, which were to be hugely influential on the Wiccan Tradition at a later date. Thelema, the Greek word for *'will'*, was the name given to a system of philosophy created by

Crowley around the central core of a text received by him in 1904 in Cairo called *The Book of the Law* (*Liber Al vel Legis*). Crowley viewed Thelema, with its emphasis on finding your own true will and exclusively pursuing it, as the religion of the new age that was dawning. Crowley and the magician George Cecil Jones, who had introduced Crowley to the Hermetic Order of the Golden Dawn in 1898, worked together on the formation of the Astreum Argenteum which was inaugurated in 1906.

A leading light of the Golden Dawn who wrote about witchcraft was the Scottish scholar magician J.W. Brodie-Innes. In an essay entitled *Witchcraft* written for the *Occult Review* in 1917, he wrote:

> *"If we will but for a moment lay aside prejudice, and look at the subject dispassionately, we shall become convinced that the cult of the witch is as old as humanity. It is as old as the world, and as flourishing today as it was in the fifteenth or sixteenth centuries."*

Even more significantly than this remark, regarding the contemporary nature of witchcraft practices, Brodie-Innes made an observation which is unerringly accurate and merits further consideration. In another essay by him entitled *Witchcraft Rituals,* also published in 1917 in the *Occult Review,* he observed:

> *"Returning for a moment to the question of the Rituals. There is little doubt of the antiquity of very many of them. We find them in the Grimoire, and in Trithemius; we search back through the pages of Virgil and Hesiod, and we seem to see the origin of the same formulae."*

The key word in this passage is *'grimoire'*. In the meticulous *Archivio di Stato* of the numerous trials of the seventeenth century Venetian witch, Laura Malapiero, there are some extremely significant details about the documents in her possession. These included the *Key*

20

of Solomon, one of the best known grimoires and one which would in time prove to be hugely influential on some of the rituals found in the modern Wiccan tradition.

> *"When Laura's house was searched by the Capitano of the Sant'Ufficio in 1654, a number of manuscripts were found. Some were rather crudely written scongiuri [spells]; others were sophisticated herbals and copies of the Clavicle of Solomon."*[1]

The State Archives also make reference to a man, Boniface Cabiano, selling magickal manuscripts near the Rialto in Venice in 1648, saying that he *"deals in C. Agrippa and a book with little signs and secret circles".*[2] The reference to Agrippa, whose work would also be influential on other grimoires and indeed on Wicca, is something we will encounter again and again as we look at the magickal practices used in this tradition.

Returning to the late nineteenth and early twentieth century, we now have to consider the magickal order which would prove to be one of the most influential to emerge during that period. The Hermetic Order of the Golden Dawn, founded in 1887, provided a meeting place for many influential figures and inquiring minds of the time. Writers such as W.B. Yeats, Algernon Blackwood and Arthur Machen, the actresses Florence Farr and Sara Allgood, the artist Pamela Colman-Smith, the writer A.E. Waite as well as the infamous magicians Allan Bennett and Aleister Crowley, all received initiation and training in this order. This would lay the foundations for much of what would follow in the subsequent decades. The Golden Dawn rituals combined strands from a variety of systems of magick and mythology, but the order also promoted equality of the sexes, previously unseen in magickal orders

---

1 Marriage or a career?, Scully, 1995
2 Marriage or a career? Scully, 1995

and placed a universal goddess more in the mainstream of esoteric consciousness, in the form of the Egyptian mother goddess, Isis.

The Golden Dawn disintegrated due to internal schisms in the early twentieth century, but it guided the way towards the creation of a number of derivative groups as well as a number of tangential orders founded by ex-members. The most significant of these derivative orders would be the *Alpha et Omega* and the *Stella Matutina*, both of which would become new melting pots of magickal and spiritual ideals, attracting many members who would also become important contributors to the development of the modern magickal community, including most significantly the occultists Israel Regardie and Dion Fortune.

Regardie, a psychologist and author, was a member of a Stella Matutina lodge in the early 1930s. In the late 1930's he published his very important work *The Golden Dawn,* initially as four volumes, which made available the rituals and teachings of the Stella Matutina (derived from those which were used in the Golden Dawn) to a wider audience, thereby ensuring its survival into the modern day.

Likewise, the author Dion Fortune who is today best remembered for her work *The Mystical Qabalah,* received initiation and training in the Alpha et Omega. She worked with both Moina Mathers (wife of MacGregor Mathers) and Brodie-Innes, before leaving the Alpha et Omega and forming her own order, which was initially named the Fraternity of the Inner Light, and later renamed the Society of the Inner Light. The Society of the Inner Light is still active today and continues to promote and practice a unique blend of Christian mysticism, Qabalah and pagan ritual.

Contemporary with these esoteric luminaries of the early twentieth century was the magickal artist Austin Osman Spare. His unique style of art led him to early success, though he turned his back on this in order concentrate on the system of sorcery and sigilisation he developed. Spare claimed that he first learned magick from a hereditary witch, Mrs Patterson, who was a descendant of the Salem witches. Spare knew Crowley, as well as Kenneth Grant, one of Crowley's successors, and it was through Grant that Spare would be introduced to Gerald Gardner in the early 1950s.[3]

A discussion on the magickal currents around the time of the emergence of the Wiccan tradition would be incomplete without mentioning the often neglected work of the pioneering rocket scientist and Thelemic magickian Jack Parsons. During the 1940's he was the head of the only active Ordo Templi Orientis lodge in America and in 1946 he published a series of essays called *Magick, Gnosticism and the Witchcraft*. This clearly illustrates, that Parsons, like Crowley, had an established interest in witchcraft. In his *Book of Babalon* which was also published in 1946, Parsons proclaimed:

> *"65. Gather together in the covens as of old, whose number is eleven, that is also my number. Gather together in public, in song and dance and festival. Gather together in secret, be naked and shameless and rejoice in my name.*
> *66. Work your spells by the mode of my book, practicing secretly, inducing the supreme spell.*
> *69. This is the way of it, star, star. Burning bright, Moon, witch Moon."*

Allowing for the fact that Parsons used the Thelemic number of 11 instead of the traditional 13 for the number of members in a coven, what he wrote is quite reminiscent of the flavours which would arise within the Wiccan tradition just a few years later. It is worth noting here that it is possible that Gardner could have been exposed to Parsons' writings around 1947 when he was visiting the United States and met with people such as Karl Germer, who was Crowley's successor as head of the Ordo Templi Orientis As an interesting aside, not at all related to our discussion here, it is also fascinating to note that Parsons is probably

---

3 Zos Speaks, Grant, 1998

the only magickian who has a crater on the Moon named after him, which is strangely appropriate when we take into consideration that his work may have had some influence on a tradition in which the Moon plays such a pivotal role. Parsons' astonishingly lucid writings are worthy of further study by anyone interested in the magickal currents of the twentieth century.

In addition to the material published by practising magickians, we also need to consider the material published by a number of other authors in the decades preceding the work of Gerald Gardner. Many of these works were written in a style suggesting that the authors were openly sympathetic to the practice of witchcraft in a way which could not be done by those who undertook its study within a scholastic context at the time.

The Book of Witches by the author Oliver Madox Hueffer published in 1908 has a significantly named opening chapter called *'On a Possible Revival of Witchcraft*. In it Hueffer makes the following rather interesting statement in regards to the likelihood of a witchcraft revival:

> *"Under these circumstances it is easy to credit the possibility of a revival of the belief in witchcraft even in the most civilised countries of the modern world. What is more, it is far from certain that such a revival would be altogether deplorable. Granted that oceans of innocent blood were shed in the name of witchcraft – the same might be said of Christianity, of patriotism, of liberty, of half a hundred other altogether unexceptionable ideals. And, as with them, the total extinction of the witchcraft superstition might, not impossibly, have results no less disastrous than, for instance, the world-wide adoption of European fashions in dress. This quite apart from any question of whether or no witches have ever existed or still exist..."*

What is additionally interesting about *The Book of Witches* is that it includes an account by Hueffer in regards to a Tuscan witch named Emilia he claimed to have had encounters with two years previous to writing the book. *The Book of Witches* was published in 1908, so presumably these meetings between Hueffer and Emilia took place around 1906. Hueffer further tells us that Emilia was living in Florence at the time and was considered to be very effective at her magick. In one of the examples given, Emilia worked towards the removal of a curse from a young lady, using charms and incantations – though Emilia did seem to place a great deal more emphasis on the secretive nature of her work than displayed by Leland's Maddalena and was unwilling to share her methods with the author.

> *"Exactly what counter-charms she used in Zita's treatment I was not privileged to know; at least, I can testify that they were entirely successful, and that within a very short time Zita was herself again..."*

As already stated Leland's material was hugely influential amongst those interested in and writing on the subject of witchcraft in the decades preceding Gardner. Another such example can be found in the book *Witches Still Live,* by Theda Kenyon which was published in 1929. Whilst discussing *Aradia* Kenyon observes of the incantations within it that:

> *"Many of these are very beautiful, and have been used from time immemorial, as they are today, and they cannot fail to clarify certain witch mysteries."*

Significantly Kenyon seems to be saying that at the time of her writing the material in the *Aradia* was being used by witches. This in itself might be easily overlooked, however as this precedes Gardner's writing (and return to England) by some years, we have to at least take into consideration that Kenyon may have been writing about something which could have contributed to or may have been a predecessor of what would become Gardnerian Wicca. At the very least it is worth considering that her claim that the material was being used may have influenced the subsequent compilers of the material which became the Book of Shadows.

These examples clearly highlight that in the decades leading up to the public birthing of Gardnerian Wicca, there was no shortage of ideas which seem to indicate that a precursor to the tradition either already existed (albeit in the shadows), or that the practices and ideas that previously existed were ready to be amalgamated into a new tradition suited to the time.

In the years from 1936-1954, Gardner was at different times a member of the Ancient Druid Order, the Ordo Templi Orientis, the Ancient British Church, the Folklore Society and possibly the Orthodox Catholic Church in England. This diversity points to a man seeking knowledge, and trying to fulfil a spiritual need. This can also be seen in the many significant figures in the magickal revival that Gardner would have contact with, such as Aleister Crowley, W.B. Crow, Margaret Murray, Ross Nichols, Madeline Montalban, Idries Shah, Kenneth Grant and Austin Osman Spare.

Gardner also had assistance from other magickians in making his important works presentable. The angel magician Madeline Montalban (Dolores North) tidied up *High Magic's Aid* for Gardner (acknowledged in a letter to Cecil Williamson from June 1951). Ross Nichols, editor of the translation of Paul Christian's classic nineteenth century *History and Practice of Magic*, was said to have edited *Witchcraft Today* with a firm hand.

> *"It's very funy. Mrs North is 'Delores'. She used to work at the Atlantis Bookshop, + she typed + put the spelling right in High Magics Aid."*[4]

---

4 Letter from Gardner to Cecil Williamson, June 1951 (also showing Gardner's bad spelling)

Gardner was the self-appointed father of this new movement, with the many high priestesses he initiated and worked with during this period of his life, the mothers who would in turn birth many covens and initiates in the decades to follow.

The 1960's, with its newfound sexual and spiritual freedom, provided the backdrop for the establishment of Wicca as a worldwide tradition, primarily through the work of Alex and Maxine Sanders. They would further promote the ideals and practices to the public arena through their involvement with the mass media and through their arduous work to establish a community. Their work would continue for many decades and it is particularly the work they did in providing training and facilitating initiations that would in turn lead the way in the worldwide pagan revival.

CHAPTER 2

BAPTISM

Since emerging into the public eye in the 1950s, the tradition which is now commonly referred to as Wicca has been known by many different names, and there has been much debate about which of the terms holds the most authenticity. Terms such as *'the witch cult'*, *'the Craft'*, *'the Old Religion'*, *'Wica'*, *'Wicca'* and simply *'Witchcraft'* are all used, exclusively and interchangeably, sometimes with varied definitions being applied, causing a great deal of confusion along the way.

During the last few years *'Wicca'* has become a buzz word amongst modern seekers of alternatives to the more established systems of religion and spirituality, which are often viewed as being patriarchal and restrictive. Although the word is used interchangeably by some with terms such as *'witchcraft'* and *'paganism'*, for the purposes of clarity and consistency within this work we have decided to use the term *'Wicca'* to describe the tradition of magick, mysticism and spirituality which was first made public through the writings and teachings of Gerald Gardner. There are some who believe that the term *'Wicca'* should only be applied to the initiatory traditions, whilst at the same time the vast majority of those applying the term to themselves today are often followers of what is commonly referred to as *'Solitary Wicca'* made popular through the writings of American authors such as Scott Cunningham, Starhawk and Silver Ravenwolf.

Further to the already confused blend of definitions and terminology we have found that a number of modern writers and teachers have incorrectly come to the conclusion that Gerald Gardner was somehow solely responsible for the revival of the term *'Wicca'* and a few who even believe him to have invented it. To address these misconceptions we will begin by exploring the use of the term in the decades preceding the publication of Gardner's first books, as well as some much earlier applications of it within its original context in Old English texts.

Our exploration begins with Gardner himself who used the term *'Wica'* to refer to the tradition, as can be seen in the example below, found in his book *The Meaning of Witchcraft*:

> *"I realised that I had stumbled upon something interesting; but I was half-initiated before the word, 'Wica' which they used hit me like a thunderbolt, and I knew where I was, and that the Old Religion still existed."*

Much has been made by some modern practitioners of the difference in spelling between *'Wica'* and *'Wicca'*, with some adopting *'Wica'* to distinguish themselves from the masses using the term *'Wicca'* for practices which often seem to have little in common with the initiatory traditions. However, this spelling of the word does not seem to have any historical significance, beyond having been used by Gardner and it is very likely that it was a deliberate variation of the spelling. Unless of course Gardner meant *'wiça'* which is the word used by the Dakota people of North America for *'man'* or in some instances *'raccoon'* – though that is probably a little bit farfetched! However, we thought this little quirky coincidence was an interesting aside nonetheless and worth including.

Looking at Gardner's writings, we see he consistently used the spelling *'Wica'* in his books, and also in his dealings with the media. The term *'Wicca'* only occurs in his last book *The Meaning of Witchcraft* in 1959, and then only in a discussion of the etymology of the word from Anglo-Saxon times. Even in the biography *Gerald Gardner: Witch*, the term used is *'Wica'*. From this it is clear that Gardner did not invent the use of the term *'Wicca'*, as we will now further demonstrate.

We will start with a use contemporary to Gardner's and which is unlikely to have influenced him, where the term was found in an early draft of J.R.R. Tolkien's book *The Two Towers*.[5] Christopher Tolkien, the son of J.R.R. Tolkien, recorded the way in which his father worked in a twelve volume set. In volume seven *The Treason of Isengard*, he mentions that J.R.R. used the term *Wicca* in reference to the characters of Gandalf and Saruman. These two characters would both be referred to as wizards and as part of the Wise throughout the rest of the trilogy. In addition to being one of the best known and loved fantasy fiction writers of the twentieth century, having penned works such as *The Hobbit* and *The Lord of the Rings;* J.R.R. Tolkien was of course also a scholar of Old English and his (unpublished) application of this term took place in 1942, only a few years before it was used by Gerald Gardner. This clearly shows a use of the term contemporary with, yet completely unrelated to its usage by Gardner, illustrating that the word was not forgotten as some would have us believe.

More than twenty years prior to Tolkien, Lewis Spence made a few passing references to the term *'Wicca'* in his book *An Encyclopædia of Occultism* published in 1920, saying (amongst other things):

> *"The Anglo-Saxon system of magic was of course Teutonic. Their pretenders to witchcraft were called wicca..."*

In the book *Gypsy Sorcery*, published in 1889 by Leland, author of *Aradia*, we find a yet earlier reference to the term *'Wicca'* where he used it in a footnote as part of a definition for the word Witch:

> *"Witch. Medieval English wicche, both masculine and feminine, a wizard, a witch. Anglo-Saxon wicca, masculine, wicce, feminine.*

---

5 Volume 2 of The Lord of the Rings Trilogy, J.R.R. Tolkien, 1954

Wicca is a corruption of witga, commonly used as a short form of witega, a prophet, seer, magician, or sorcerer."

Again this shows a use of the term, this time by an author, whose work, as we will see later in this volume, had and continues to have, a huge impact on the Wiccan tradition. Also we must comment that Gardner himself referred to the book *Gypsy Sorcery* in his work *The Meaning of Witchcraft*. This illustrates that even more than fifty years before Gardner would use the term, it had not fallen into complete disuse, and that Gardner was probably aware of earlier uses. In fact, Leland seemed to think that it was *"commonly used"*, and indeed he seems to have been right. We have found dozens of references spanning the entire nineteenth century which refer to the term, too many to list here and besides, many are repetitive and quite basic. We will however include a couple just for those readers who are curious to see examples of its usage.

In 1856 we find the term mentioned in *The History of the Anglo-Saxons* by Thomas Miller:

> *"Scarcely an obscure English province is without its wise-man, or cunning fortune-teller, those lingering remains of the Wicca of the Saxons..."*

In 1854 the term moreover appeared in *Hereward of Brunne*, a short story, published in *Ainsworth's Magazine*, as a term used for a wise-woman healer who is considered to be witch:

> *"At the sound of his voice the creature slowly rose, and the young man drew back aghast, while the word 'Wicca' escaped from his lips. 'Wicca! - ay, Wicca!' sneered the hag. 'Start ye wat my winsome face? Is your purpose less ugly than I am? Come ye for a witch's med'cine - ratsbane is the best! Come ye for her blessing - better have another's curse."*

Some have suggested that the term *'Wicca'* might be a corruption of the Saxon witega, which in turn means *'prophet'* or *'seer'*. This is now widely disputed and some scholars are suggesting that it might come from the Indo-European root-word *'wek'* which means *'voice'*. This idea would then define a witch as someone who invokes or summons supernatural power through the use of their voice.

J.A. Picton in his work *Hall, Wych, and Salt Works* in *Notes and Queries*, 1874, suggested a different meaning for the word *'wicca'* based on the Low German rather than the Anglo-Saxon.

> *"He derives the term wich from Low German wijck or wicca, sacred, devoted, alleging that the Northern nations attached great sanctity to salt springs from their healing qualities."*

There are many examples of the term *Wiccan* being used throughout Old English Christian texts, usually to describe practitioners of witchcraft, in most instances specifically female and in a non-complimentary manner. In other words the *Wiccan* was usually viewed as someone who was involved in diabolic and necromantic magick. One such example can be found in the tenth century writings of Ælfric of Eynsham (955-1010CE):

> *"Gyt farað <u>wiccan</u> to wega gelæton and to hæþenum byrgelsum mid heora gedwimore and clipiað to ðam deofle, and he cymð hym to on þas mannes gelicnysse þe þæ lið bebyrged swylce he of deaðe arise, ac heo ne mæg þæt don þæt se deada arise hire drycræft."*

> *"Witches still travel to where roads meet and to heathen graves with their illusory skill and call out to the devil and he comes to them in the guise of the person who lies buried there, as if he would arise from*

the dead – but she cannot really make it happen, that the dead man should arise through her wizardry."[6]

Here we need to take note that the *wiccans* are working their necromancy at the crossroads, a place where the bodies of those who committed suicide or who, in some other manner were considered to be unclean were buried. Ælfric evidently did not believe in their ability to raise the dead either, instead he believed it to be some form of illusion or that the *wiccan* herself was being tricked by the devil into believing that she was raising a dead man. It is worth noting that although necromancy does not form a part of the Wiccan Tradition today, a variation of its practices are as popular as ever in the form of modern spiritualism, though graveyards play a far lesser role.

The term *wiccan* also makes an appearance in texts such as *The Sermon of the Wolf to the English* which was composed by Wulfstan II, the Archbishop of York and Bishop of Worcester around 1014 CE. He wrote it under the penname Lupus, meaning *'wolf'*. In it he named wiccans alongside other unpleasant characters such as plunderers, thieves, pledge-breakers, perjurers and murderers, to name but a few. Once again this indicates the use of the term to describe people who are not considered to be of an agreeable character.

Thus it is clear that the term *'Wiccan'* has historical precedence, and is not a modern invention, even though it would seem that it was not in use by practitioners in the 1950's. However, in 1958 the term *'Wiccen'* was introduced into the modern public arena, through an article entitled *The Craft of the Wiccens*, by Charles Cardell, published in *Light* magazine. Cardell was initially friendly with Gardner, but the two men fell out in 1958. Cardell subsequently published much of the Gardnerian Book of Shadows as an exposé in his book *Witch* in 1964, and also republished Leland's *Aradia* in the early 1960s. Beyond a derogatory use by Robert Cochrane in an article in *Pentagram* magazine

---

6 Leechcraft, Stephen Pollington, 2000

no.2 in 1964 when he referred to *"the illusionary world of Ye Olde English Wiccen"*, this term was never widely used.

By the seventeenth century witchcraft was widely linked with more specifically demonic magick, hence the French librarian and bibliographer Gabriel Naudé wrote in 1625 distinguishing four types of magick: divine, theurgic, goetia or witchcraft, and natural magic.[7] Goetia, which literally means *'howling'* and also refers to a specific grimoire for summoning demons and fallen angels, is considered illicit magick, unsanctioned by the divine, and by association the same is true of witchcraft. This was not a new association, as the term *goes* was used in ancient Greece to describe a wizard or sorceror, and was itself derived from the term *goetia* which was equated to witchcraft even then.

Likewise in the grimoires, when reference was made to witches, it was as associates of the devil, perpetuating the accepted medieval stereotype. Pictures found in the grimoires reinforced this view, showing magickians inside magick circles for protection, whilst witches wandered freely amongst the demons outside the circle, having already sold their souls to the devil, such as in the fourteenth century *MSS Cotton Tiberias A VII*.

It was not only the monotheistic religions which had an issue with witches. In the thirteenth century *Poetic Edda*, Odin's dislike of witches is made clear when he describes how he kills the astral bodies of witches in spirit flight by preventing them from returning to their physical bodies. He said:

> *"If I see witches riding through the air*
> *I do something to make them lose their way*
> *And they never find their own skin again*
> *And they never find their own spirit again."*

---

7 Apologie pour tous les grands personages qui ont esté faussement soupçonnez de magie, Naudé, 1625

This negative attitude to witches is seen elsewhere in Norse writings, such as the description in *Diplomatarium Islandicum* (1281) that *"they would enchant [seiði] or work witchcraft [magni troll upp] to ride men or cattle"*, and *Norges gamle Love* (Norway's Old Law) that *"No man shall have in his house a stave [stafr] or altar [stalli] or witchcraft [vitt] or sacrifice [blot] or anything that is known to be heathen custom."*

It should be apparent from what has been shown thus far that the term *'wiccan'* is simply an old word meaning *'witch'* when translated into modern English. As such there is no reason why these words should not be used interchangeably from an etymological point of view. The word *'wicca'* does thus provide us with a term, which has been given a new meaning based loosely on the old, and is understood in a wider sense to mean what we know as the practices and beliefs of the Wiccan Tradition as it stands today. The classification of all magickal practices which incorporate a high percentage of natural magick as *witchcraft* is one which has been with us for some time. The term *'witch'*, although different definitions are being applied within modern pagan circles, is still widely recognised by the general population, in the English language and through its corresponding words in other modern languages, as being descriptive of an unpleasant person who uses magick for evil and negative purposes.

The expression *"Witch Cult"* was probably drawn from the title of Margaret Murray's book *The Witch Cult in Western Europe*. This term was widely used from the 1920s onwards, being found not only in works like *Witches Still Live* by Kenyon in 1929, but also having its own entry in *The Encyclopaedia of Freemasonry* (1946).

The *'Old Religion'* is a term used to describe both witchcraft and Catholicism. Leland used the phrase *'la vecchia religione'* meaning the old religion to describe witchcraft in his work *Etruscan Roman Remains in Popular Tradition* in 1893. Robert Graves would also use the term the *'Old Religion'* referring to the *"witch cult in Medieval Britain"* in his work *The White Goddess*, first published in 1948. Graves described this work as *"A historical grammar of poetic myth"*, however the significance of this

35

statement often seems to have been lost in Graves' presentation of his ideas as fact and truth. Many people have believed Graves and imported ideas into the Wiccan tradition which have no historical basis and have only served to muddy the waters rather than adding anything to the tradition.

However over three hundred years earlier Reginald Scot also used the term *'the Old Religion'* to describe Catholicism in his classic *Discoverie of Witchcraft* in 1584. To Protestant reformers, Catholicism was:

> *"an organised system of magic designed to bring supernatural remedies to bear upon earthly problems."*[8]

The magickal nature of Catholicism was a reality to the populace in medieval Britain, to such an extent that it could be argued that Catholicism was the predominant magickal system for some centuries in Britain. People were encouraged to use the prayers and rites magickally, and ritual items were seen as highly effective for both amuletic and talismanic purposes. Attendance at Mass was believed to give benefits such as ease in childbirth, protection whilst travelling and recovery of lost goods. Holy water could be drunk to cure sickness, or sprinkled on houses for protection or crops for good yields. Saints with their associated powers formed a pantheon whose seasonal rituals filled the year. It is somewhat ironic that Catholicism, which had produced so much anti-witchcraft literature and fervour should be seen in a similar light as a similar *'evil'*.

This dismissal of the *'pagan'* Catholic practices is well illustrated in the seventeenth century Scottish manuscript, *Memorialls*, where old folk practices and Catholicism are intermingled in a description of the practices good upstanding Church-going folk abandoned:

---

8 Religion and the Decline of Magic, Thomas, 1971

"They solemnly renounce – Lammas-day, Whitsunday, Candlemas, Beltan, cross-stones, and images, fairs named by saints, and all the remnants of popery; Yule, or Christmas, old wives fables and bye-words, as Palm-Sunday, Carlin-Sunday, the 29th of May, being dedicated by this generation to profanity; Pasch-Sunday, Hallow-even, Hogmynæ-night, Valentine's-even."

The obvious connection between the name *'The Craft'* and Wicca is that *'Craft'* is a contraction of *'Witchcraft'*. The use of the term also occurs on a regular basis in the grimoire tradition in which it is used as a general term to refer to art of performing magick. To illustrate this, what follows is an extract from *Sloane MS 3847*, the earliest known *Key of Solomon* which dates to 1572:

"Heare begineth the prologue of ye Booke of Clavicles of Salomon contayninge the secrets of all secrets of all crafts magicall of Nigromancy, the which booke of craftes as, Ptolomeus the most wisest philosopher in Greece, doth testify…"

However, the term also enjoyed a long history of use in Freemasonry. Taking into consideration that there is much in Wicca that has been drawn from the rites and practices of Freemasonry this connection would also seem significant, providing us with yet another possible source for its use. Freemasonry too received its share of persecution and accusations similar to those levelled against witchcraft. For example, Freemasons were accused of dedicating their children to the Devil when receiving the Mason's Word in their initiation ceremonies and continue to be accused of numerous occult affiliations to this day[9] The nineteenth century Masonic author and scholar Albert Mackey made an intriguing connection between the use of the words *'Craft'* and *'Mystery'* in the context of Freemasonry in his major work *An*

---

9 A Short History of Freemasonry to 1730, Knoop & Jones, 1940

Encyclopaedia of Freemasonry (1879), which could hint at a reason why the term Craft was applied to Wicca:

> *"In this secondary sense we speak of the 'Mystery of the Stonemasons as equivalent to the 'Craft of the Stonemasons.'"*

When we look at the records of the inquisition we find that often practitioners of magick, who did not consider themselves to be witches, would be labelled as such. A good example of this is the Italian Benandanti, or the *'Doers of Good'*, who considered themselves to be the balancing force, battling the evil-doers who practiced witchcraft. The Benandanti were actively opposed to witchcraft, yet they were also labelled as witches by the inquisition.

Magickal practitioners such as British cunning folk, the Italian Benandanti, the German Hexenbanner and the Livonian werewolves used their powers to combat the malefic magick of witches, and effectively occupied a middle-ground between church and witch, for they used scripture and grimoire-derived material in their work. Their magick might be Christian in provenance, but it was definitely not approved of by the church due to its magickal nature. The use of magick to protect from witches and their magick can be found throughout history and examples can be found going back many thousands of years. What follows is an example from ancient Babylonia, in which an exorcism is performed on a simulacrum representing a witch:

> *"But I by command of Marduk, the lord of charms,*
> *by Marduk, the master of bewitchment,*
> *Both the male and female witch*
> *as with ropes I will entwine,*
> *as in a cage I will catch,*
> *as with cords I will tie,*
> *as in a net I will overpower,*

as in a sling I will twist,
as a fabric I will tear,
with dirty water as from a well I will fill,
as a wall throw them down."[10]

Similar examples of a separation between good and bad (evil) magick can be found in many cultures today, in which the negative magick is usually associated with witchcraft. For example, in Latin America today, a definite separation is made between those who use magick to heal (healer or *Curandero*) and those who use it for evil purposes (witch or *Brujo*).

Yet, modern pagan witches insist on using the term, often saying that it is their right to use the term, and that they are working towards reclaiming it as a positive term. This is an extraordinary contradiction, as the practices associated with witchcraft when viewed from a global perspective, are in exact opposition to the magick worked by followers of the Wiccan Tradition, who as we have already seen use the term to describe themselves and their practices.

Indeed, when even writers of the past have categorised witches into a range of different categories, from Nicolàs Eymerich in the fourteenth century to Francis Hutchinson in the early eighteenth century, we realise that the term witch is likely to always remain a loaded one with many negative connotations.

"A Hebrew Witch, a Pagan Witch, a Lapland Witch, an Indian Witch, a Protestant Witch, and a Popish Witch, are different from one another; some in Honour, and some in Disgrace."[11]

---

10 The Religion of Babylonia & Assyria, Jastrow, 1893, also quoted in The Book of Witches, Hueffer, 1908
11 An Historical Essay Concerning Witchcraft: With Observations Upon Matters of Fact, Hutchinson, 1718

So, was *'witchcraft'* ever a term used by practitioners to describe positive forms of magick they practiced? It would seem that historically it was not, nor is it a term which is generally understood to be that today, with the exception of its use within the modern pagan community. The term was often used to describe any practitioner of magick in an effort to vilify them and demean their magick to the same level of those who practiced witchcraft, which was considered the lowest form of magick.

It should be clear by now that it can be argued that both the words *"wiccan"* and *"witch"* (which, as we have seen, historically have the same meaning) are completely inappropriate terms for the practices and beliefs of the modern Wiccan movement, in which magick is predominantly used for positive ends such as for healing, divination and for self-improvement. Both the terms *'witch'* and *'wicca'* have had severely negative connotations attached to them from the earliest times of their use, however we also need to take into consideration that these are terms which were there from the first popular stirrings of the Wiccan movement, whether or not revivalist or a continuation of an earlier tradition.

It is ironic perhaps that the practices of modern Wicca have more in common with those of the temple religions of the ancient world, combined with the Qabalistic and ceremonial practices of the medieval through to Victorian period, yet they perpetuate the use of the very word that the oppressors of these practices used in an effort to suppress them. This is a strange and unfortunate twist in the development of the tradition, and possibly one of the greatest stumbling blocks for those who wish to have it recognised and accepted as a world religion today.

Returning to the word *'wicca'*, we see that Doreen Valiente, in her book *An ABC of Witchcraft*, published in 1973, omitted an entry for the term *'wicca'*, although she was familiar with it as illustrated by her use of it in another entry. This would seem to indicate that the term was simply not considered significant enough by Valiente at the time of her writing to warrant its own entry. Gerald Gardner himself referred to the practices he wrote about and taught as *"The Witch Cult"* or *'witchcraft'* not Wicca, other than in saying that those who initiated him referred to themselves as the *'wica'* and using the term infrequently to refer to the practitioners of the Witch Cult in his writings. Likewise, earlier books written by prominent initiates of the tradition also seemed to use the term *"Witch"* or *"Witchcraft"* rather than *"Wicca"* as their preference as the norm well into the 1980's. For example What <u>Witches</u> *Do; A <u>Witches</u> Bible; An ABC of <u>Witchcraft</u> Past and Present; and Mastering* <u>Witchcraft.</u>

Of course, as all practitioners of magick will know, names have a great deal of power, and as such the names we use for ourselves can define and also sometimes constrain us. The names we use for the traditions we follow, our practices and beliefs likewise define us and should be given due consideration. Whilst Gardner might have preferred *'the witch cult'* and *'wica'*, it is clear that these terms are not appropriate for the tradition as it is practiced and perceived today. At the same time the terms *'Wicca'* and *'Witchcraft'*, whether used singularly or interchangeably, are both possibly historically inappropriate, yet useable today, as is *'Craft'*. The latter is possibly a less loaded term, and more fully representative of the tradition when applied to the initiatory esoteric variants thereof.

CHAPTER 3

BOOK OF SHADOWS

The term *'Book of Shadows'* (often abbreviated to *BOS*) is a very evocative one, but what does it mean and where does it come from? The Book of Shadows is the core document of the Wiccan tradition. It contains the key liturgy of the tradition including the ceremonies of initiation and that of the seasonal festivals, as well as information on other significant practices. Each initiate copies their initiator's Book of Shadows by hand and is oathbound not to share it outside the tradition.

In this way the core rituals and techniques are preserved and perpetuated down the initiatory line. Additionally, each initiate may add and evolve the material within their Book of Shadows as they progress in knowledge, experience and understanding. The result of this is that different initiatory lines may possess slightly different Books of Shadows with an identical core and unique variations. This principle is elucidated by the author and witch Frederic Lamond in his book *Fifty Years of Wicca,* when he recounts being told by Gerald Gardner that:

> *"The Book of Shadows is not a Bible or Quran. It is a personal cookbook of spells that have worked for the owner."*

This practice of preserving a tradition through hand copying the material has parallels in earlier magickal traditions. One of the earliest books of the grimoire tradition, the thirteenth/fourteenth century *Liber Juratus or The Sworn Book of Honorius,* gave instructions in its prologue for the preservation of its knowledge through copying its contents:

42

*"and therefore we being somewhat moved, made this oath among
ourselves: First, that this book should be delivered to no man until
such time as the master of the art were in jeopardy of death, and
that it should be copied but to three at the most."*

Liber Juratus was essentially the first *Liber Spirituum* (*'Book of
Spirits'*) of the grimoire tradition, being a magickal book of practice.
Many of the subsequent grimoires in the following centuries would give
details of how to make and consecrate a Liber Spirituum. The *Key of
Solomon* went so far as to detail the nature of its contents, these being
*"the prayers for all the operations, the Names of the Angels in the form of
Litanies, their seals and Characters"*.

Many centuries earlier in ancient Egypt there were books of spells
and ceremonies which were jealously guarded by the priesthood. These
books, such as *The Book of the Heavenly Cow*, were never shown to
anyone outside the priesthood, lest the uninitiated should profane the
magick within and render it ineffective. However the first reference
specifically to a *'witch's book'* may be seen in the writings of the Roman
poet Horace, recorded in his *Epodes* in 30 BCE from his dialogue with
the witch Canidia:

*"And by the inflexible divinity of Diana, and by the books of
incantations able to call down the stars displaced from the
firmament"*

The Greek geographer Pausanias also recorded the use of a
magickal book in his second century *Guide to Greece*. He referred to a
magickian making dry wood catch fire after he, *"in his native language
had sung hymns, and pronounced certain barbarous words, out of a book which
he held in his hand."*

The origin of the name *'Book of Shadows'* seems to be contemporary
with Gardner's novel *High Magic's Aid*. A copy of the magazine *The
Occult Observer* from 1949 contained the term *'Book of Shadows'* in an

article by the palmist Mir Bashir about an ancient Sanskrit divination manual of the same name. Significantly, *The Occult Observer* was published by Michael Houghton, the then proprietor of the Atlantis Bookshop in Bloomsbury, London, which also published *High Magic's Aid* by Gerald Gardner in the same year under its publishing imprint of Neptune Press.

Earlier uses of the phrase do occur, though the only esoteric occurrences are in Christian works which are clearly unrelated to the Wiccan tradition, such as this reference from a few years earlier in 1942:

> *"According to Charles Wesley, the Old Testament is a book of shadows, of which Jesus is the substance."*[12]

In her autobiography, *High Priestess*, Patricia Crowther refers to the Book of Shadows as also being called the *Black Book*. This is an interesting observation, as Gardner had a manuscript copy of the *Grimoire of Honorius* in his collection, which was alternatively known as the *Black Book*.[13] The *Grimoire of Honorius* is essentially a spell book with techniques for circle casting and conjuration, with a curious mixture of angelic and demonic entities summoned. Considering Gardner's description of what the Book of Shadows should contain, it is easy to see why the term *Black Book* might have been appropriated.

As an aside we may note the Scandinavian tradition of *Black Books* of magick, which have some similarities to the Book of Shadows, and speculate as to whether any influence from these works found its way into the tradition. Black Books were generally hand-copied books of herb lore, charms and incantations. These books, of which more than two hundred have been identified, date from 1480 – 1920, with the majority from the period 1750 – 1850.[14]

---

12 The Evangelical Doctrines of Charles Wesley's Hymns, Rattenbury, 1942
13 Secret Lore of Magic, Idries Shah, 1957
14 Narratives of magic and healing, Stokker, 2001

Returning to the connection between the grimoire tradition and the Book of Shadows, there is one more source which we need to consider here. Extracts from grimoires and popular Renaissance works on magick were commonly used by British cunning folk in the seventeenth to nineteenth centuries as their 'source of power' for their textual amulets. Contrary to some popular views, cunning men were often literate, this being a major indication of magickal power in a time of high illiteracy. In this the cunning men were continuing the medieval tradition of religious beneficial magickal textual amulets which still permeated the church until at least the fifteenth century.[15]

Popular influential occult texts amongst cunning folk included the *Key of Solomon*, Albertus Magnus's *Book of Secrets*, Cornelius Agrippa's *Three Books of Occult Philosophy* & *Fourth Book of Occult Philosophy*, Giambattista della Porta's *Natural Magic*, John Heydon's *Theomagia* and Reginald Scot's *Discoverie of Witchcraft*. It was a common phenomena for a cunning man to have a unique book containing their successful charms and spirit names, whose contents they kept entirely secret and would only pass on to a worthy successor. Here again we see the same approach as subsequently found in the Wiccan tradition with the Book of Shadows.

It is clear that the use and copying of grimoires and spell books was not restricted to Britain. As previously discussed in *Emergence*, the Venetian witch Laura Malapiero, on her arrest in 1654 was found to possess a number of magickal manuscripts for copying, including the *Key of Solomon* and many other books containing magickal incantations and spells.

The hand copying magickal documents was also a standard practice in the Hermetic Order of the Golden Dawn where the initiate had to swear in the Neophyte ritual that they would:

---

15 Binding Words: Textual Amulets in the Middle Ages, Skemer, 2006

"Neither copy nor allow to be copied, any manuscript until I had obtained permission from the Second Order, lest our Secret Knowledge be revealed through my neglect..."

This demonstrates that the transmission of the practices and beliefs of the magickal tradition by hand was still in common use just a few decades before the emergence of the same practice in the Wiccan tradition.

We should also point out an interesting use of terminology with regard to the *Key of Solomon*, as a Hebrew version of this manuscript dated circa 1700 has the sub-title of *Sefer ha-Levanah* – the *'Book of the Moon'*.[16] Considering the lunar emphasis in the Wiccan tradition this is another curious synchronicity. It has been suggested that this book is the same *Sefer ha-Levanah* mentioned by the Jewish Kabbalist Rabbi Nahmanides in the thirteenth century in his work *Commentary on Deuteronomy*, which potentially provides us with a significantly earlier date of origin.

Like the books of the old cunning folk, the first known version of the Book of Shadows, contained a mish-mash of material from different sources, including the *Key of Solomon*. It was believed to have been compiled by Gardner, and called Ye Bok of ye Art Magickal (BAM for short), a bad example of pseudo Old English which happily was dropped at some point in favour of Book of Shadows. Subsequent variants of the early Book of Shadows in the 1950s discarded much of the material in Ye Bok of ye Art Magickal, with minor changes being made to each version, which are sometimes referred to as Text A, Text B and Text C. However we will not use this nomenclature in the current volume, as the thrust of our work is in the opposite direction back in time.

As has been shown, copying a book of techniques which form the core of a system was in continuous practice from the thirteenth century

---

16 Oriental MS 6360, Anon

onwards with first the grimoires and subsequently the Cunning folk and members of the Hermetic Order of the Golden Dawn. The use of the hand-copied Book of Shadows in the Wiccan tradition can thus be seen as a likely continuation of a common European magickal practice, amongst members of a variety of practices – including that of witchcraft - and suggests its use may well have been derived from such practices.

CHAPTER 4

INTO THE MYSTERIES

The Wiccan Tradition contains three key initiation ceremonies which form part of its core mysteries, the liturgies of which are contained in the Book of Shadows. It is through the first of these initiations that a person becomes a Wiccan initiate and a member of a coven. The second and the third initiations mark further points of learning and understanding which in turn qualify the initiate to teach and initiate others. It is customary for Wiccan initiation to be passed on from a man to a woman, and from a woman to a man.

Today, although the initiatory lineage and priesthood of Wicca no longer represents the majority of those interested in and practising the tradition, it nonetheless remains important. Through the initiated priesthood, practices have been continued and inspired dozens of thriving new traditions of Witchcraft since the 1950's and have also been adopted, adapted and moulded for use in many of the modern Pagan and Goddess traditions. Sometimes the adaptations can be considered to be progressive and in other instances, due to lack of understanding or misinformation, they are truly regressive in their application. Regardless, the practices and beliefs remain preserved and available within the bounds of some of the esoteric traditions, passed on from one generation of initiates to the next, as they were intended to be – and in the same way that the inner beliefs and practices of the ancient mystery traditions were passed on from initiator to initiate.

'Initiation' comes from the Latin word for 'origin' or 'beginning'. As a word it can have a number of connotations, and so it is as well to be clear what we mean when we discuss initiation in the context of the Wiccan tradition where the term is used to refer specifically to the process of formally admitting a new member to the coven or to the tradition.

Within the tradition propagated by Gardner there are three degrees of initiation. These are generally referred to simply as first degree, second degree and third degree, with each having an accompanying title, conferred upon the initiate during the respective ceremonies.

1st Degree	Witch & Priest/Priestess
2nd Degree	High Priest/Priestess
3rd Degree	High Priestess & Witch Queen/High Priest & Magus

With time variations have developed in these titles, and there are also traditions which do not use a three degree system.

The first degree is the entry into the coven and Wiccan tradition, sometimes referred to as a rebirth and commonly accompanied by the giving of a new name which is only used during ceremonies in the magick circle. This name is known as a *'witch'* name or craft name. Gardner does not follow this pattern in the details he records in *High Magic's Aid*. In that novel the hero, Jan, is given a new name during his second degree initiation. Gardner used the name Janicot for his hero, which he subsequently recorded as being a name for the god of the witches. Curiously, an earlier nineteenth century reference by the French historian Michelet in his work *La Sorcière* attributed the name Janicot as being an alternative name for Jesus.

There is a clear precedent for this idea of the witch name in the medieval witch trials, where the idea of being given a new name on becoming a witch was a common theme in the records of confessions. We are aware that some of the witchcraft confessions are disputed, but all the same we also need to take into consideration that the early practitioners of Wicca, would have been familiar with the trial records and may have been influenced by them – regardless of the accuracy contained within and for this reason it is probable that these records may have provided some form of inspiration, at the very least. In one such example from Scotland in 1644 we find a woman from Lauder confessing to being an initiated witch, even though she was offered the opportunity to set herself free:

> *"She had been fyled[17] as a witch, she said, and as a witch she would die. And had not the devil once, when she was a young lassie, kissed her, and given her a new name."[18]*

Likewise, the story of the famous Scottish witch Isobell Gowdie is described in the same book under the heading of *The Witches of Auldearne*. She was invited by the devil to meet with him at night at the parish church of Auldearne. Promising she would, Isobell met with him accordingly and:

> *"...he baptized her by the name of 'Janet' and accepted her service."[19]*

The taking of a new magickal name for use within ceremonies was a common practice in magickal groups such as the Hermetic Order of the Golden Dawn and Ordo Templi Orientis, where a new name or motto which represented the aspirations of the individual was taken upon initiation.

In addition to the medieval precedent for witch names, there is also reference to witches undergoing three initiation ceremonies. Murray referred to Reginald Scot's *Discoverie of Witchcraft* (1584) when she recorded in *The God of the Witches*:

---

17 Fyled is an old Scottish term meaning 'soiled' or 'fouled'.

18 Witch Stories, Lynn Linton, 1861, 'Sinclair's stories'

19 Witch Stories, Lynn Linton, 1861, 'The Witches of Auldearne'

"In short, they were set apart to perform the duties and ceremonies always associated with priests and priestesses, and must be regarded as the priesthood of the Horned God. It is probably this body to which Reginald Scot refers when he mentions that the witch went through three admission ceremonies. The first was when she accepted the Devil's invitation to join the society."

During the first of the three Masonic initiation ceremonies, we encounter a whole range of techniques which may well have translated into the Wiccan first degree. In the Masonic ceremony of the first degree, the postulant is tied up and blindfolded, and stripped to the waist. All of this is of course echoed in Wicca. The cord around the neck to lead the candidate, referred to as the cable tow, is used in exactly the same manner to lead the candidate in Wicca. The Masonic candidate is then described as being *'properly prepared'*, again a term used in regards to the candidate in Wicca. Before entering the room for initiation, a sword is held to the bare breast of the Masonic postulant and he is challenged. Again the parallel here to Wiccan practice is obvious. At this point the candidate is given their first instructions, which could be translated into the *First Instruction* which is used by some traditions of Wicca today. After being admitted the postulant is presented to the four cardinal directions of East, South, West and North[20] – yet again a clear correlation of this can be found echoed at the corresponding part of the Wiccan first degree ceremony.

The term *'properly prepared'* is likely to be one which was inherited by the Craft of Wicca from the Craft of Freemasonry. It plays a significantly important role within both traditions and particularly with regards to initiation. Within the Wiccan tradition only someone who is *'properly prepared'* may be considered for initiation. There are the physical preparations which are made and which the candidate undertakes during a first degree ceremony, all of which may be

---

20 Freemasons' Guide and Compendium, Jones, 1956

considered to be part of the test of *'properly prepared'*, a full discussion of this is outside of the scope of this work as there are variations between traditions in regards to its application.

Interestingly, the phrase is also found in the Second Degree rite of the Ordo Templi Orientis where the Saladin (a title given to one of the initiating officers) questions the Wazir (who is the sponsor) saying: *"Do you vouch that he is properly prepared?"*[21] This provides us with another possible source for its inclusion in Wiccan ceremonies. The Ordo Templi Orientis, as a quasi-masonic order, most probably inherited the term from Freemasonry. Gardner was proud of his involvement with the Ordo Templi Orientis of which he was made a member by Aleister Crowley in 1947. There were no active lodges in the UK at the time of Gardner's initiation by Crowley and therefore we have to assume that Gardner's experience of the order was limited; regardless of the degrees he was awarded, though he may have been given copies of the rituals.

It is also believed that Gerald Gardner had some involvement with Freemasonry or Co-Masonry and this is often cited as the reason for the inclusion of this term. However, it is also worth noting that many of the other characters whose work may have contributed to or influenced the practices of Wicca were familiar with or had involvement with either Freemasonry or Co-Masonry, including Aleister Crowley as we have already seen. As such the term would have been a familiar one and its use in Wicca could be ascribed to anyone familiar with basic Masonic practices, not just Gerald Gardner.

The phrase *'properly prepared'* is one which has a history of use in regards to magickal thought, though of course not necessarily in the same context as found in the Wiccan Tradition, we will still consider them here for the sake of completion.

Proclus, the last of the great Greek philosophers, in his classic work *Metaphysical Elements* circa fifth century CE mentioned it when discussing the concept of the ultimate divine being, writing:

---

21 The Secret Rituals of the O.T.O, Francis King, 1973

"That also, which is most admirable and laudable in this theology is, that it produces in the mind properly prepared for its reception the most pure, holy, venerable, and exalted conceptions of the great cause of all".

We also see the phrase in Mathers' edition of the *Key of Solomon the King* when we find the following in the introduction chapter:

"Therefore, O my son! Thou mayest see every experiment of mine or of others, and let everything be properly prepared for them, as thou shalt see properly set down by me, both day and hour, and all things necessary; for without this there will be but falsehood and vanity in this my work; where are hidden all secrets and mysteries which can be performed..."

Here the writer of the *Key of Solomon* is instructing his son Roboam on the magickal arts. Although not a formal initiation ceremony, this instruction may be considered as part of Roboam's formal introduction to the magickal arts and therefore it is interesting to note that *'properly prepared'* is stressed here, as it is in other instances in the *Key of Solomon* in regards to the preparation for ceremonies.

In the instance of the *Key of Solomon* the writer is instructing his son. In Wicca, as already stated, initiations are always conducted woman to man, and man to woman. Contrary to some of the modern suggestions that this cross-gender transmission was the result of social and sexual attitudes of the 1940s and 1950s, we find that it might instead have its roots in old folk beliefs. One such example clearly illustrates a belief held in the Devonshire and Cornwall areas, that it was important to pass the power of charms between the sexes. This was reported in *the Pall Mall Gazette* newspaper of 23rd November 1868, in which a witness in the inquest of the death of a child refers to a charm which she was told about many years before by a man for use on burns, saying that:

"A man may tell a woman the charm,
Or a woman may tell a man;
But if a woman tells a woman,
Or a man a man,
I consider it won't do any good at all."

But we must return again to Freemasonry for clues about other aspects of the practice of initiation in the Wiccan tradition. Freemasonry has three main grades, which is also true for Wicca – although the names given to each degree differs completely. For the stripped-down ceremonial form of Wicca three degrees is much more appropriate than the tenfold Qabalistic system of orders such as the Golden Dawn and Ordo Templi Orientis.

The vows made in the Golden Dawn Neophyte ritual can be seen to have clearly influenced those in the first degree initiation ceremony of the Wiccan tradition. Elements can be seen to have been drawn from vows such as:

"I now ask you, are you willing to take a solemn Obligation in the presence of this Assembly, to keep the secrets and Mysteries of our Order inviolate."[22]

"I, [Name], in the Presence of the Lord of the Universe .... Do, of my own free will ... most solemnly promise to keep secret this Order ... from every person in the world who has not been initiated into it ... Furthermore, if I break this, my Magickal Obligation, I submit myself, by my own consent, to a stream of Power."[23]

The vows used in the Ordo Templi Orientis first degree initiation ceremony, whilst clearly influenced by the Golden Dawn and thus being

---

22 The Golden Dawn, Israel Regardie, 1989
23 The Golden Dawn, Israel Regardie, 1989

something of an intermediary, can also be seen to be moving towards the Wiccan first degree initiation in the wording used.

> "I, [Name] in the presence of the Powers of Birth, visible and invisible … most solemnly promise and swear never to reveal … unless it be to a true brother … or else in session of such a camp as this within whose border I stand."[24]

An earlier oath is seen in the thirteenth century grimoire *Liber Juratus*, where each person who came into possession of the book was not only tested for a year, but also obliged to swear:

> "That it should be delivered to no woman, nor to any man except he were of lawful age, and he should also be both Godly and faithful, whose Godly behaviour had been tried for the space of a whole year, and that this book should no more hereafter be destroyed, but that it should be restored again to the honour, or to his successors, and if there cannot be found an able and a sufficient man to whom this book might be delivered, that then the master bind his executors by a strong oath to bury it with him in his grave."

In the mystery cults of ancient Greece, the distinction was made between those who were initiates and the uninitiated, or magickal practitioners and non-practitioners.[25] Likewise oaths of secrecy or a specific course of action sworn with dire consequences were common phenomena in the ancient world. The use of persuasive analogy in this manner is described in some detail by the modern Classics professor Fritz Graf in his study of magickal practices from the sixth century BCE through to late antiquity, *Magic in the Ancient World*, clearly demonstrating the practice of imprecation and consequence.

---

24 The Secret Rituals of the O.T.O, Francis King, 1973
25 Magicka Hiera, Faraone & Obbink, 1991

However, the concept of initiation itself is much older and examples of it, with components which are still found today in Wiccan initiation ceremonies, can be found throughout the ancient world. Such connections often occur in association with the mysteries of the deities which are still important in modern Witchcraft.

> *"The mysteries of the Cabiric worship were celebrated also at Thebes and especially at the Isle of Samothrace. They are said to have taken place at night. The candidate for initiation was crowned with a garland of olives, and wore a purple band round the loins. He was prepared by sacred ceremonies, probably hypnotic, and was seated on a brilliantly lighted throne, around which the other initiates danced in a mystic measure."* [26]

There are parts of the Wiccan ceremonies which clearly do not originate within Freemasonry, but for which we must look further back into history and to other sources. The second degree ceremony contains in essence the Sumerian myth of the descent of the goddess Inanna into the underworld, but in an adapted form. Gardner published a version of this in his book *Witchcraft Today* in which he referred to it as the *"Myth of Witchcraft"* and made no reference to it being used for an initiation. He seemed to think that the story may have originated from that of Ishtar or Siva, but went on to say that he thought it might be Celtic.

In his book *Witchcraft and the Black Art*, first published in 1920, Wickwar made a reference which may be significant to those familiar with the second degree initiation ceremony, which at its core contains the apostolic succession rites of one initiate to another, giving the candidate undergoing the elevation the right to initiate others into the first degree of the Wiccan tradition:

---

26 The Mysteries and Secrets of Magic, Thompson, 1927

"The actual initiation into the mysteries of witchcraft must have been an exciting experience ... and then the presiding Master of the Ceremonies or Chief Devil would proceed with the service as follows: Placing one hand on the crown of the head of the candidate and the other on the sole of the foot, he would declare that from now henceforward all that was betwixt and between his two hands - body and soul - were at the Devil's service."

Traditionally when a person is initiated into the Wiccan tradition it is as a member of a coven. The word coven is one which Murray used in her work, referring to it in *The God of the Witches*.:

"The word coven was used both in England and Scotland to designate a band of people of both sexes, who were always in close attendance to their god, who went to all the meetings, large or small, who performed the ceremonies either alone or in company with the Grandmaster, and who were conspicuous in the ritual."

This is an interesting point to keep in mind as it implies the predominance of men as the leaders of groups of witches working together, rather than women, which is more often found in contemporary covens today. We find a reference to this term in Pitcairn's *Criminal Trial of Scotland* (1662) saying:

"Ther wold sometimes meat a Coeven, and in ilk Coeven ther is threttein persones"

The tools are a pertinent part of the tradition of Wicca, being both symbolic and functional – some of the tools play a vital role in the majority of ceremonies, whereas others are only used in some specific instances. In the Wiccan tradition there are eight key tools, excluding the chalice. These eight tools are presented as part of the first degree initiation all initiates experience.

Interestingly the first mention made by Gerald Gardner to the presentation of the tools is in his novel, *High Magic's Aid* when the character of the high priestess, Morven, presents six of the tools to the hero Jan during his initiation, starting the presentation by saying:

"...'Now I present thee with the working tools of a witch.'..."

The tools included in this fictitious initiation ceremony were the magick sword, the athame, the white handled knife, censer of incense, the scourge and the cords. Here we find an absence of the pentacle, the wand and the chalice, which although it may seem to be significant may just be poetic license or a deliberate blind, as of course this is a work of fiction containing identifiable elements rather than an account of a real initiation!

In some traditions the purification of the soul is achieved through scourging. This practice is one which was advocated by Gerald Gardner, not only for purification, but also towards the achievement of a variety of altered states of consciousness. He first mentions it in *High Magic's Aid* where Morven tells Olaf, after his initiation:

"Water purifieth the body, but the scourge purifieth the soul"

This seems to hark back more to the practices of the medieval Christian flagellants using self-inflicted pain to alter consciousness and *'purify'* their souls than on cleanliness of the body itself.

The use of the scourge in the Wiccan tradition as purification also forms part of the initiation rites. Gardner's fictional initiation account in *High Magic's Aid* gives us an example of this in which the initiate is scourged forty times for this purpose:

"Thou first must be purified. Taking the scourge from the Altar, she struck his buttocks, first three, then seven, then nine, then twenty one strokes with the scourge..."

This sequence is the same as that which is found in accounts of initiation in various Books of Shadows both in published and unpublished sources.

There are also recorded examples of initiates of medieval witch coven's allegedly being scourged by the Devil during ceremonies. In most instances it is not clear from the accounts why the scourging is taking place, other than that it might be a form of punishment for disobedience. One example is recorded in the 1678 accounts of Katherine Liddell of Scotland where it is said curious details were given including:

> *"that he (the devil) was cold to the touch, and his breath like a damp air, and that he scourged them oft, and was a most 'wicked and barbarous master'..."* [27]

Many reasons have been given for the use of forty strokes during the scourging. For instance within the tradition this number corresponds to the number of knots on a traditional scourge (8x5) which in turn equals the so called eight paths of power multiplied by the number of points on the pentagram. Scourging and flagellation have a long history of use throughout the ancient world and examples can be found from Rome, Greece and in the later Christian practices. The precedent for the use of forty strokes may be found in the Bible when St Paul said in *Corinthians* 11:24-25:

> *"Of the Jews five times received I forty stripes save one."*

The reason for the *'save one'* is that it was illegal under the laws of the time to give more than forty strokes, hence to avoid any misunderstandings with this law, it was customary to give one stroke less. It may also be of interest to some that the person who was

---

27 Witch Stories, Lynn Linton, 1861

scourged in this way, would be tied to a low pillar for the duration of the scourging to ensure that they would be leaning forward. This practice was described by Cyprian in his third century work *The Life of Cæsarius Arelatensis* and seems to parallel the descriptions given by some modern authors of how some covens perform scourging during the first degree initiation rite. As an aside to this, it is curious to note that after Solomon, Cyprian is probably the most often attributed author of grimoires, including the black book *Clavis Inferni*, which deals with the control of the demon princes of the four cardinal directions.

CHAPTER 5

DO AS YE WILL

Today many Wiccans adhere to the ethical code known as the Wiccan Rede, which is typically expressed in the eight words *"An it harm none, do as ye will."* Although the Rede does not seem to have been part of the early Wiccan tradition, it quickly evolved as a popular ethical code, fulfilling the role of moral compass which is found in different magickal traditions.

> Witches *"… are inclined to the morality of the legendary Good King Pausol, 'Do what you like so long as you harm no one…'"*.

Gardner's comments in *The Meaning of Witchcraft* indicate that he took at least some of his inspiration from *King Pausol*. But who was King Pausol? Searching for him revealed Pierre Louÿs's work of 1901, *The Adventures of King Pausole* which seems to be what Gardner was writing about, making an error in the spelling of his name. In this book the character of King Pausole recommends that one should: *"Do no wrong or harm to thy neighbour, and observing this, do as thou please."*

Another concept for the Wiccan Rede however, seems to emerge from one of Gardner's Books of Shadows in the line *"And for long we have obeyed this law, Harm none"*. This appeared at the end of the so-called *"Craft Laws"* which contain the laws of conduct presented to covens. These laws are generally believed to be a later addition to the Book of Shadows.

However, how plausible is it that the Wiccan Rede originates with the obscure writings of Louÿs? From various accounts we know that Gerald Gardner also met, on more than one occasion, with Aleister Crowley. In 1904 Crowley received *The Book of the Law* through his wife Rose whilst in Cairo. *The Book of the Law* was a transmitted text that declared a new aeon, the new age, was upon us. Herein we find the core axiom of Crowley's later work:

> "39. *The word of the Law is THELEMA.*
> 40. *Who calls us Thelemites will do no wrong, if he look but close into the word. For there are therein Three Grades, the Hermit, and the Lover, and the man of Earth. Do what thou wilt shall be the whole of the Law.*"

And a few lines later:

> "57. *Invoke me under my stars! Love is the law, love under will. Nor let the fools mistake love; for there are love and love. There is the dove, and there is the serpent. Choose ye well!*"

The lines *"Do what thou wilt shall be the whole of the Law. Love is the law, Love under will"* were to become one of the most famous occult doctrines of the entire twentieth century and continue to be so today. Some believe that though *The Book of the Law* was said to have been dictated by a praeterhuman entity, named Aiwass, it is possible that Crowley was inspired in his use of the term by Francois Rabelais' novel *Gargantua*, which was first published in 1534 and in which we find the following:

> "*Do as thou wilt because men that are free, of gentle birth, well bred and at home in civilized company possess a natural instinct that inclines them to virtue and saves them from vice. This instinct they name their honour.*"

Crowley himself, in the essay *The Antecedents of Thelema*, briefly credits the influence of St Augustine's phrase *"Love, and do what thou wilt"*, found in *Homilies on the First Epistle of John*, VII.8 as an earlier prequel to the law of Thelema; he then goes on to give far more credit to Rabelais as painting the vision of what was to come with Thelema.[28] Parallels between the two are clearly visible. Crowley started the *Abbey of Thelema* in Sicily, Italy. Rabelais wrote of the *"Abbey of Theleme"* which was build by the giant Gargantua. The two abbeys of Thelema, the fictional one in the satirical writings of Rabelais and the real life one of Crowley, both encouraged *"Do What Thou Will"* as their central tenet.

Crowley did not make any reference to other influences on the channelled doctrine of *"love is the law, love under will"*, but we may note a possible predecessor in Lew Wallace's epic novel of 1880, *Ben-Hur: A Tale of the Christ*. Chapter VI of the book makes two references to love and law in conjunction which could have inspired a fertile mind. These are, *"The law of the place was Love, but Love without Law,"* and *"Better a law without love than a love without law."* This is an obscure possibility, but then Crowley was an avid reader, so who knows.

The concept of the power of the will was expressed clearly by the seventeenth century theologian Joseph Glanvill, in a manner which may well have influenced Crowley's later views, remembering that Crowley came from a strict Christian upbringing in the Plymouth Brethren with a preacher father. Glanvill also wrote the work *Saducismus Triumphatus* in 1681 supporting the existence of witches and their powers and attacking sceptics. On the will he said:

> *"And the will therein lieth, which dieth not. Who knoweth the mysteries of the Will with its vigour? For God is but a great Will pervading all things by nature of its intentness. Man doth not yield*

---

28 The Revival of Magick, Aleister Crowley, 1917

himself to the angels nor to death utterly, save only through the weakness of his feeble will."[29]

In Crowley's writings, the law of Thelema is explained in terms of True Will, the ultimate spiritual essence of the individual, the part of us that makes each one of us unique and that through finding the goal of this essence (True Will) we can reach fulfilment by following the path in life that we are meant for. Finding your True Will is hard work, it is not an easy path, it demands that you respect your own True Will at all times, but also that you respect the True Wills of others.

Many believe that the Rede as we know it originated with Doreen Valiente, who first mentioned the Rede in the form it is best known today. Valiente referred to it as the *'Witches' Creed'* instead of *"Rede"* in some of her writings, as the following example from her book *Witchcraft Today* clearly illustrates:

> *"Eight words the Witches' Creed fulfil: If it harms none, do what you will!"*

Valiente's use of the term *'Witches' Creed'* is significant when we consider its earlier uses. The term *'witch creed'* was widely used in early psychology to refer to the demonization of negative qualities to witches, which may be significant when we remember Valiente was involved with the psychologist and witch Charles Cardell and his branch of witchcraft in the late 1950s. The term *'witch creed'* was also used in classic works such as Walter Scott's *Letters on Demonology and Witchcraft* (1831) to describe practices of identification and counter-magick against witches. That is was a commonly known term in the nineteenth century can be seen by its use in the 1860 work by Walter Thornbury, *Turkish Life and Character*:

---

29 Also quoted by Edgar Allan Poe at the beginning of his short story Ligeia.

"It is just a fossil bit of Paganism, like our English witch creed, our amulets, and our charms."

The first public reference to the Rede was also by Doreen Valiente, in a speech given on October 3, 1964 at an event sponsored by the *Pentagram* newsletter. The text of this speech was subsequently published in number 1 of *Pentagram* later in 1964:

"Demanding tolerance between covens as well as toward the outside world, Doreen spoke the Anglo-Saxon witch formula called the Wiccan Rede or wise teaching: Eight words the Wiccan Rede fulfil, An' it harm none, do what ye will."

In 1975, Gwen Thompson, a high priestess of an American Welsh tradition, claimed in *Green Egg* magazine that her grandmother Adriana Porter had passed the Rede on to her, and that her copy predated both Gardner and Crowley. Her long poem entitled *The Rede of the Wiccae*, which ends with the familiar Rede couplet, has confusingly become known to many as the Wiccan Rede, which is not the case. We may note with interest however that Ms Thompson was said to be a subscriber to Joseph Wilson's magazine *The Waxing Moon*, which reprinted Valiente's words in 1965-6.

Although we cannot definitively state the source of the Rede, it does seem likely that it was derived from the works of Crowley, who himself drew on earlier writings. The need for a practical ethical code has always been paramount in magickal and spiritual systems, so it is perhaps no real surprise that the Wiccan Rede, which did not play a major part in the initial public dissemination of the Wiccan tradition, has gone on to become one of the best known and most definitive statements of Wicca and the Pagan revival.

CHAPTER 6

NAKED IN OUR RITES

Ritual nudity plays an important role in the practices of Wicca. This state of being naked in a magick circle is often referred to as being 'skyclad'. Being naked might be a natural state for us to be in, but it is not one which is usually part of our ordinary world. By being naked the practitioners remove any reference to status or mundane occupation, which might be interpreted from their clothes and accoutrements. There is also an element of breaking social taboos and demonstrating trust in the other practitioners by being in the uncovered state of nudity.

Reference to nudity can be found in the earliest versions of the *Charge of the Goddess* and in most of the versions of the Book of Shadows.

> *"And ye shall all be freed from slavery,*
> *And so ye shall be free in everything;*
> *And as the sign that ye are truly free,*
> *Ye shall be naked in your rites, both men*
> *And women also: this shall last until*
> *The last of your oppressors shall be dead..."*

This extract from *Aradia Gospel of the Witches* became incorporated into the Wiccan tradition, at least in part, by its adaptation and amalgamation into the *Charge of the Goddess*. In it the goddess Diana addresses her daughter Aradia, giving her instruction on how to teach witchcraft to humanity. Ten years earlier Leland had commented specifically on witches practicing their witchcraft naked under the full moon in *Gypsy Sorcery*:

> *"Moon-worship is very ancient; it is alluded to as a forbidden thing in the Book of Job. From early times witches and other women worked their spells when stark-naked by the light of the full moon"*

The reasons given in *Aradia Gospel of the Witches* are very different from those which are given by Gerald Gardner in *Witchcraft Today*. He wrote on the subject of ritual nudity recalling the witches' rationale that it was the only way that they could release the power residing within their bodies. He went on to say:

> *"... this power they believe exudes from their bodies, clothes impeding its release..."*

To be fair to Gardner in this respect, he did go on to observe that it is difficult to say how much of this belief is real and how much is down to the imagination. The same explanation also appears, sometimes slightly adapted, in various versions of the Book of Shadows. In *Witchcraft Today* he also speculated about the power which could be released by a group of witches working naked vs. those working wearing bikinis, saying:

> *"At the same time one might heed the witches' dictum: 'You must be this way always in the rites, 'tis the command of the Goddess.' You must be this way so that it becomes second nature; you are no longer naked, you are simply natural and comfortable."*

Ceremonies and rituals honouring the Gods have been performed in the nude for thousands of years, and when not naked special costumes, setting those leading and participating apart from the *'mundane'* seem to be the norm, in the manner of robes and cloaks today.

Countless examples of rituals and magick being performed naked can be found throughout Africa, for example, but in reality our gaze need not be distracted from our own green British Isles for precedents of ritual nudity. In many instances the examples from the British Isles seem to point to preparation for war, where the clothes were removed, and the bodies painted as part of the preparation for fighting the enemy and ensuring victory. Such examples are recorded in Pliny's *Natural History*, where he also recorded the practice of ancient British women performing their rituals naked.

Medieval reproductions of witches often showed them naked. This can be seen in such classic images as *The Witch* by Albrecht Durer (1500) and *Witches Sabbath* and *Departing for the Sabbath* by Hans Baldung Grien (1510, 1514). Durer's painting of *The Four Witches* (1497) is significant in that it shows the women still wearing their headgear, which clearly indicates their different social classes from peasant to aristocrat, a distinction that disappears in the naked state. This is a point often made in modern writings centuries later.

Lastly, we suggest that the term *'skyclad'* is most likely borrowed from the Sanskrit word *'Digambar'*, the name of a sect of Jains. The term translates as *'sky-clad'* and was certainly well recorded throughout various publications during the late nineteenth century. The use of ritual nudity during Wiccan ceremonies has so many precedents within other religions that we have concentrated our attention on those sources of most direct relevance to the Wiccan tradition, in this instance the classical witch of the medieval period.

CHAPTER 7

A REAL WITCH'S WEAPON

In the Wiccan tradition one of the key tools is the black-handled knife, also known as the athame. The athame is unique amongst the tools in being symbolic of the individual witch, and as such is also referred to as *"the real witch's weapon"*. The athame is used for the casting of the magick circle, for invocations (e.g. the guardians of the watchtowers) and for consecrations (e.g. salt and water; cakes & wine; other ritual tools). It is never used for cutting physical objects, but might be used to cut doorways into the magick circle or for other such magickal uses.

Before we consider the probable origins of the athame and its use in the Wiccan tradition, we will also for a moment ponder on a modern tendency, found amongst some practitioners to use a blunt bladed athame, mentioned by Stewart and Janet Farrar in their book *The Witches Way*. The athame represents the will of the practitioner. Thus to have a blunted athame, representing your will, is also to have a blunted (or unfocused) will, which symbolically could represent being ineffective in directing your intent. The athame is used in a similar way to the sword, which is said to be used in the Wiccan tradition to command and direct both spirits and power. A deliberately blunted weapon on a symbolic level simply would not be able to command the same level of power for this use.

Many people have assumed that the use of knives in the Wiccan tradition comes from Gardner's exposure to the use of kris knives whilst living in Malaysia. In fact Gardner was so fascinated with these knives, which are also used for ceremonial purposes, that he wrote an entire book about them entitled *Kris and Other Malay Weapons,* first published in 1939. The assumption is that Gardner introduced the use of the athame because of his interest in the kris, but there are however clues which clearly demonstrate that this was not the case.

Firstly the waved (*lok*) shape of the blade itself is not one commonly used in Wiccan circles, where the blade is usually double edged and straight. Then the kris has a long history of use as a weapon of physical self defence, whilst the athame in the Wiccan tradition should never be used to draw blood.

Lots of myths do however exist around the kris as a magickal weapon with supernatural powers. In one such story a man commanded his kris dagger to shapeshift into a venomous snake which bit a beautiful girl putting her into a coma; she was then saved by the antidote he possessed and they lived happily ever after. This story accounts for the shape of the blade, as it is said that craftsmen took their inspiration from the story and set to work creating the blade in the shape of a small snake with an extremely sharp bite. Other magickal powers were ascribed to these knives too, including the power to turn the owner invisible, to protect the owners from a surprise attack and even the ability to fly long distances at night to attack and kill the enemies of the owner.

A letter from Austin Osman Spare to Kenneth Grant, dated 25 August 1954 shows the near-fanatical importance placed on magickal knives during the early development of Gerald Gardner's witch cult. The letter made reference to one of Gardner's friends, later identified as Diana Walden (Ameth), who claimed to be the head of the sole surviving witch-cult in Britain. The context in which she was discussed would indicate that Spare did not think much of her, nor her knowledge of witchcraft at the time of writing in 1954:

> *"Dr. Gardner of the Isle of Man sent along his deputy, a myopic stalky nymph…with two magickal knives that she insisted on*

showing me! Harmless and a little tiresome...what she was really interested in I don't think she herself knew. She believed the Witches Sabbath was some sort of Folk dance of pretty young things...I agreed that a Maypole may have symbolism-"[30]

The modern esoteric scholar Joseph Peterson has traced the word athame to one of the French manuscripts of the *Key of Solomon,* showing a range of alternative spellings including *arthame, arthane* and *artave,* English spellings of *arthanus* and *arthany,* and Latin spelling of *artavus,* the latter meaning *'penknife'.* The use of the word athame may well originate from this range of variant spellings in the *Key of Solomon.*

> *"The variability is easy to explain: Artavus is a Medieval Latin term, not found in most dictionaries. It is clearly described by Du Cange as 'a small knife used for sharpening the pens of scribes'."[31]*

Interestingly the spelling of *arthame* was also used by Grillot de Givry in his book *Witchcraft, Magic and Alchemy* first published in the French language in 1929 and in English in 1931. In this book de Givry discusses and quotes from a *Key of Solomon* manuscript, which he found in the *Bibliotheque de l'Arsenal* in Paris:

> *"The circle must be nine feet in diameter: this space is ample for comfortable room. It must be traced with the arthame, or consecrated knife, and says the manuscript, 'thou shalt make four Pentacles with the names of the Creator, and beyond these two circles thou shalt make a circle within a square by means of said arthame, as the circle here drawn will show and demonstrate to thee'."*

---

30 Zos Speaks, Kenneth and Steffi Grant, 1998
31 Joseph Peterson

The term *arthame* was subsequently used by authors such as the horror writer Clark Ashton Smith, who used it in a number of his short stories and novels, the first of which was *The Master of the Crabs,* published in 1948. Smith also referred to the kris knife in a number of his works, including his first published short story, *The Malay Krise,* published in 1910 in the magazine *Overland Monthly.* The combined use of the terms *arthame* and kris by a well known author prior to Gardner is an interesting synchronicity, and we must speculate as to whether Gardner may have drawn inspiration from Smith's work.

> *"for the Master wore his one-horned hat, and his cloak was girdled tightly about him, with the ancient arthame depending from the girdle in its shagreen sheath that time and the hands of many magickians had blackened."*[32]

In 1927, C.J.S. Thompson published the term *arthana* for the knife in his work *Mysteries and Secrets of Magic.* He was quoting from Sloane MSS 3847, the earliest known *Key of Solomon* manuscript (dated 1572), which also uses the terms *arthano, arthanos* and *arthany,* all for the same tool. Significantly this early manuscript advocates the use of the *arthana* for cutting:

> *"and bind all these herbs in a rod of hazel that must be cut off at one cut, with Arthana, as we have spoken of in the chapter of the knife"*

Another similar word found in the grimoires is the term *Athemay.* This word is used as the name of the Sun in summer in the fourteenth century *Heptameron,* and subsequently reproduced in Barrett's *The Magus.* Considering the association of the Sun with the will, and the athame's association with the will of the witch, this similarity is worthy of note.

---

32 The Master of the Crabs, Smith, March 1948 in Weird Tales

An alternative origin for the name athame was suggested by the Sufi writer Idries Shah in his 1961 book *Secret Societies*. Shah's suggestion was that athame was derived from the Arabic term *al-dhamme*, meaning *'blood-letter'*. Shah also claimed that Wicca and witchcraft derived from a medieval secret society in Moorish Spain, a claim which does not seem to be substantiated by any of the practices, as there is a lack of evidence linking them to that part of the world. However some traditional witches do claim a link between Arabic practices and witchcraft, though conclusive evidence of this is still outstanding.

A more interesting and plausible possible origin for the word athame was given by James Baker in his article *White Witches*, published in the book *Magical Religion and Modern Witchcraft* in 1996. Baker suggested the Old French word *attame*, meaning *'to pierce'* or *'to cut'* as the origin of the term athame.

The precedents for the use of the athame in the Wiccan tradition today probably originate within the grimoire tradition. The most obvious source of inspiration would have been the *Key of Solomon*, however it is important to keep in mind that the black-handled knife is also found in a number of other grimoires, including *The Grimoire of Honorius*. An important point to make here is that the images of black handled knives in the *Key of Solomon* show a single-edged blade, not a double-edged dagger as has become popular in modern times. However *The Grimoire of Honorius*, which we know was possessed by Gardner, does show a double-edged black-handled knife like a dagger rather than the single-edged type shown in the *Key of Solomon*.

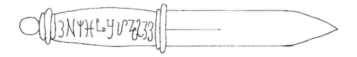

(The markings on the black-handled knife of Pope Honorius)

Reference was made by a number of authors in the late nineteenth and early twentieth century to the grimoire use of black handled knives. A.E. Waite referred to this in his *Book of Black Magic*, which was first published in 1898, saying:

> *"That with the black handle, destined to describe the circle and intimidate the spirits, and for performing other similar things..."*

The first source for the athame in Gardner's writings is his novel *High Magic's Aid*. An examination of the symbols shown on the illustration of the athame in *High Magic's Aid* clearly indicates Mathers' *Key of Solomon* as his primary source. We know that Gardner reproduced his illustrations from Mathers published *Key of Solomon* because they include a change made by Mathers and not found in any of the source manuscripts Mathers drew upon. In the preface of his *Key of Solomon*, Mathers wrote:

> *"In some places I have substituted the word AZOTH for 'Alpha and Omega,' e.g., on the blade of the Knife with the Black Hilt."*

Gardner's illustration of the athame blade contains the word Azoth, as substituted by Mathers, and the Hebrew divine names Yah (IH) and Elohim (ALHIM). These three words comprise the shorter top line of the two lines of names found on the blade of the black-handled knife in Mathers' *Key of Solomon*. Although subsequent images of the athame markings do not include any lettering on the blade, it is nonetheless relevant to look at these divine names and explore their significance.

(The black-handled knife markings as given for both the hilt and the blade in Mathers' Key of Solomon)

Azoth is a composite word used in medieval alchemy and subsequently in the magickal traditions of the Western Mystery Tradition. Its symbolism lies in its use of letters, representing the beginning and end. It is usually written with a Hebrew Aleph, the first letter of the Hebrew alphabet corresponding to the English letter 'A' and the Greek letter Alpha. The letter Z is next, followed by the Greek Omega (Ω) and the Hebrew Tav. All of these letters are the last in their respective alphabets. Azoth thus symbolises the beginning and end, and as a result all that lies within. It represents perfection and for this reason it is easy to see why Mathers should have substituted it for the divine name of *'Alpha and Omega'*, which also represents beginning and end (as the letters of the Greek alphabet). In alchemy this term also represented the Mercurial essence, part of the process of creating the Philosopher's Stone.

(Azoth as written on the blade of the black-handled knife by Mathers)

Next on the athame blade is the Hebrew letters Yod Heh (IH), pronounced *Yah*, which is the divine name of the sephira of Chokmah on the image of the Qabalistic Tree of Life. Chokmah means *'wisdom'* and this sephira is attributed to the zodiac and the masculine principle as the *'great father'*. Yah is also known as the *'inner chamber'*, as being the first part of the unpronounceable name of god, Tetragrammaton. In this context it is considered a symbol of sexual union between the masculine letter Yod and the feminine letter Heh as father and mother. In some ways it is a shame these names have been dropped, as they are particularly symbolically appropriate to the Wiccan tradition.

The other divine name on the athame blade is Elohim. Elohim is the pronunciation of ALHIM (Aleph Lamed Heh Yod Mem), and means *'gods'*. It is significant as a divine name in that it is a feminine singular noun with a masculine plural ending. So not only does it combine masculine and feminine, but it also combines singular and plural. From a Wiccan perspective it could be interpreted as the mother goddess (singular feminine beginning) giving birth to the gods (masculine plural ending). Elohim is also part of the divine names of all three of the Sephiroth on the Black or Feminine Pillar of Severity on the Tree of Life. Significantly the name Elohim can also be linked to the Lords of the Watchtowers, as we will show in the later chapter *The Mighty Ones*. The names of Yah and Elohim thus both combine divine masculine and divine feminine symbolism, which is highly appropriate for the athame in the Wiccan tradition.

As with the attributions of symbols and divine names around the magick circle, Gardner transposed the symbols on the handle of the black-handled knife from those found in Mathers' *Key of Solomon*. Thus the top line of symbols in the *Key of Solomon* became the bottom line in *High Magic's Aid* and vice versa, excluding the eight-rayed star figure at the end of the hilt nearest the blade. According to the Farrars in *The Witches' Way*, Gardner then subsequently divided these two lines of symbols in the Book of Shadows with his top line of symbols going on the left hand side of the hilt and the bottom line on the right hand side of the hilt. The Farrars also printed Valiente's version of the markings, together with her explanation of why she replaced some of the symbols with different ones.

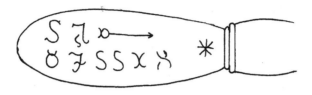

(The hilt of the black-handled knife as portrayed in Gerald Gardner's High Magic's Aid)

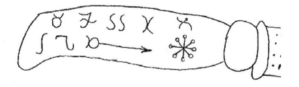

(The hilt of the black-handled knife as portrayed in Mathers' Key of Solomon)

What follows is a table with the symbols used by Gardner, the meanings of these symbols as published by the Farrar's on Doreen Valiente's information. In addition we also give the interpretation of the symbols as they are found in magickal documents and symbolic language throughout the centuries preceding Gardnerian Wicca. This clearly indicates a lack of basic understanding of the symbols being used by Gardner and Valiente as in all instances the symbolic meanings given by them have little or no bearing on what they were used for historically.

Symbol	Gardner	Symbolic interpretation
♉	Horned God	Taurus (fixed Earth) Muriel (angel of the Moon & Cancer) [33] Cauda Leonis (*'the tail of the lion'*) [34] Alzarhpa or Azarpha (the 12th of the 28 Mansions of the Moon which gives prosperity to harvests)[35] The alchemical principle of Salt[36]
⨍	Initial of his name[37]	Sun[38]
S	Kiss and Scourge	Venus[39] Air[40] Sand[41]

---

33 Three Books of Occult Philosophy, Agrippa, 1531

34 Anulorum Experimenta, Abano, 1303

35 Harley MS 6482, Thomas Rudd, 1712

36 Encylopédie Receueil de Planches, sur les Sciences et les Arts, Diderot, 1763

37 The Farrars point out in The Witches Way that this glyph is similar to the letter 'F' in the Theban Script. However they are mistaken in this, as a cursory glance will show that it does not resemble any of the letters of the Theban Script. Valiente chooses in her list of symbols to replace it with the ankh, misreading a Venus symbol. This may be because she has actually used the wrong bladed weapon as her basis! Study of her symbols and the differences from Gardner's athame markings reveals a different tool with the symbols used by Valiente, the poniard. However, although she has used the wrong tool, if we look at the weapons in the Key of Solomon, the poniard looks much more like the double-edged dagger that most people associate with the shape an athame should be.

38 Collection of medical observations, Tables of Sigils and Alchemical Receipts, Shelton, Sloane MS 997, 17th century

39 De aspectibus planetas ad Lunam, Scaliger, 15th century

40 Calendarium, Brahe, 1582

41 Lexicon Pharmaceutico-Chymicum, Sommerhoff, 1701

χ	Waxing and Waning Moon	Capricorn (the goat)[42] Pisces[43] Hanael (angel of Venus)[44] Prima Materia (the first material of alchemy from which life springs) [45] Realgar (arsenic sulphide, which burns with a brilliant white flame) [46]
$\varkappa$	Initial of her many names in Hebrew script[47]	As the first letter of the Hebrew alphabet it is attributed to the divine as the beginning, and also corresponds to the element of Air.
$*$	Eight ritual occasions, eight weapons	Gnostic symbol for Christ[48]
$\bowtie\!\!\!\longrightarrow$	Power flowing from the horned god	Mercury (planet) [49]
$\mathcal{L}$	Sickle, symbol of death[50]	Capricorn[51]

---

42 Three Books of Occult Philosophy, Agrippa, 1510

43 Astronomical and Astrological Tracts, Herne, 15th century

44 Calendarium, Brahe, 1582

45 Lexicon Pharmaceutico-Chymicum, Sommerhoff, 1701

46 Lexicon Pharmaceutico-Chymicum, Sommerhoff, 1701

47 Valiente replaces it completely with the astrological symbol for Scorpio as the sign of death and the Lord of the Underworld, and the dark half of the year in counterbalance to the light half of the year represented by the Taurus symbol.

48 Il Simbolism dei Giudeo-Christiani, Testa, 1962

49 A New and Complete illustration of the Occult Sciences, Sibley, 1790

50 Valiente changes it completely so it becomes the two sets of straight line figures which she calls 'the perfect couple'.

51 Greek Horoscopes, Neugebauer, 1959

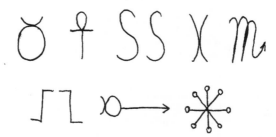

(*The markings on the athame according to Doreen Valiente, quoted in*
The Witches Way by Janet and Stewart Farrar)

(*The different knives used in the earliest known*
Key of Solomon, Sloane MS 3847)

So from the evidence it would seem that the idea of the athame, or the black-handled knife, is another practice which made its way into the tradition of Wicca straight from the *Key of Solomon*. We would point out that the earliest known manuscript of the Key of Solomon dating to 1572, Sloane MS 3847, has three different knives in it, the black knife (*'cuttellus niger'*), white knife (*'cuttellus albus'*) and arthany (a possible root of the word athame). Thus the terms were originally distinct and subsequently were equated. Additionally this manuscript does not distinguish between black and white handled knives in their function, saying:

"with such a knife as the circles should be made with, if it be grievous for you to make such a knife, finde some knife of the foresaid fashion, with a haft all white or all blacke,"

The markings given for the knife in this manuscript are completely different from those seen in the Mathers *Key of Solomon* and subsequently on the athame. They are:

(Sloane MS 3847)

Thus the symbols seen on the handle of the athame in Wicca, derived from the version of the *Key of Solomon* published by Mathers (which draws on seven manuscripts of which five are French), once again indicate a French connection to a practice found in the Wiccan tradition.

Many authors and researchers have suggested that due to the lack of perceived evidence for the use of such a knife in witchcraft practices prior to the twentieth century, this was a late addition to the practices of witchcraft and that as such it should be dismissed. However, there is plenty of evidence to suggest that a dagger with a black handle has a long history in use within the folk magick traditions of Europe prior to the time of Gerald Gardner, which supports the claims by Gardner that it was a traditional practice. The knife was rarely called by the name athame however, but that doesn't make it a different tool as it is still described in the same manner, and often used for similar purposes as one would expect from the athame.

We have already explained that the *Key of Solomon* was a text which was widely available to practitioners of magick, both *'high'* and *'low'* varieties, including the practitioners of folk magick such as the English and Welsh cunning folk. There is no reason why, considering that they were inspired by other practices found in the *Key of Solomon*, that they may not also have gleamed the use (or indeed additional uses) for the black-handled knife found in this text.

There are many examples of the use of a black-handled knife in pre-Gardnerian Witchcraft practices. A number of these examples come to us from Ireland, and some of the evidence would suggest that knowledge of the use of such knives was widespread. On the 22nd of April 1895, the *London Spectator* (newspaper) related details of the murder of a Mrs Cleary in the County of Tipperary (Ireland). Mrs Cleary was burned to death by her husband, who was convinced she was in fact a fairy changeling that had been substituted for his wife. He and his neighbours believed they would be able to rescue the real Mrs Cleary from the fairies.

> *"Again, after the burning, many of the men of the locality sat up all night in a 'fort' (earth embankment of ancient Irish village,) armed with black-handled knives. These poor people thought that a fairy procession would pass by; that in its midst would be Mrs Cleary riding on a gray horse, and that if anyone rushed forward and cut her bonds with a black-handled knife, (a potent weapon against all evil spirits,) she would at once be restored to the world."* [52]

This use against fairy folk was not restricted to Ireland. Wirt Sikes' 1880 book *British Goblins* described the use of the black-handled

---

[52] London Spectator, 22nd April 1895

knife for protection from Welsh fairies amongst the most effective amulets:

> *"The more worldly exorcisms, such as the production of a black-handled knife."*

In a footnote found in the story of Betty Sullivan published in the *Dublin University Magazine* of 1849, and described in more detail in the subsequent chapter on the *Magick Circle*, we find the following explanation for the use of the black-handled knife, once again linking it to the practices of magick a hundred years before Gardner's writings. Interestingly it also links its use to ceremonies performed on All Hallows Eve, which is of course known by the name of Samhain to modern Wiccans:

> *"A black-handled knife is an indispensable instrument in performing certain rites, and we shall have occasion to describe its virtues by-and-by. It is employed in the ceremonial of Hallow-Eve, and also in the mystic ceremonies performed at the rising of the new moon, as well as in certain diabolic mysteries made use of to include love etc."*

The black-handled knife turns up again and again in Irish folklore of the nineteenth century. In yet another legend, *The Man who killed a Spirit* recorded by Florence M'Carthy in 1843 for *The United States Democratic Review*, a wise woman by the name of Ould Molly gave instructions to a young lady called Mary which involved the use of a black-handled knife to help free her love, Tom Malloy from the possession of an evil spirit. Mary rewarded the wise woman with a generous gift of tea (which was a commodity of great value at the time). She obtained a black-handled knife and took it to the suffering Tom with instructions on how to use it against the spirit. Following the instructions, Tom struck the spirit through the heart once (and only

WICCA MAGICKAL BEGINNINGS

once) whilst on holy ground. Tom succeeded in ridding himself of the spirit and was able to continue his life with Mary as his wife.

A modern dictionary of Hiberno-English refers to a black-handled knife as a *Scian* saying:

> "...'*Scian na coise duibhe*' - a black-handled knife (regarded as a protection against the spirit world)..."[53]

In ancient Egypt knives were used as a symbol of protection and retribution. Malevolent creatures were often shown in images being cut with knives to render them powerless, giving a good example of the use of the knife in that culture, many thousands of years preceding that of the Irish folk magic uses, yet remarkably similar.

George Hill in *Notes and Queries* quotes from a newspaper from January 17, 1942 on the use of a black-handled knife by sailors in the Mediterranean.

> "In his 'Description de toute l'isle de Cypre' (Paris, 1580, fo 212) the Dominican Father Estienne de Lusignan describes a spell by which certain mariners have the power of dispersing tornadoes or whirlwinds.
>
> It is a custom of the mariners of the East, when they see whirlwinds approaching them, to take a knife, with which they make the sign of the Cross in the air, uttering these words of the Gospel of St John, 'In principio erat verbum, et Verbum erat apud Deum, et Deus erat Verbum:[54]' and incontinently the whirlwinds are broken up and divided. I have seen this remedy used twice, and the second time was when I came from Cyprus to Italy. In this procedure I find no superstition, except it be that the knife must have a black handle."

---

53 A Dictionary of Hiberno-English, Terrence Patrick Dolan, 1999

53 A Dictionary of Hiberno-English, Terrence Patrick Dolan, 1999
54 "In the beginning was the Word, and the Word was with God, and God was the Word." John 1:1.

The newspaper article goes on to say that similar spells were used against waterspouts, again using a black-handled knife to cut the waterspout, quoting Thevenot's work, *Voyage au Levant*.[55] This practice was also recorded in nineteenth century fiction, such as the novel *The Strange Adventures of Captain Dangerous* published in 1863.

> *"Our Sailors, to conjure it away, had recourse to the Superstitious Devices of cutting the air with a black-handled knife, and reading the first chapter of St John's Gospel, accounted of great efficacy in dispersing these Spouts."*

The suggestion that black-handled knives were a late addition to witchcraft is clearly inaccurate, as can be seen from the examples we have quoted. The black-handled knife has also been used for folk spells in Greece, including protection from nightmares. This was recorded comparatively by Robert Lawrence in *The Magic of the Horseshoe*:

> *"In Morocco it is customary to place a dagger under the patient's pillow, and in Greece a black-handled knife is similarly used to keep away the nightmare."*

Another example detailed by Lawrence was a charm using the black-handled knife to get rid of insects:

> *"The following charm against insects is in vogue in Lesbos: In the evening a black-handled knife is stuck in some spot where the insects congregate, and certain Greek verses are repeated, of which the following is a translation:--*

---

55 Voyage au Levant, Thevenot, 3rd edition, 1727

I got three naughty bairns together,
One a wasp, one caterpillar,
And a swarming ant the other.
Whate'er ye eat, whate'er ye drink,
Hence, hence avaunt,
To the hills and mountains flee,
And unto each fruitless tree.

The knife is to remain in the same spot until the next morning, and is then to be removed. This completes the charm, and the insects are expected to depart at once."

An early and particularly interesting source for the use of the black-handled knife is in connection with the *'princes of the thumb'*, a name given to specific demons summoned to stand on the palm of a young virgin boy within a magick circle to answer divinatory questions in sixteenth and seventeenth century Jewish magickal texts. This practice is referred to in Codex Gaster 315, where it describes tracing a circle in the earth with a black-handled knife and placing the young boy in the circle. His thumbnail and forehead are anointed with pure olive oil, and a conjuration whispered into his ear whilst he gazes at his thumbnail. This practice has much earlier antecedents than all the other sources, going back to the eleventh century, as described by Trachtenberg in his work *Jewish Magic and Superstition.*

> *"Rashi, in the eleventh century (San 67b), mentions that a black-handled knife is required in invoking the 'princes of the thumbnail'; three MSS from Spain, Tunis and the Orient, dating from the 16th to 18th centuries (Daiches 54, 18, 22), do not fail to include the black-handled knife!"*

So far from being a contemporary inclusion by Gardner in the Wiccan tradition, we can clearly see that the black-handled knife has a well documented history of magickal use in a number of traditions in a range of countries which dates back at least a thousand years. We also see that many of these uses involve the creation of magick circles or protection from spiritual creatures, functions which are still seen with the Wiccan athame. These include the grimoires and Irish and Welsh folk magick, showing that the use of the black-handled knife was a well-known practice in the British Isles long before the emergence of Wicca. So although the name athame may be a more recent usage, nevertheless the black handled knife as a magickal tool is definitely not.

CHAPTER 8

MAGICK CIRCLE

The magick circle is one of the most quintessential aspects of Wiccan practice, defining the space where all the ceremonies are performed. The magick circle is usually cast by the High Priestess of the coven. Typically the athame or sword is used for the casting, though the wand may also be used in some circumstances. The person casting the magick circle walks a complete circuit in a sunwise direction around the circle speaking words of conjuration, whilst tracing the boundaries of the magick circle.

When considering the origins of the magick circle, there are a number of factors we need to explore. These factors include the size of the magick circle, the use of tools and words in constructing the magick circle, the form of the magick circle, and the use of the circle to contain power and to exclude unwanted influences.

In his book *Witchcraft Today*, Gardner wrote that the magick circle should be nine foot in diameter, unless it was created for a very specific purpose. He went on to say that:

> "There are two outer circles, each six inches apart, so the third circle has a diameter of eleven feet."

The same instruction for a nine foot circle, with two subsequent outer circles, each a foot greater, can also be found in some of the earlier Wiccan Books of Shadows. This would give a diameter of eleven foot for the outermost Circle, as stated by Gardner.

This practice is taken directly from the *Key of Solomon* which we will subsequently demonstrate as providing much of the ritual of purification and consecration of the magick circle. Mathers' publication of the *Key of Solomon* records that you should:

> *"take thou the Sickle or Scimitar of Art and stick it into the centre of the place where the Circle is to be made; then take a cord of nine feet in length, fasten one end thereof unto the Sickle and with the other end trace out the circumference of the Circle, which may be marked either with the Sword or with the Knife with the Black hilt. Then within the Circle mark out four regions, namely, towards the East, West, South, and North, wherein place Symbols; and beyond the limits of this Circle describe with the Consecrated Knife or Sword another Circle ... Beyond this again thou shalt describe another Circle at a foot distance with the aforesaid Instrument."*

There is absolutely no doubt in our minds that this is the source of inspiration for the creation of the magick circle as found in the Wiccan tradition. However, it is not correct to say that the magick circle used by Gerald Gardner has been taken directly from a *Key of Solomon*. Considering the magick circle as recorded by Gardner in his novel *High Magic's Aid* we find some rather strange differences to those given in the Mathers edition of the *Key of Solomon*. The magick circle shown in *High Magic's Aid* is the same one which Gardner had in the Witchcraft Museum in Castletown, in the Isle of Man, as illustrated in photographs from the time which have been reproduced in books such as Doreen Valiente's *The Rebirth of Witchcraft*.

The magick circle reproduced by Gardner in *High Magic's Aid*, is often described as Solomonic, but it is in fact a composite with a number of errors introduced into it, possibly through a lack of understanding of Hebrew by the copier of the image or as a deliberate blind.

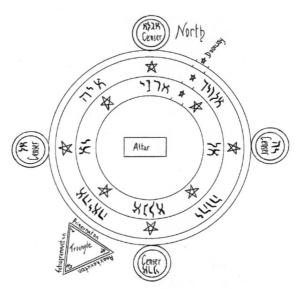

(The Magick Circle as portrayed in Gardner's novel High Magic's Aid)

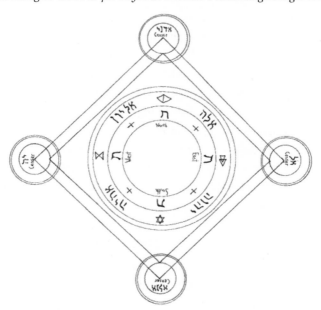

(The Magick Circle as given in the Mathers' Key of Solomon)

In fact this magick circle is based on the one in the frontplate of Mathers' *Key of Solomon,* with a number of changes made to the original image which produce a new magick circle not found in any of the grimoires. These changes are as follows:

The four small outer circles containing censers have had the divine names transposed North-South and East-West. Thus we see:

Direction	Key of Solomon	High Magic's Aid
North	ADNI	AGLA
East	AL	IH
South	AGLA	ADNI
West	IH	AL

In the inner circle, where there are four equal-armed crosses on the cross-quarters in the *Key of Solomon* magick circle, these are replaced in *High Magic's Aid* with pentagrams. Likewise, in the second circle in the *Key of Solomon,* where there are the four hexagram permutations of two triangles at the cardinal points, these are also replaced in *High Magic's Aid* with pentagrams. Gardner also introduced pentagrams in the north north-east of the magick circles to represent the entrance, which is not included in the *Key of Solomon* circle.

The inner circle of the *Key of Solomon* magick circle has the Hebrew letter Tav at the cardinal points, which are replaced in the *High Magic's Aid* magick circle with the divine names attributed to the cardinal points in the censers (not transposed this time). However there is an error here with the western name written as IA instead of IH.

The second circle in the *Key of Solomon* magick circle has other divine names at the cross-quarter points. Two of these are miscopied (South-West and North-West) and two are transposed (North-East and North-West) in the *High Magic's Aid* magick circle. Thus we have:

Direction	Key of Solomon	High Magic's Aid	Correction to HMA
North-East	ALH	ALVIK	Should be ALHIM, Heh (H) miscopied as Vav (V), Mem (M) miscopied as Kaph (K)
South-East	IHVH	IHVH	
South-West	AHIH	AHIAH	Should be AHIH, additional Aleph (A) added
North-West	ALHIM	AIH	Should be ALH, Lamed (L) miscopied as Yod (I)

If we now turn our attention to the triangle on the diagram in *High Magic's Aid*, this was taken not from the *Key of Solomon* but from the *Goetia*. The original source was Sloane MS 2731, which is reproduced in Crowley's *Goetia*. The copyist has again made an error, this time in only partially copying the name of the archangel Michael in the inner corners of the triangle. This reads Mi-CH-L, and should read Mi-Cha-El. We may also note that the triangle is not shown next to the circle in any of the grimoires, and should be further away (two foot away). By its position the implication is that this triangle was used for an operation to summon one of the *Wandering Princes*, either Icosiel or Soleviel, both of whom are described as good spirits.

The final addition to the *High Magic's Aid* magick circle, not seen in any images of a magick circle from grimoires like the *Key of Solomon* or *Goetia,* is a central altar. The altar is important to Wiccan practice, being the working table used during ceremonies. Grimoires such as the *Key of Solomon* and *Goetia* did not make use of an altar, as all the tools were carried by acolytes or placed on the floor. However if we look at the *Book of Abramelin*, which was contemporary to these grimoires, we see the use of an altar in which the tools are stored:

"The altar, which should be made of wood, ought to be hollow within after the manner of a cupboard, wherein you shall keep all the necessary things, such as the two robes, the crown or mitre, the wand, the holy oils, the girdle or belt, the perfume; and any other things which may be necessary."

It is significant in the *Key of Solomon* that the magick circle *"may be marked either with the Sword or with the Knife with the Black hilt"*, as this clearly introduces the idea of casting the circle with the sword or athame. The use of magick tools to cast circles has a long history extending back to the ancient world. The use of the wand for this purpose, which is given as an option in the Wiccan tradition, is prominent in the history of magick circles.

In the fifteenth century the German Abbot Johannes Trithemius described the use of an ebony wand to trace the circle whilst speaking the conjuration in *The Art of Drawing Spirits into Crystals*. This short booklet was a small part of the material included by Francis Barrett in his famous work *The Magus* in 1801, which provided a wealth of material from the grimoires, Qabalah and on natural magick in an accessible printed book in English for the first time.

In the *Grimoire of Pope Honorius* the writer suggested that the magick circle should be marked with charcoal which has been blessed with salt, or as an alternative with chalk, the latter being the more popular choice for later magickians.

One of the later grimoires makes specific reference to the use of the knife to trace the existing magick circle upon entry within. This is the *Grimorium Verum ("The True Grimoire")*, a latecomer to the grimoires, being dated to 1817 in its earliest form. It is largely derivative of earlier grimoires like the *Key of Solomon*, but the knife reference is interesting in the context of Wiccan practice in its use to trace the circle which has already been drawn:

"Once inside, trace your ring (or circle) with the knife of the art."

In her book *Magic in Ancient Egypt,* the prominent modern Egyptologist Geraldine Pinch has postulated that wands were used in Ancient Egyptian practices, to draw magick circles:

> *"Abrasions on the pointed ends of some wands suggest that they were used to mark out lines, probably a protective circle, in sand or clay."*

We also find a further precursor for the use of a magick circle marked on the ground in ancient Assyria, with a recorded example of an Assyrian sorceror using lime and corn flour found in R. Campbell Thompson's 1908 work *Semitic Magic*:

> *"I have completed the usurtu (magick circle), with a sprinkling of lime I have surrounded them. The flour of Nisaba (the corn god), the ban of the great gods I have set around them."*

The ancient Greeks used the wand as a primary tool in their magick, a theme that was to continue for many centuries, from ancient Egypt all the way through to the grimoires and into the modern magickal traditions.

> *"Hubert thus describes the ceremonial and apparatus employed by the Greek magician. The most important implement was the wand, without which no magician was completely equipped."*[56]

As well as magickal tools, words are part of the construction of the magick circle. In many of the grimoires there is no mention of words being spoken during the construction of the magick circle, a practice which is very much used in the Wiccan tradition. There are however exceptions which hint at possible origins for this practice. In the *Grimoire of Pope Honorius*, dating back to 1670, we find instructions on

---

56 The Mysteries and Secrets of Magic, Thompson, C.J.S, 1927

words to be spoken whilst making the magick circle. Although the phraseology bears no resemblance to the words used in Wicca, the heading of *"That which must be said whilst making the protective circle"* is clearly descriptive of the union of words with actions and can also be seen to contain recognisable themes expressed in the Wiccan circle casting. Here we may note that Gardner possessed a manuscript copy of the *Grimoire of Pope Honorius* in his collection. The grimoire gives the following wording:

> *"I make this circle to bind and restrain the evil spirits, in the Name of the Father + and of the Son + and of the Holy Ghost + that it may be impossible for any of the evil spirits to enter into the circle or to work evil to any who may be present in any way whatsoever"*

Significantly more than a century earlier, Trithemius in *The Art of Drawing Spirits into Crystals* gives words to be spoken whilst tracing the magick circle, with a black ebony wand as previously discussed. Again the protective nature of the magick circle is stressed:

> *"In the name of the blessed Trinity, I consecrate this piece of ground for our defence; so that no evil spirit may have power to break these bounds prescribed here; through Jesus Christ our Lord. Amen."*

Another grimoire, the Munich Manuscript (Clm 849), is covered in detail by the author and researcher Richard Kieckhefer in his book *Forbidden Rites*. This fifteenth century German grimoire, written in Latin, contains interesting examples of a pre-*Key of Solomon* circle casting with many of the same components later seen in the Wiccan magick circle. The conjuration of the spirits at the end is repeated at each cardinal point, summoning the spirits in a similar manner to the guardians of the watchtowers.

"...*in a secret place outside of town, under a clear sky, on level ground, trace a circle such as appears here, with a magnificent sword, writing these names and everything shown along with them ... when you have done this, take blessed water and sprinkle yourself and the circle, saying 'Asperges me, Domine ...' [Ps 50:9]. When you have done this, kneel facing the east, and in a strong voice say, 'I, so-and-so, conjure you, O Fyriel, Mememil, Berith, Taraor, powerful, magnificent, illustrious spirits',*"

The location of the magick circle was also another important consideration. Isolation was extremely important, to avoid being discovered and then subject to punishment. In his *Discoverie of Witchcraft,* Scot went into some detail on this subject:

"*As for the places of Magickal Circles ... either in Woods or Deserts, or in a place where three wayes meet, or amongst ruines of Castles, Abbies, Monasteries, &c or upon the Seashore when the Moon shines clear, or else in some large Parlour hung with black, and the floor covered with the same, with doors and windows closely shut, and Waxen Candles lighted.*"

More than two centuries earlier, in 1323, French judicial records describe the actions of a band of monks and canons near Paris who wished to recover stolen money. They planned to stand in a circle made from the skin of a cat, and from within the magick circle to invoke the demon Berith to answer their inquiries.[57] However the use of magick circles went beyond clerical nigromancy in the following centuries. The *Directorium Inquisitorum* of the Catalan Dominican Nicolàs Eymerich, printed in 1376 described three types of witchcraft, and the third of these has clear parallels to the practices regarding the '*princes of the thumb*' referred to in the previous chapter, *A Real Witch's Weapon,* and

---

57 Life in the Middle Ages, Coulton, 1928

96

links witchcraft to the magick circle and the sword at a very early date. Eymerich refers to:

> *"The witchcraft of those who summon up devils by tracing magickal signs, by placing a child in the middle of a circle, by using a sword or mirror."*

A few decades later in 1452 a woman was charged with witchcraft in Provins in France, of conjuring the devil with her associated group of witches by tracing three concentric circles on the ground.[58] This clearly parallels the magick circles found in grimoires such as the *Key of Solomon*.

The use of a triple circle in folk magick was also to be found in Russia in the Middle Ages. In his definitive volume *The Bathhouse at Midnight*, Ryan records a livestock protection ritual performed on January 6th:

> *"The owner was to bring home some water from the Blessing of the Water ceremony, put a sheaf of mixed cereal crops in the form of a cross in the farmyard, and then drive in the livestock. The owner's wife was to put on her sheepskin coat inside out, draw a circle with an axe three times round the sheaves and livestock while holding in the other hand an icon and a candle. The owner followed her sprinkling the blessed water over the sheaves and animals with a bunch of head of rye. The wife then threw the axe over the animals."*

In referring to the witch trial of Mrs Samuel in 1593, Richard Boulton reproduced an interesting image in his 1715 work *A Compleat History of Magick, Sorcery and Witchcraft*. The picture shows a witch in a double magick circle, containing candles. She has a book (Liber

---

58 Quellen und Untersuchungen zur Geschichte des Hexenwahns und der Hexenfolgung im Mittelalter, Hansen, 1901

Spirituum) at her feet and waves a wand at the devil she has conjured. This image is striking as it shows a witch in a double magick circle conjuring a demon, which she has clearly summoned using the book lying at her feet. To put this into perspective, this image shows a witch performing grimoire magick, giving a clear convergence of the two forms of magick in the early eighteenth century.

(Mrs Samuel, The Witch, in Richard Boulton's
A Compleat History of Magick, Sorcery and Witchcraft, 1715)

A major functional difference between the Wiccan magick circle and the magick circles of the grimoires and others discussed above is the concept of *'being between the worlds'* when working within it. This seemingly modern concept of being *'between the worlds'* may derive from the ancient Egyptian concept of there being no time when within a sacred space. This was because for the Egyptians stepping into a sacred space was seen as returning to the beginning of time, to enable the priest to tap into the energies of creation. This was expressed very clearly by the religious historian Mircea Eliade, who wrote in his book *The Sacred and the Profane*:

> *"by its very nature sacred time is reversible in the sense that, properly speaking, it is a primordial mythical time made present. Every religious festival, any liturgical time, represents the reactualisation of a sacred event that took place in a mythical past, 'in the beginning'."*

It is clear that the use of the magick circle in the Wiccan tradition initially appears to derive from the Grimoire Tradition. Considering the examples given previously of magick circles being linked to medieval witchcraft at a time when the earliest grimoires were starting to appear, the possibility of magick circles entering into witchcraft via a different route cannot be ignored.

The use of the magick circle predates the grimoires by many centuries, and we need to explore the earlier use of magick circles further to understand their passage through time into the Wiccan tradition. Examples of the use of the magick circle can be found going back at least five thousand years, sometimes with remarkable resemblance to the way in which it is used and created in the Wiccan tradition. For example, sprinkling with water, censing, and even sweeping with a broom were all components of preparing the space which were used in Ancient Egypt, as described by Pinch in her work *Magic in Ancient Egypt*:

> *"The area where a rite was to take place was also purified. The floor was sprinkled with water and swept with a special broom. A layer of clean sand might be spread and the area fumigated with incense smoke."*

Idries Shah, who wrote on grimoires and oriental magic in the late 1950s, gave an interesting example from Assyria of the magick circle in his book *Oriental Magic*. Giving a translation of a *Surpu* tablet dating to around 1600 BCE the book records a magick circle charm used to describe a holy defence which the gods were believed to provide to the faithful against the powers of darkness, as an impenetrable barrier. The long piece starts:

> *"Ban! Ban! Barrier that none can pass,*
> *Barrier of the gods, that none may break,*
> *Barrier of heaven and earth that none can change,*
> *Which no god may annul"*

Idries Shah's connection to Gerald Gardner has long been understated. In addition to being the ghost writer of *Gerald Gardner: Witch,* the biography attributed to Jack Bracelin and published by Shah's own publishing house Octagon Press; he also acted as Gardner's secretary for a period of time in his latter years. Although Shah would later become famous as the most influential Sufi writer of modern times, we can only speculate what influence he may have contributed to the evolution of the Wiccan tradition through his extensive knowledge of grimoires and obscure oriental magick.

In the ancient Babylonian myths we find a reference to a magick circle created by the magick god, Ea (also known as Enki). Ea created this magick circle in order to thwart the murderous designs of his father, the god Apsu who planned on killing all of his children due to their boisterous behaviour! It is believed, based on both the style of the writing and other cultural evidence that this story may in fact date up to a thousand years earlier than the recorded date of 1000 BCE, dating it to at least 2000 BCE.

> *"The one of supreme understanding, the skilful (and) wise,*
> *Ea, who understands everything, saw through their plan.*

He made and established against it a magickal circle for all."[59]

Elsewhere, in Jewish mythology, we find the story of *Honi, the circle drawer* from around the first century BCE. The story, recorded in *M. Taanit 3:1*, tells of Honi who was approached by his community to pray for rain.[60] Honi prayed, but the rain did not fall, and he decided to take more drastic action. He drew a circle and standing inside it addressed God asking for rain on behalf of the people. Rain started falling in small drops. Honi once again addressed God and asked that the rain should fall sufficiently so that it would fill the pits, ditches and caves. Now the rain fell in *'anger'* (i.e. heavily) and again Honi addressed God saying he did not ask for such heavy rain, but for rains of benevolence, blessing and generosity. Upon this the rain started falling as required.

The use of a magick circle also turns up frequently in the folk practices of Ireland, often in association with the fairy or other spirits. In 1849 *Dublin University Magazine* described the case of a woman by the name of Betty Sullivan, who died in childbirth. She was laid out for a wake and mourners cried over her body for two days and nights. At this point her husband dreamed that Betty wasn't dead at all, but that she had in fact been carried off by some of the *'good people'* to nurse the child of the fairy king, Donn Firinne. In the dream Betty's husband was told that if he still had feelings for her he could rescue her if he adhered to the following instructions at the cross-roads of Ballinatray at midnight:

> *"and there performing certain incantations, as precisely at that hour she was to pass by with a grand cavalcade of fairy ladies and gentlemen. He was to know her by seeing her mounted on a white horse at the rear of the whole party. First of all he was to provide*

---

59 Babylonian Genesis, Tablet I.60-1
60 New Testament Background: Selected Documents, Barrett, 1956.

himself with some holy water and a prayer-book, as well as some
sprigs of yarrow, which should be cut by moonlight with a black-
handled knife, certain mystic words having been first pronounced on
the herb..."

Once he arrived at the appointed place he was to sprinkle it with the holy water, using the yarrow and then draw a circle round him on the road, large enough for the fairy procession to pass through. Then using a hazel wand he had to draw a cross in the circle, starting at the eastern point and ending at the Western. Having repeated certain prayers facing the Moon he had to fix his eye on the white horse his wife was on and pull her off, if possible, once she was near enough without leaving the circle himself. If he failed, Betty would be lost to him forever; luckily for the couple he succeeded and rescued her.

There are several elements of note in this story when exploring the origins of Wiccan magickal practices. Not only the midnight magick circle, but also the use of the black-handled knife and the hazel wand. The hazel wand is a significant tool in the *Key of Solomon*, with a description given on how to make it:

"and the Wand of hazel or nut tree, in all cases the wood being virgin,
that is of one year's growth only. They should each be cut from the
tree at a single stroke, on the day of Mercury, at sunrise. The
characters shown should be written or engraved thereon in the day
and hour of Mercury."

A curious novel written in 1838 entitled *The Jew's Daughter or The Witch of the Water-side* contains a description of the creation of a magick circle and also the use of a steel wand (which would be as effective as a sword for use in controlling spirits), together with the use of chanting and salutations to the East, which is the traditional place for the casting of the circle to start from in the Wiccan tradition. The witch Myrza uses herbs, her wand and the power of the elements to great effect through the story:

> *"She took her long steel wand into her hand, and, after pointing it to the east three times, and bowing herself to the ground, drew from a recess a number of living snakes, which she placed just within the edge of the circle that she had drawn around her. She then waved her branch of mistletoe, and again stretching out her wand to the east, bowed herself thrice, chanting all the time a monotonous measure, the import of which was to remind certain unseen beings of her past necromantic adventures."*

We have included these examples to illustrate the widespread knowledge of the use of the magick circle, both in folklore and literature as well as in the magickal texts of previous centuries.

Those familiar with the personal recorded history of Gerald Gardner, will know that he spent a great deal of time in Malaysia prior to his return to retirement in England. It is generally believed that during his time amongst the Malay people, Gardner learned a great deal about their magickal practices and that this in turn would inspire some of his own work years later. An example of this is recorded in *Gerald Gardner: Witch*:

> *"Gardner himself frequently visited the séances which were held in kampongs close to Mawo Estate"*

Though not constructed in the same way, circles are still considered auspicious shapes by the Malay magickians, who Mircea Eliade records employing them when conducting séances in his classic work *Shamanism*:

> *"The séance proper takes place inside a round hut of a magic circle, and the object of most séances is cure, the discovery of lost or stolen*

objects, or knowledge of the future. Usually the shaman remains under a covering during the séance. Censing, dancing, music, and drumming are the indispensable preparatory elements in any Malayan séance"

Another consideration in regard to the magick circle is that of the use of ritual movement within it. In a Wiccan magick circle all movement is performed sunwise (deosil) unless it is for the purposes of banishing, in which case movement is performed anti-sunwise (widdershins). The immediate precedent for this is to be found in Aleister Crowley's classic work *Magick*, where he observes of spirals that *"like the circumambulation, if performed deosil they invoke - if widdershins they banish."* The magickal use of the terms deosil and widdershins together in Crowley's work is significant, indicating again the use of his writings as possible source material, though the terms also turn up at times separately in older texts.

Margaret Murray used the term *'widdershins'* in her *The Witch Cult in Western Europe*, relating it to the rites of the witches:

"In Lorraine the round dance always moved to the left. As the dancers faced outwards, this would mean that they moved 'widdershins', i.e. against the sun."

At this point we should consider the actions which correspond to moving deosil and widdershins in a circle. A deosil circle will be walked with the left hand side of the body on the outside and the right on the inside. This means the natural tendency would be to use the left hand to cast the magick circle, rather than reach across the body with the right hand. Although deosil is *'sunwise'*, most Wiccan magick circles are cast at night, so the movement of the sun is not that relevant a factor, unless the ritual is specifically focused on a solar deity. The use of the left hand side would be symbolically appropriate for several reasons.

The use of the term deosil may be a later incidental addition to the more significant factor of the practice of using the left, or sinister, side of the body. Negative or *'black'* magick is commonly called *'the left-hand path'*. This is a very old association, seen from the Latin word sinister meaning both *'left'* and *'evil'*, and even earlier in the ancient world where movement to the right was seen as propitious and to the left as unfavourable. This combination of the left with black magick was also extended to women and the moon. It became established Christian doctrine that Eve was formed from the smallest rib on Adam's left side, supporting the identification of woman with the left and evil.

This connection between the left side of the body and magick is seen particularly in the Celtic mysteries, e.g. with the corrguinecht (*'heron/crane-killing'*) posture adopted by several of the Celtic deities. It is first recorded in the ninth century, being used by the god Lugh in *The Second Battle of Moytura* (*Cath Maige Tuired*) against the opposing army of the Fomorians. It is also used by the goddess Badb in the twelfth century tale of the *Destruction of Da Derga's Hostel* (*Togail Bruidne Da Derga*) and the goddess Morrigan in the fifteenth century *Destruction of Da Choca's Hostel* (*Bruiden Da Chocae*). This posture, used for prophecy and cursing, involved standing on the left leg, pointing with the left arm and closing the right eye, thus entirely concentrating the body's energy in the left side.

The association with the left is also seen in Tantra, which is known as the *Vama Marg*, or *'Left Hand Path'*. It is so called because of the emphasis placed on unconventional and taboo areas of Indian religious life. Thus Tantra places more emphasis on sex, death and individuality, and being outside the boundaries, whereas conventional Hinduism has very clearly defined boundaries.

In using the term widdershins Murray was recording a phrase which saw popular use long before her work. In a report of the case of Johanne Feane (Cwninghame) schoolmaster of Saltpans, Lothian, who was arraigned for witchcraft and high treason on the 26th of December

1590, which appeared in the book *Witch Stories* by Lynn Linton first published in 1861 we find the following:

> *"A further count was, that once again he consorted with Satan and his crew, still in North Berwick church, where they paced round the church wider shins (wider sheins), that is contrary to the way of the sun..."*

The term widdershins also frequently turned up in prose during the eighteenth and nineteenth century, one such example being in the book *Popular Rhymes, sayings and Proverbs of the county of Berwick* which was published in 1856, in a poem entitled *'Betty Bathgate the Witch'*

> *"...Widdershins, widdershins,*
> *How she runs widdershins!*
> *She's sunken Geordie Houldie's ship*
> *And drown'd his men in it;*
> *She, and her devilish squad*
> *Hae gar'd Tom Burgon's nag rin mad;*
> *She' shaken a' Pate Trumbul's bere,*
> *And kill'd the cow o' Robin Weir!*
> *Now she rins widdershins,*
> *Nine times round the grey stane,*
> *Nine times round the riddle!"*

There are much older examples of this principle to be seen in ancient Egypt, where all movement in the magick space was conducted sunwise (deosil), in the direction of the daily journey of the Sun god Re. Any anti-sunwise movement was considered to be inviting *isfet* (chaos and disorder) and was avoided at all costs. This principle of creation being associated with sunwise movement and disorder or negativity being associated with anti-sunwise movement is still adhered to today in the Wiccan tradition five thousand years later.

Recording the witch trials in his book *Saducismus Triumphatus* (1681), Joseph Glanvill recorded the 1664 confession of the witch Elizabeth Styles, who said that when they parted from their meeting the witches said *"A Boy! Merry meet, merry part"*, which may be the origin of the *"merry meet, merry part, and merry meet again"* at the end of ceremonies. However the words spoken at the end of the old second degree Masonic initiation could also be the root of this phrase, being *"Happy have we met, happy have we been, happy may we part, and happy meet again!"* In fact it would seem some form of merging between the two is likely for the words spoken at the end of some Wiccan ceremonies.

In discussing the use of the magick circle we drew attention to its function to contain the power raised and also to exclude any unwanted influences. In his book *Fifty Years of Wicca*, Frederic Lamond quotes Gerald Gardner as saying:

> *"Ceremonial magickians draw a circle to keep out the spirits they summon. Witches draw a circle to keep the power we raise in."*

This is a simplistic generalisation, as in fact the magick circle in the Wiccan tradition fulfils both of these purposes. Let us consider the antecedents of the magick circle being used to contain power. Anglo-Saxon leech-craft made use of circles to keep power in at times, and may be the source of this belief. Although it contained a merging of Heathen and Christian belief, the significant magickal practice which occurred was the drawing of circles around wounds or infections to *contain* the affliction. This principle was also applied to the picking of some plants, where a circle was drawn on the ground with a knife to contain the healing power of the plant within it when it was picked.[61]

A recurrence of the same principle is seen in Renaissance alchemy, where we find examples such as the drawing of *"a circle around a pestilential carbuncle with a sapphire, the carbuncle will soon turn black and*

---

61 Anglo-Saxon Magic, Storms, 1948

fall off."[62] Similarly circles were drawn around the eye with a sapphire to preserve the sight in cases of measles and smallpox.

This idea of the magick circle being used to focus power has much earlier roots however, showing far earlier precedents for the subsequent Wiccan practice. Kieckhefer makes an interesting observation in his work *Forbidden Rites* when he states:

> *"The circle as a locus of power, enhancing the power of the operator, is ancient; it appears, for example, in the early Jewish story of Honi the Circle-Drawer and in the Greek magical papyri."*

A variant of this can also be found in India, as recorded in the book *Witchcraft in Western India* by Kapur, who describes in a necromantic rite how:

> *"A magic circle is drawn around the particular grave, which is then opened. The corpse brought out of it kept within the circle – with its head facing east. The black magician touches the body three times with a wand of human thigh bone or his sacrificial knife, and commands it, in the name of Kali, to rise and answer."*

Next we need to consider the purification and consecration of the space in which ceremonies are performed. This is done through the consecration of a bowl each of water and salt, usually by the High Priestess, sometimes with the assistance of the High Priest.

The consecrations of the salt and water in Wiccan ceremonies have been widely published and with minor variations usually follow a style like those given below:

> *"I exorcise thee, O creature of Water, that thou cast out from Thee all the impurities and uncleanness of the Spirits of the World of*

---

62 Prodromus chamiae rationalis, de Maets, 1693

Phantasm, this I do in the holy and most potent names of our Lady and our Lord."

"Blessings be upon thee creature of Salt, let all malignity and hindrance be cast forth from thee, and let all good enter herein, wherefore I bless thee and invoke thee, that thou mayest aid me in the holy and most potent names of our Lady and our Lord."

The wording of these consecrations is drawn directly from the *Key of Solomon* where we find the following exorcism of the water and benediction of the salt:

"I exorcise thee, O Creature of Water, by Him Who hath created thee and gathered thee together in one place so that the dry land appeared, that thou uncover all the deceits of the Enemy, and that thou cast out from thee all the impurities and uncleanliness of the Spirits of the World of Phantasm, so that they may harm me not, through the virtue of God Almighty Who liveth and reigneth unto the Age of the Ages. Amen"

"The blessing of the Father almighty be upon this Creature of Salt, and let all malignity and hindrance be cast forth hencefrom, and let all good enter herein, for without Thee man cannot live, wherefore I bless thee and invoke thee, that thou mayest aid me."

This not only shows a provenance for the words used, but also for the *'exorcism'* of the water and the *'blessing'* of the salt as it is found in the Wiccan tradition. However, the use of the salt and water consecrated in this way found in the *Key of Solomon* confusingly does not relate to the consecration or purification of the magick circle. Instead it relates to the ritual bathing which is performed as part of the personal purification prior to the ceremonies found in the *Key of Solomon*:

> *"The Bath is necessary for all Magickal and Necromantic Arts;*
> *wherefore, if thou wishest to perform any experiment or operation,*
> *having arranged all things necessary thereunto according to the*
> *proper days and hours, thou shalt go unto a river or running*
> *stream…"*

The *Key of Solomon* also provide us with the practice of sprinkling the circle with water and salt, instructions on how this should be done are found under the heading of *'Of the Water, and of the Hyssop'*. The magician is instructed therein to take a vessel made of brass and to fill it with *"the most clear spring water"* and salt. A consecration is said over the salt:

> *"Tzabaoth, Messiach, Emanuel, Elohim Gibor, Yod He Vau He; O*
> *God Who are the Truth and the Life, deign to bless and sanctify this*
> *Creature of Salt, to serve unto us for help, protection and assistance*
> *in this Art, experiment, and operation, and may it be a succour unto*
> *us"*

This done, several Psalms are read over the salt and a sprinkler is made by bundling the following herbs, gathered in the day and hour of Mercury, whilst the Moon is waxing: vervain, fennel, lavender, sage, valerian, mint, garden-basil, rosemary and hyssop. The herbs should be tied together using a thread spun by a young maiden and various inscriptions are to be made onto the handle. The *Key of Solomon* goes on to say that once this is done this water may then be used whenever necessary, by sprinkling it with the specially made sprinkler and that:

> *"wheresoever thou shalt sprinkle this Water, it will chase away all*
> *Phantoms, and they shall be unable to hinder or annoy any. With*
> *this same Water thou shalt make all the preparations of the Art"*

Through this we find a further precedent for Wiccan ceremony in the *Key of Solomon* – that of the actual practice of sprinkling the magick circle in order to cleanse and purify the space for use during ceremonies.

It can be demonstrated that the material found in the *Key of Solomon* existed as part of an even older tradition of magickal texts. For example, the *Heptameron* which was first published in 1496, attributed to the Italian physician Peter de Abano (1250-1317), contains material which clearly influenced the *Key of Solomon*. Thus in the *Heptameron* we see for example the use of water for the purification of the magick circle:

> *"When the Circle is rightly perfected, sprinkle the same with holy or purging water, and say, Thou shalt purge me with hyssop (O Lord) and I shall be clean: Thou shalt wash me, and I shall be whiter than Snow."*

The *Heptameron* was also included as part of *The Fourth Book of Occult Philosophy* which was allegedly written by Cornelius Agrippa and was first published in English in 1565. In it we find instruction on how the magick circle should be consecrated, which includes:

> *"you must bless the place with the sprinkling of Holy-water..."*

These consecrations may have their roots in medieval Christianity, where we discover a Benediction of the Water in a text entitled *'Of the Ordeal of Boiling Water'* which dates to the twelfth or thirteenth century:

> *"I bless thee, O creature of water, boiling above the fire, in the name of the Father, and of the Son, and of the Holy Ghost, from whom all things proceed; I adjure thee by Him who ordered thee to water the whole earth from the four rivers, and who summoned thee forth from the rock, and who changed thee into wine, that no wiles of the devil or*

magic of men be able to separate thee from thy virtues as a medium of judgment..."[63]

The magick circle can be seen to touch on a whole range of different traditions from the ancient world through to the grimoires. The range of different components from different sources is quite extensive when considering the apparent simplicity of the creation of the magick circle, showing that divergent strands can be successfully synthesised into a simple and effective process when understanding and experience are present. The Wiccan magick circle is a good example of this, blending functionality and effectiveness from a variety of sources, and continuing a tradition which extends back many thousands of years. Although the first obvious source may be the Lesser Banishing Ritual of the Pentagram, it is clear that all of the components of Wiccan circle casting may be found in the grimoires, and their synthesis to create the Wiccan formula of the magick circle is the most likely origin of the practice.

---

63 The Breviary of Eberhard of Bamberg ed. Zeumer in MG.LL. Sec V, Formulae, 1898

CHAPTER 9

THE MIGHTY ONES

Once the magick circle has been cast, consecrated and purified the guardians of the watchtowers are invoked. They are referred to in early published works as *'the Mighty Ones'* or the *'Lords of the Watchtowers'*. They are invoked at each of the four cardinal points of the circle, starting in the East and progressing to the South, then the West and ending in the North. Although there are variants in different texts, the invocations are usually something like:

> *"I summon, stir and call ye up, ye Lords of the watchtower of the East to guard this circle and to witness our rites."*

The use of the term *'watchtower'* in the Wiccan tradition needs consideration. The term was used by the Golden Dawn, who in turn drew from the work of the Elizabethan magus and astrologer Dr John Dee. Dee recorded the term watchtower in his diaries from June 1584, reproduced by Meric Causabon in his work *A True & Faithful Relation* in 1659.

The term was used to describe a vision seen by Dee's skryer Edward Kelley, of four towers at the corners of the universe, from which came various figures of spiritual creatures. The watchtowers were described by Dee as symbolising the Four Angels of the Earth. A drawing of Kelley's vision was also included in the book, with towers set on the cardinal points of a circle. Dee had a gold disk made with this image on.

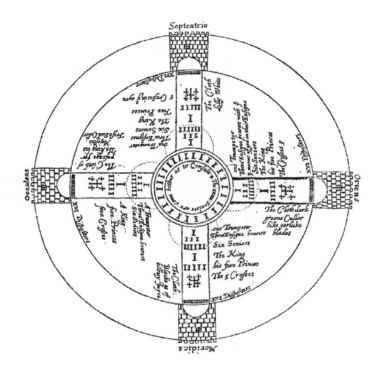

(Edward Kelley's vision of the Watchtowers, 20th June 1584, reproduced as a gold talisman, currently in the British Museum,[64] London)

The Golden Dawn applied the term watchtower to the four Enochian tablets, squares of 12x13 letters which are used to derive the names of the Enochian hierarchy of spirits, and attributed to the directions. These Enochian tablets were also the result of skrying work carried out by Edward Kelley on behalf of Dee.

As an aside, it is interesting to note that some translations of Virgil's *Aeneid* include the word *watchtower* in connection with a

---

64 Collection reference P&E MLA 1942,5-6,1

goddess and woods. Whilst it may have no direct bearing on the use of the term in the Wiccan tradition, we decided to include it as it provides an intriguing link between the word and a goddess at a much earlier date:

> *"But the grim goddess, seizing from her watchtower the moment of mischief, seeks the arduous roof, and sounds the pastoral signal from the highest summit of her abode, and strains her Tartarean voice on the twisted horn, which made the entire forest tremble, and echo through the deep wood."*

Considering the original meaning of the term watchtower as applied by Dee, the use of archangels as the Lords of the Watchtowers is entirely correct by his definition, as they are literally the Lords of the Angels! However, if the Golden Dawn meaning of the term were used, then they would be the Lords of the Enochian Tables, making them Enochian Angels being called at the cardinal points, which is not part of the Wiccan tradition.

The Enochian Angels corresponding to each of the cardinal points are Bataivah, the King of Air in the East, Edelperna the King of Fire in the South, Raagiosel the King of Water in the West, and Ikzhikal the King of Earth in the North.

However, when considering Dee's use of the term watchtower, we should bear in mind that he was a deeply religious man. Therefore his use of the term may well have been influenced by the Old Testament, specifically *Isaiah* 21 describing the news of the fall of Babylon.

> *"Prepare the table, watch in the watchtower, eat, drink: arise, ye princes, and anoint the shield."*

To understand the practice of invoking guardians at the four cardinal points there is a range of sources which we need to consider in order to trace the magickal beginnings. The first and most recent source which is also most often cited by modern authors as being the ultimate source for the practice of calling the Lords of the Watchtowers is that of the Lesser Banishing Ritual of the Pentagram.

This ritual was created by members of the Hermetic Order of the Golden Dawn in the late nineteenth century and has become one of the most popular and significant rituals in ceremonial magick. It is also one which was adopted by some Wiccans, notably Alex Sanders and those who followed in his footsteps, and incorporated in full or in part into Wiccan ceremonies. This is also a practice which we find in Ye Bok of ye Art Magickal in the early writings of Gardner.

The Lesser Banishing Ritual of the Pentagram comprises four parts, of which the relevant parts for consideration are the second and third. The first part, the Qabalistic Cross, is a centring exercise, and is repeated as the fourth part of the ritual. The second part is the vibration of divine names, where a banishing pentagram of Earth is drawn at each cardinal point with the vibration of Qabalistic divine names. A banishing pentagram of Earth is one which starts at the bottom left point and begins with an upward stroke to the top point. The opposite of this is the invoking Earth pentagram used in the invoking version of the Lesser Banishing Ritual of the Pentagram, and also in calling the Lords of the Watchtowers. A blue circle of fire is also traced with the hand and visualised joining the four pentagrams set as wards at the cardinal points.

The third part of the ritual is the calling of the elemental archangels, starting in the East with Raphael, invoking in turn also Gabriel (West), Michael (South) and Uriel (North) as guardians at the cardinal points. This does not follow the deosil invocations subsequently seen being used in the Wiccan tradition, and the archangels invoked correspond to the four elements.

Name	Element	Colour of Robe
Raphael	Air	Yellow
Michael	Fire	Red
Gabriel	Water	Blue
Uriel	Earth	Green

From these archangels we thus see the four colours which are most often used in the Wiccan tradition today to correspond to the four elements and their respective directions. Some covens prefer to call on these archangels as the guardians of the cardinal points rather than the traditional Lords of the watchtowers.

Eliphas Levi's writings were the source of a lot of the early Golden Dawn material and his attribution of the elemental beings to specific directions is likely to be the source for the attributions used by the Golden Dawn and tabulated above. In his most famous work *Transcendental Magic,* Levi explained:

> *"It must be borne in mind that the special kingdom of Gnomes is at the north, that of the Salamanders at the south, that of Sylphs at the east, and that of Undines at the west."*

Thus once again we have the same directional attributions to the same elements, only with the elemental beings associated with that element, rather than the archangels found in the later Golden Dawn material. It is clear that the Golden Dawn substituted the appropriate elemental archangel with the elemental being attributed here by Levi:

Direction	Element	Origin: Elemental Being
East	Air	Sylphs (beings of Air)
South	Fire	Salamanders (beings of Fire)
West	Water	Undines (beings of Water)
North	Earth	Gnomes (beings of Earth)

The drawing of a magick circle, pentagrams at the cardinal points and calling of guardians at the cardinal points are all part of the Wiccan casting of the magick circle, and could at first glance appear to be derived from the Lesser Banishing Ritual of the Pentagram. However there are differences which indicate that although the Lesser Banishing Ritual of the Pentagram may have played a role in influencing Wiccan ceremony, it is by no means the complete source for the origins, nor even for the invocations of the guardians at the cardinal points.

First we should consider the Supreme Invoking Ritual of the Pentagram, an expanded and more elaborate version of the Lesser Banishing Ritual of the Pentagram also created by the Golden Dawn. This version of the ritual goes through the directions in the sunwise sequence and also uses all the elemental pentagrams, combined with the names of the Enochian Kings of the Elements.

The Opening by Watchtower Ritual is another Golden Dawn ritual which needs consideration. It begins with the Lesser Banishing Ritual of the Pentagram and other components, including parts drawn from the *Chaldean Oracles of Zoroaster*, and is significant as the first ritual to include invocations of the angels of the watchtowers of the cardinal points:

> *"In the names and letters of the Great Southern Quadrangle, I invoke ye, ye Angels of the Watchtower of the South."*[65]

The calling of the Lords of the Watchtowers is sometimes known as *"Calling the Quarters"*. This expression may well have been drawn from the grimoire tendency to draw two lines in the magick circle dividing them into quarters, or influenced by the use of the term in the *Key of Solomon*:

> *"Let the Magus of the Art .... Lead them into the Circle of Art and station them therein towards the Four Quarters of the Universe."*

---

65 Ceremonial Magic, Regardie, 1980

The *Grimoire of Honorius* also has an interesting reference to conjurations of the Kings of the Directions which are made after the circle has been created, though the sequence is not the one used commonly elsewhere in ceremonial magick. In the section entitled *"General Conjuration of Spirits"*, it says:

> *"After this general conjuration you must make the four specific conjurations which follow; first to the King of the East, 2nd to the King of the West, 3rd to the King of the North and 4th to the King of the South."*

This sequence of East, West, North, and South is one seen in the positioning of the Enochian Tables when they are combined, and in the invocations of Enochian angels found in the seventeenth century magickal work which continued Dee's practices.[66]

Interestingly the term *"Kings"* for the rulers of the Watchtowers does appear in some of the writings of Wiccan Elders. The *'kings of the directions'* referred to in the late seventeenth century *Grimoire of Honorius* may have appeared in the writings of Patricia Crowther as the *'kings of the elements'*. As previously mentioned, it was also Crowther who recorded the use of the term *'black book'* for the Book of Shadows, a term previously used for the *Grimoire of Honorius*. Crowther, who was one of Gerald Gardner's initiates and High Priestesses, wrote in her book *Lid off the Cauldron* that:

> *"In the Craft, the intelligences behind the elements are called the 'Lords of the Outer Spaces', or the 'Kings of the Elements'"*

Although they used the term ruler interchangeably with king, the Golden Dawn gave these beings names, calling them:

---

66 The Practical Angel Magic of Dr John Dee's Enochian Tables, Skinner & Rankine, 2004

Element	King of the Element
Air	Paralda
Fire	Djin
Water	Niksa
Earth	Ghob

Furthermore, these names are also previously found in Levi's *Transcendental Magic* with prayers to the elementals and consecrations of salt and water so they undoubtedly have a long history of use, predating that of the Golden Dawn.

The origins of these names are fragmentary. We do not know for certain where the names Ghob and Paralda originate, though we can trace Djin and Niksa to diverse sources. Djin comes from the Arabic name for a type of fiery spirit, popularised in the West as genie. Niksa is derived from nixie, a type of shapeshifting water spirit found in German mythology and folklore. Ghob, as an earthy name, may be taken from the name of the mountainous region between Hirat and Ghazni in Afghanistan.

A possible answer to the reason the names of the Elemental Kings as used in the Golden Dawn are not found in Wicca (apart from as later additions by High Priests and High Priestesses who have taken their inspiration from the Golden Dawn) is that it may be that the original material was inspired not directly by the Golden Dawn, but instead by Dion Fortune, who wrote about the kings of the elements in her book *The Mystical Qabalah*. Dion Fortune was, as previously mentioned a student of the Alpha et Omega, one of the offshoots of the Golden Dawn.

It is interesting that Fortune moved away from the elemental emphasis of the Golden Dawn, as can be seen by comments she made in regard to the Qabalistic Sephira of Tiphereth (the Sun). In her book *The Mystical Qabalah* in 1935, she wrote:

"It is through this Vision of the Harmony of Things that we are made one with Nature, not by means of elemental contacts."

This fits in with the lack of elemental emphasis in early Wicca. Fortune further observed the emphasis on working with the elements through the presiding kings.

"The nature contacts are made through the Angelic Kings of the Elements in the Sphere of Tiphereth, in other words, through the realisation of the spiritual principles behind natural things, and the initiate then comes to the elemental beings in the name of their presiding King."

As an aside we may note the connection here to the angels of Tiphereth, the *Malakhim,* whose name means *'Kings'.* It is no coincidence that there is a connection of kingship with Malkuth, sphere of the Elements, one of its Divine Names being *Adonai Malakh,* meaning *'Lord King'.*

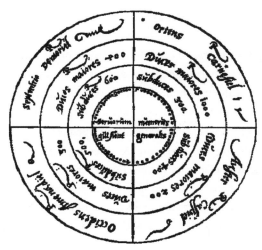

(The Magick Circle from the Steganographia of Trithemius, 1500)

121

There is an interesting illustration in Trithemius' work *Steganographia* from around 1500, which shows a magick circle quartered, with the Latin words for East, South, West and North (Oriens, Auster, Occidens, Septentrio) in the four quarters, along with the names of the spirits associated with the respective directions. This image graphically displays the idea of calling spirits from the four cardinal points.

Now we need to return again to the fourteenth century grimoire, the *Heptameron*. In the circle casting described in the *Heptameron*, pentagrams are marked on the floor outside the outer circle at the cardinal points as wards. This practice may be the source of the subsequent marking of pentagrams at cardinal points in the magick circles in later grimoires, and even the drawing of pentagrams at the cardinal points in the Lesser Banishing Ritual of the Pentagram. Another significant component of the magick circle casting in this important work is the calling of the:

"angels from the four parts of the world that rule the air".

An interesting aspect of this calling of angels is that they are ones that *"rule the air"*. All four of the angels from the different directions are of one type, who *"rule the air"*. Looking at other grimoires we see the same is true of other rulers of the directions. In Dee's writings the four kings of the watchtowers are all angels of earth. The four demon kings ruling the directions who are called for assistance in some of the grimoires are likewise all specifically airy beings (fallen angels).[67]

Considering the early public Wiccan texts, there is no obvious reference to any elemental connection to the lords of the watchtowers. Not only are there no obvious elemental references, but all four of the lords of the watchtowers are invoked using the same pentagram, which is the one attributed to invoking earth. Now this pentagram is

---

67 The Keys to the Gateway of Magic, Skinner & Rankine, 2005

appropriate if either the invocation is of earthy spirits, or it is rather an evocation, calling airy spirits to become more manifest, i.e. earthy.

Continuing this line of thought, the term *'mighty ones'* makes this unity of type amongst the kings of the watchtowers an interesting one. It is found throughout the Bible, being an old translation for the Hebrew divine name Elohim, which also means *'gods'*.

> *"Who, among the mighty ones, is like thee, O Lord? Who, among the mighty ones, like thee?"*[68]

In a commentary on this verse in 1794, a Dr Geddes correctly observed *"Mighty ones, others would render gods."*[69] The significance of the name Elohim from a Wiccan perspective has already been discussed in the chapter *A Real Witch's Weapon*. This terminology is far removed from elemental guardians, which do not appear to have been part of the early Wiccan magickal practices.

Going off on a tangent just for a moment, we find that in Wiccan practises today, the guardians called at the cardinal points are sometimes called by the names of the four winds from ancient Greece, i.e. Eurus, Notus, Zephyrus and Boreas. In ancient Greece these winds were personified as gods, the Anemoi (*'wind-gods'*), being the children of the dawn goddess Eos (*'Dawn'*) and the stellar god Astraios (*'Starry'*).

Originally there were three Anemoi – Notus, Boreas and Zephyrus. Each one of these gods was connected with one of the ancient Greek Seasons (they had three not four) and then Eurus was later added for Autumn. Boreas, the purple-winged god of Winter does have some associations which could be indicative of the element of Earth, but the other wind-gods do not correspond. For example, the South wind Notus is the storm-bringing god of wet weather

---

68 Exodus 15:11
69 Geddes's translation of the Bible, 1794, The British Critic and Quarterly Theological Review

corresponding to late Summer and Autumn, which does not indicate any associations with the element of Fire for which he is sometimes invoked in modern paganism.

Boreas is the only wind-god originally included in some Book of Shadows invocations of the Guardians, and as this is for the north it also supports the idea that the lords of the watchtowers were not elemental beings. Another interesting point to make here, as an aside, is that beyond the mountain dwelling place of the North wind Boreas is Hyperborea, the place of eternal Spring in the North, according to Greek legend. Hyperborea can never be touched by the North wind's icy air, and equates to the Wiccan idea of the *'Summerlands'*.

However it is easy to see the benefits of summoning protective deities at the cardinal points. This was done in ancient Egypt with goddesses called at the cardinal points, these being Serket in the East, Isis in the South, Neith in the West and Nephthys in the North.[70] The ancient Egyptians not only called deities at the cardinal points, they also called up spirits, as observed by Geraldine Pinch in *Magic in Ancient Egypt*:

> *"A spell which simply invokes the four spirits who watched over Osiris to watch over the magician's client, seems similar to the standard Christian prayer invoking the four evangelists or four archangels to surround and protect a sleeper."*

At the end of a Wiccan magick circle the guardians of the cardinal points are dismissed, with words to the effect of:

> *"Mighty Ones of the (East, South, West, North), I thank you for attending, and ere you depart for your lovely realms, I say Hail and Farewell."*

---

70 Magic in Ancient Egypt, Geraldine Pinch, 1994

There is no comparable dismissal in the grimoires, where the magician would perform a license to depart, ensuring all and any spiritual creatures in the vicinity left, making it safe to leave the magick circle. However, a phrase in the *Grimoire of Honorius* may also have influenced this part of the ceremony. When dismissing spirits, the phrase *"Now go ye hence to your abodes and let peace be between us"* is given as part of the instruction. Though not the same as the words above, it certainly does remind of the formulae used by some traditions today.

Thus when we look at the origins of the Mighty Ones in the Wiccan tradition, we can see that groups of gods or an individual type of spiritual creature are the norm, not the elemental beings often called today. The use of the term watchtower can be dated to the magick of John Dee in the late sixteenth century, although it was subsequently made popular by the Hermetic Order of the Golden Dawn in the late nineteenth and early twentieth century. Thus although we cannot conclusively determine the origins of the Mighty Ones, we can date the terminology to the Hermetic Order of the Golden Dawn and possibly Dee.

The function of these Mighty Ones is also something to consider, whether it is the original guarding and witnessing, or if the beings are expected to contribute to the magick circle, and if so, what incentive are they given?

CHAPTER 10

DRAW DOWN THE MOON

The process known in Wicca as Drawing Down the Moon is one of invocation, of drawing down a goddess into a priestess. Both the terminology and the practices associated with it today, have a long history of use by priestesses, priests and witches. Drawing Down the Moon is actually performed by the High Priest, who through his words and actions focuses the coven's attention on the High Priestess in preparation for the Charge of the Goddess.

The use of the term *'draw down the moon'* had a different meaning in classical times to the Wiccan usage today. It literally meant the descent of the Moon close to the earth (or an eclipse). The witches of Thessaly in ancient Greece were particularly famous for being able to draw down the moon from the heavens, and were described as using this technique for malefic emotional magick such as sexual control. References are made in many ancient works to their ability to do this, such as those of the first century BCE poets Propertius[71] and Virgil.[72]

It is likely that the phrase *Drawing Down the Moon* was derived from early English translations of Plato's work. For example in *Gorgias* in 380 BCE he wrote:

> *"Like the Thessalian witches, who, as they say,*
> *draw down the Moon from heaven."*

---

71 Elegies I.1, Propertius, 1st century BCE
72 Eclogue 8, The Sorceress or Pharmaceutria, Virgil, 1st century BCE

The fame of the Thessalian witches and their drawing down of the moon was such that they endured as a theme in ancient literature for centuries. One of the first such references was by the Greek playwright Aristophanes, who wrote in 423 BCE in his comedy *The Clouds*:

> *"Suppose I purchased a Thessalian witch,*
> *And made her draw me down the moon by night;*
> *Then shut it up, as if it were a mirror,*
> *In a round bonnet box, and kept it there"*

Indeed so well known was this association that the fourth century BCE poet Sosiphanes of Syracuse had a character in his lost tragedy *Meleager* remark that:

> *"Every chit of a girl in Thessaly can command the moon down from heaven by magic incantations – believe that if you will."*[73]

This practice was linked with eclipses in ancient times and seen as fooling the credulous. The writer Menander was said to have written a play specifically about this theme entitled *The Thessalian Women*, but no copy is known to have survived.

> *"According to Pliny, Menander, who was skilled in the subtleties of learning, composed a Thessalian drama, in which he comprised the incantations and magic ceremonies of women drawing down the moon. Pliny considers the belief in magic as the combined effect of the operations of three powerful causes, medicine, superstition, and the mathematical arts..."*[74]

---

73 Tragicorum Graecorum Fragmenta 12 92 F1
74 The Southern Literary Messenger, Rhododaphne, Volume IX

In more recent centuries writers made a point of explaining the connection with predictive astronomy and the occasion of eclipses. Thus in *A New Pantheon* written by Samuel Boyse in 1753 we find footnoted:

> *"Aglonice, a Thessalian, being acquainted with the cause and time of eclipses, gave out, upon their approach, that she was going by her enchantments to draw down the Moon to the Earth, at the same time directing the Thessalian Women to join her in making a hideous noise, to cause her to reascend. Taking the hint from this, they no sooner perceived the beginning of an eclipse, than they made a clattering noise with pans and kettles, and such like instruments to prevent her (the Moon) hearing the incantations of the Thessalian sorceress."*

Another interesting reference to the practice of drawing down the moon can be found in the *Mythology and Fables of the Ancients*, by Antoine Banier, in 1739:

> *"The Priests instituted for that purpose, invented Stories, and published Apparitions of their pretended Deities, to keep up thereby a gainful Worship. They made People believe, for example, that Diana had fallen in love with Endymion, and that the cause of her Eclipses, was owing to the Interviews she had with her Gallant on the Mountains of Caria; but as ill luck would have it, these Amours could not last for ever, and this put them upon the hard shift of accounting for her Eclipses another way. They gave out that Sorceresses, especially those of Thessaly, (where poisonous Plants were more common, by reason of the foam of Cerberus had dropt there, when he was brought from Hell, according to another Fable) had power by their Enchantments to draw down the Moon to Earth."*

The association with the act of drawing down the moon and lunar eclipses is further emphasised in the book *The British Poets* published in 1822. Here we find a note saying:

"It was related in an ancient legend, and believed by popular superstition, that enchantresses used to draw down the moon by their sorceries. The witches of Thessaly, in particular, were said to have possessed extraordinary powers of this kind; and among others, Aglonice, the daughter of Hegemon. The true meaning of the story is, that she, being skilful in astrology, was enabled to foretell when the eclipses of the moon were to happen; on which account she was supposed, by the ignorant people among whom she lived, to bring to pass the alarming phenomenon which, in fact, she only predicted. This woman was involved in misfortunes; for killing one of her domestics, and being prosecuted for her crime, she gave rise to the saying, 'They draw down the moon:' to denote unfortunate persons. The ancients believed implicitly in the extraordinary powers of sorcery. We find in the classics innumerable passages that refer to the force of magickal incantation, to draw down the moon from her sphere. This was done to favour those rites which were supposed to require an hour of solemn darkness, or the ascent of departed shades and demons, who were thought to have strong objections to the glare of light."

George Granville Lansdowne has his character Arcabon in *The British Enchanters* or *No Magic Like Love* a dramatic poem published in 1732 speak saying:

"Ah there's the fatal wound,
Which tears my heart-strings - but he shall be
Yes, ye infernals, if there's power in art (found)
These arms shall hold him, as he grasps my heart,
Shall I, who can draw down the Moon, and keep

The stars confin'd, enchant the boist'rous deep,
Bid Boreas halt, make hills and forest move,
Shall I be made a whining fool to love?"

This is an intriguing piece, especially in that he specifically mentions Boreas, who is also uniquely mentioned at times in the early Wiccan tradition as part of the invocation of the guardians of the watchtowers.

In the early nineteenth century the German writer Goethe also referred to the practice of bringing down the moon in association with the Thessalian witches in his masterpiece *Faust*. His reference though was more negative in its nuances, and indicative of the anti-magick theme which runs through the whole work, when he said:

"by praying the moon to remain with her calm light in heaven and not to be jerked down by magic of Thessalian witch."

However there was a practice which involved reflecting the full moon into a bowl or jug of water, and this may well have been what was referred to as drawing down the moon. The Greek poet Petronius has the character of a witch describe this in his play *Satyricon*, where she says:

"The image of the moon descending, brought down by my incantations."

Aristophanes may also have been hinting at a form of reflection when he linked a mirror to the drawing down of the moon, when his character in the play *The Clouds* says of the drawing down the moon that he would:

"Then shut it up, as if it were a mirror, in a round bonnet box, and kept it there"

Whether the ancient drawing down the moon was cunning use of eclipses or a reflective technique, the manner in which Drawing Down the Moon is used in the modern Wiccan tradition would be more accurately described as invocation in the proper sense, i.e. of *"calling into"* which is derived from the Latin *"in-vocare"*.

The idea of assuming the qualities of a deity is not new, as can be seen from ancient Egypt where magickians would identify with deities to draw on their powers. The Egyptian papyri are full of such identifications, from the identification with Osiris to successfully join the gods in the afterlife recorded in the epic texts like the *Papyri of Ani* (commonly known as *The Book of the Dead*) to the huge range of spells recorded in works like *The Leiden Papyrus*. These spells often contained a combination of spoken word and action, in a manner similar to that seen in the Wiccan tradition millennia later. For example, in a spell identifying with Horus to protect the magician for the coming year, the magician would walk sunwise (deosil) around his house carrying a club saying:

> *"Retreat disease demons! No breeze will reach me so that passersby would pass on, to rage against my face. I am Horus who passes along the wandering demons of Sekhmet. Horus, sprout of Sekhmet! I am the unique one, the son of Bastet – I will not die on account of you!"*[75]

The assumption of god-forms was also practised by the Golden Dawn in the late nineteenth century, who saw it as the deity literally *"stepping into"* the body of the magician. The Golden Dawn emphasised the assumption of Egyptian deity god-forms, as being appropriately sharp images of deities with clearly defined roles. They also emphasised being *'clothed with the god-form'* during initiation ceremonies, so there would be a genuine divine contact for the aspirant, ensuring the most profound effects in the initiation. This use of divine

---

75 Ancient Egyptian Magickal Texts, Borghouts, 1978

contact is subsequently seen in a similar manner in the Wiccan tradition with Drawing Down the Moon always being performed in initiation ceremonies.

In his instructional masterpiece *Liber O*, Crowley gave more concise instructions for assuming god-forms based on those he had learned in the Golden Dawn.[76] Considering the influence Crowley's material had on the ceremony of Drawing Down the Moon, it is possible that his instructions may also have had an influence.

Having looked at the antecedents, we shall now examine the origins of the ceremony used in the Wiccan tradition, attributed to the Book of Shadows. We shall look at the components of the ceremony in turn to provide the clearest view of the origins of the respective components. The Charge of the Goddess, which is usually considered in direct conjunction with Drawing Down, will be considered separately in the next chapter *Adore the Spirit of Me*.

Drawing Down the Moon begins with the High Priest invoking the goddess into the High Priestess. He does this with a combination of words, gestures and intent. The invocation to the goddess used for the Drawing Down the Moon ceremony, now widely published, goes something like this, with minor wording variations:

> *"I invoke Thee and call upon Thee, Great Mother of us all,*
> *Bringer of all fruitfulness,*
> *By seed and root and bud and stem,*
> *By leaf and flower and fruit,*
> *By life and love do I invoke Thee*
> *To descend into the body of this*
> *Thy servant and High Priestess."*

This was clearly part inspired by Crowley's *Gnostic Mass* which contains the phrase *"By seed and root and stem and bud and leaf and flower*

---

76 Liber O, Magick, Crowley, 1929

and fruit do we invoke Thee".[77] It is likely that Crowley took at least some of his inspiration in writing this piece from the poem *Song of Proserpine* by the early nineteenth century poet Percy Bysshe Shelley:

> *"Sacred Goddess, Mother Earth,*
> *Thou from whose immortal bosom*
> *Gods and men and beasts have birth,*
> *Leaf and blade, and bud and blossom,*
> *Breathe thine influence most divine*
> *On thine own child, Proserpine."*

Another possible source for some of the wording in this opening invocation of the goddess is the Qabalah. The phrase *'mother of us all'* which is used in the invocation refers to the Shekinah, or divine feminine, and may be drawn from MacGregor Mathers' nineteenth century work *The Kabbalah Unveiled*:

> *"From Her do they receive their nourishment, and from Her do they receive blessing; and She is called the Mother of them all."*

Another component of the Drawing Down the Moon ceremony which follows on from the invocation is a speech sometimes known as the *'Hail Aradia'* speech. This is based directly on a poem by Crowley entitled *La Fortuna* and dedicated to Tyche (the Greek goddess of Fortune), published as part of his 1907 work *Rodin in Rime*, written in praise of the artist's work, and illustrated by Rodin, with whom Crowley was friends:

> *"Hail Tyche! From the Amalthean horn*
> *Pour forth the store of love!*
> *I lowly bend before thee:*

---

77 Gnostic Mass, Crowley, 1913

I invoke thee at the end
When other gods are fallen and put to scorn.
Thy foot is to my lips; my signs unborn
Rise, touch and curl about thy heart; they spend
Pitiful love. Lovlier pity, descend
And bring me luck who am lonely and forlorn."

The position assumed by the High Priestess, often described in contemporary works as the *'Osiris position'*, is in fact not much like the position seen in depictions of the Egyptian god Osiris at all. In drawing down the arms are crossed, holding the wand and scourge at a diagonal. In the depictions of Osiris he holds his crook and flail in his hands in front of his body without them being crossed, i.e. left hand in front of left side of ribs and right hand in front of right side of ribs. He holds the crook and flail vertically upwards. Also the crook and flail are agricultural tools, symbolising the livestock (crook) and grain (flail), and are definitely not a wand and scourge!

It is also interesting to note that in Gerald Gardner's writings he referred to this position as the *'Skull and Crossbones'*, not the *Osiris Position*. His explanation in the context of Wiccan ceremonies, in particular that of initiation makes a great deal more sense. He begins by saying that he has never seen skulls and other *'repulsive objects'* used in ceremonies, but that he was told that in the old days a skull and crossbones would sometimes be used to represent the god if the High Priest of a coven could not be present at a ceremony. He then goes on to explain that the High Priestess assumed the position of the skull and crossbones for ceremonies, thus symbolising death and proceeded to move into the pentagram position, representing resurrection.

The primary goddess being invoked in the *Hail Aradia* invocation is as the wording suggests Aradia, the name given to the daughter of the goddess Diana in Leland's *Aradia*. According to *Gospel of the Witches* Aradia is born from Diana and Lucifer and then sent to the Earth to teach witchcraft to mankind so that they would be able to free themselves from their oppressors.

The name Aradia occurred in the ancient world as that of a Phoenician town. This town is mentioned by Gibbons in reference to the Punic Wars in volume one of his classic 1806 work *The History of the Decline and Fall of the Roman Empire* (which we may note is listed in the bibliography of *The Meaning of Witchcraft*). It is interesting to observe that it is referred to in an Italian work on the history of Tuscany, as this was one of the Phoenician colonies. The Phoenician influence was felt by the Etruscans who subsequently ruled there:

> *"and arriving at Canton, in China, opened a regular commerce between that kingdom, Aradia, Persia, and Egypt,"*[78]

So if the name Aradia was known in the ancient world in connection with the Phoenicians, is it too much of a speculative leap to wonder if somehow the name became conflated with the worship of one of their chief goddesses, Astarte?

As a tangential aside of some relevance, we may note that the architect of the temple in Freemasonry (another tributary contributing to the Wiccan river), Hiram Abiff, came from Tyre, i.e. was a Phoenician. This is referred to in the *Old Testament* in *II Chronicles,* and ties Hiram in with King Solomon, another legendary figure whose attributed work has influenced Wicca. *II Chronicles 13* says:

> *"And now I have sent a cunning man, endued with understanding, of Hiram Abiff."*

Further consideration may shed some light on the roots of Aradia, by exploring the name of Herodias, who Leland equated to Aradia. Herodias was the sister-in-law of King Herod, who persuaded her

---

78 The History of Tuscany, Browning, 1826

daughter Salome to ask for John the Baptist's head in exchange for her dance.[79] In medieval Italian, Herodias became *"Erodiade"*, which could have been corrupted to Aradia. A significant early reference to Herodias is in the tenth century work of Raterius of Liegi, Bishop of Verona (890-974 CE). Raterius lamented that many believed Herodias was a queen or a goddess, and said that one third of the earth was under her charge.[80] In fact Aradia's mother Diana has been associated with witchcraft for thousands of years. In the *Canon Episcopi*, which is believed to date to the ninth century CE, although it may have roots going back to as early as the fifth century CE, Diana's associations were highlighted:

> *"This also is not to be omitted, that certain wicked women, turned back toward Satan, seduced by demonic illusions and phantasms, believe of themselves and profess to ride upon certain beasts in the night time hours, with Diana, the Goddess of the Pagans, and an innumerable multitude of women, and to traverse great spaces of earth in the silence of the dead of night, and to be subject to her laws as of a Lady, and on fixed nights be called to her service."*

Bartholomew Iscanus, the Bishop of Exeter (1161-84) revealed his own knowledge of what would seem to be a cult of Diana in England when we find amongst the many superstitions he condemned the following:

> *"whosoever, ensnared by the Devil's wiles, may believe and profess that they ride with countless multitudes of others in the train of her whom the foolishly vulgar call Herodias or Diana, and that they obey her behest. Whosoever has prepared a table with three knives for the*

---

79 Matthew 14:3-12
80 Caccia alle streghe, Bonomo, 1959

*service of the fairies, that they may predestinate good to such as are
born in the house..."*[81]

Here we find that Diana is linked to witchcraft, Herodias and
fairies, more than seven hundred years before Leland published *Aradia,*
in which we find *"The Children of Diana or How the Fairies were born"* as
an appendix to the book, where Diana is considered to be the mother of
the fairy folk:

> *"We are moon-rays, the children of Diana," replied one:--*
> *"We are children of the Moon;*
> *We are born of shining light;*
> *When the Moon shoots forth a ray,*
> *Then it takes a fairy's form."*

Considering the link between Diana and Herodias in this early
writing, it is interesting that Leland should subsequently link Herodias
to Aradia, the daughter of Diana. Diana's popularity endured and she
was referred to by a number of writers through the Middle Ages and
Renaissance. The Italian philosopher and magician Giordano Bruno
wrote in 1585 of the goddess Diana in his *Heroic Furors*:

> *"Diana is one, the entity itself, the entity that is truth itself, truth
> which is intelligential nature in which the Sun and splendour of
> higher nature shine, according to the distinction of unity between the
> generated and the generator, or the producer and the product."*

It is noteworthy that Christian anti-witch writings frequently
singled out the goddess Diana for special attention as the goddess of the
witches. This may well be because of the references to Diana in the *New
Testament*, in *Acts 19*:

---

81 MSS Cotton. Faust. A. viii, fol. 32

"19:24 For a certain man named Demetrius, a silversmith, which made silver shrines for Diana, brought no small gain unto the craftsmen;

19:27 So that not only this our craft is in danger to be set at nought; but also that the temple of the great goddess Diana should be despised, and her magnificence should be destroyed, whom all Asia and the world worshippeth.

19:28 And when they heard these sayings, they were full of wrath, and cried out, saying, Great is Diana of the Ephesians.

19:34 But when they knew that he was a Jew, all with one voice about the space of two hours cried out, Great is Diana of the Ephesians.

19:35 And when the townclerk had appeased the people, he said, Ye men of Ephesus, what man is there that knoweth not how that the city of the Ephesians is a worshipper of the great goddess Diana, and of the [image] which fell down from Jupiter?"

The use of the term Drawing Down the Moon thus has no connection to the ancient practice, and is used in the Wiccan tradition as the poetic description of the process of invocation of the goddess into the High Priestess.

In recent decades the ceremony of Drawing Down the Moon to invoke the goddess has been supplemented by the ceremony of Drawing Down the Sun to invoke the god. So as a final observation on the ceremony of Drawing Down, we may note that this too is not a new idea or term, as the ancient Greek philosopher Plutarch wrote many centuries ago:

"What is this but, like the Thessalian women, to call down the Sun and Moon by enchantments from the skies"[82]

---

82 Morals, vol 3, Plutarch, circa 100 CE

CHAPTER 11

ADORE THE SPIRIT OF ME

For many people today the Charge of the Goddess is synonymous with the Wiccan tradition. The Charge of the Goddess is essentially a piece of sacred prose read or recited by the High Priestess following the ceremony of Drawing Down the Moon.

The term *"Old Charges"* was used in Freemasonry for recited texts used in the degree initiations describing the secret signs and mythology and history of Freemasonry. This term can be dated to at least the 1680s and gives us the most probable source for the use of the term *'Charge'* in the Wiccan tradition, though of course in Freemasonry it was not used to represent the words of a deity. The following extract from an old charge of Freemasonry demonstrates the emphasis on moral behaviour and personal choice found in these texts:

> *"but Masonry being found in all nations, even of divers religions, they are now only charged to adhere to 'that religion in which all men agree,' (leaving each Brother to his own particular opinions), that is to be Good Men and True Men of Honour and Honesty, by whatever Names, Religions or Persuasions they may be distinguished."*[83]

Before we delve into the origins of the Charge of the Goddess, we will consider what Gerald Gardner, who first part published it, had to say. In his book *Witchcraft Today* Gardner suggested possible

---

83 The Freemasons Quarterly Magazine and Review, 1846

explanations for the origins of the *Charge*. He quoted part of the text and explained that it was read before initiations and then continued saying: *"The charge I think came from the time when Romans or strangers came in; it explains a little which would not be known to all in the old days..."* This seems a strange claim as it is incredibly unlikely that he was unfamiliar with the *Aradia* from which part of the text he quoted originated. For this reason we must conclude that he was either genuinely unaware of the origins of the *Charge of the Goddess*, in which case someone else must have provided him with it, or that he was involved in the construction of the *Charge of the Goddess* and was trying to provide the *Charge* with a fake history.

Like the Wiccan Tradition generally, the *Charge of the Goddess* draws from a number of sources. Although the *'Lift Up the Veil'* charge which is found in some early Books of Shadows was probably from around 1948 or 1949; it is the subsequent charge, commonly called the *Charge of the Goddess*, which is the best known today.

The *Lift Up the Veil* charge was clearly pre-Valiente, as she was not initiated until 1952/3. Valiente claimed that she rewrote the *Lift Up the Veil* charge to produce the *Charge of the Goddess*, removing Crowley's influence, as she put it, *"cutting out the Crowleyanity as much as I could"*[84] However, as you will discover this is simply not true, as most of the material used in the *Charge of the Goddess* draws from material published in *The Aradia, Gospel of the Witches* by Charles Leland and from a variety of original works by Aleister Crowley – with a few additions from the Golden Dawn and Christian liturgy.

We have chosen to use a version of the *Charge of the Goddess* which has been widely reproduced both in printed and online literature. It varies slightly from the versions we have had passed down to us in our tradition, but the variations are not in our opinion of great importance as they are usually just a difference in a word here or there, possibly

---

84 The Rebirth of Witchcraft, Valiente, 1987

through scribal errors along the way or through being written down from memory at times.

We have noted differences between this version and those published by Gardner and Valiente elsewhere. The underlined text represents the words spoken by the High Priest and High Priestess, whereas the writing that follows indicates the source, or possible source material(s) used, together with commentary where appropriate. When we have been unable to establish the source we have assumed it to be original material written by the person (or persons) who compiled it and have stated as such. In some instances, we have included our own speculations on possible, but circumstantial material which may have been the inspiration for a particular line or part of this *Charge*.

Textual Analysis of the Charge of the Goddess

> "HP: Listen to the words of the Great Mother, who of old was also called among men, Artemis, Astarte, Dione, Melusine, Aphrodite, Ceridwen, Diana, Arianrhod, Bride, and by many other names."

The opening introductory statement by the High Priest is clearly presenting the idea of a universal goddess. This piece seems to be original, though there is a historical basis for the concept and name of the Great Mother, as can be seen in the writings of the Roman historian Lucian, in the second century CE, who wrote of the goddess in his work *De Dea Syria* (*'The Syrian Goddess'*) as:

> "She is our Mother Earth, known otherwise as the Mother Goddess or Great Mother. Among the Babylonians and northern Semites she was called Ishtar: she is the Ashtoreth of the Bible, and the Astarte of Phœnicia. In Syria her name was 'Athar, and in Cilicia it had the form of 'Ate ('Atheh). At Hierapolis, with which we are primarily

141

concerned, it appears in later Aramaic as Atargatis, a compound of
the Syrian and Cilician forms ... for in one way and another there was
still a prevailing similarity between the essential attributes and
worship of the nature-goddess throughout Western Asia."

The Roman historian and magician Apuleius, a contemporary of
Lucian, expressed a similar theme. In his novel of initiation, *The Golden
Ass*, he has Isis describe herself as the goddess of whom all others are
aspects.

"For the Phrygians call me the mother of the gods: the Athenians,
Minerva: the Cyprians, Venus: the Candians, Diana: the Sicilians,
Proserpina: the Eleusians, Ceres: some Juno, others Bellona, others
Hekate."

The Qabalah also needs to be considered when we look at the idea
of the great mother goddess. There is a very mistaken concept amongst
those who have not studied its mysteries that the Qabalah is entirely
patriarchal. This is not the case and it never was. The *Sefer ha-Zohar*
(*"Book of Splendour"*) places great emphasis on the Shekinah or divine
feminine, and it brought sexual polarity very much to the forefront of
Qabalah at the time of its publication in 1290, and the subsequent
publication of the *Sefer ha-Bahir* (*"Book of Brilliance"*) in 1310, when the
Hermetic and Neoplatonic texts were also being translated, resulted in
both traditions feeding into alchemy, the Grimoires and other magickal
traditions of the Middle Ages and Renaissance. Significantly this also
predated the main period of the witch trials, and the conflation of
prejudice against Jews, heretics and witches.

"From Her do they receive their nourishment, and from Her do they
receive blessing; and She is called the Mother of them all."[85]

---

85 Kabbalah Unveiled, Mathers, 1887

The word Shekinah is from the root *Shakhan* meaning *'to dwell'*, and refers to her presence within all humanity. In the ninth century the German branch of Qabalists described the Shekinah as the circle of fire around God, their union causing the throne, angels and human souls to come into being.[86] The Shekinah has been seen as manifesting in two ways. As the Lesser or Exiled Shekinah she is perceived as being the world soul, somewhat akin to the concept of Gaia as postulated by James Lovelock. However as the source of souls, Shekinah is also present in every person, as the spark that seeks to reunite with the Greater Shekinah, the great goddess.

> *"Her ways are of pleasantness, and her paths are peace.*
> *She is a tree of life to them that lay hold upon her; and happy is every*
> *one that retaineth her."*[87]

The Kabbalistic Shekinah, the Gnostic Sophia and the classical goddesses all enjoyed notable attention through the Renaissance, and it could convincingly be argued that the deities of Wicca are expressions of an inevitable resurgence of the divine powers seeking an outlet, as they have done for the last fifteen hundred years.

This idea of a universal goddess or great mother goddess was to continue through the Renaissance, as can be seen in writings by authors such as the German humanist Konrad Mutian (1471-1526). In correspondence he observed, in a manner which would have been seen as sacrilegious by the Church at the time:

> *"There is but one God and one Goddess,*
> *But many are their powers and names:*
> *Jupiter, Sol, Apollo, Moses, Christus,*
> *Luna, Ceres, Proserpina, Tellus, Maria.*

---

86 Kabbalah, Ponce,1974
87 Proverbs 3:17-18.

But have a care in speaking these things.
They should be hidden in silence as
are the Eleusinian Mysteries;
Sacred things must be wrapped in fable and enigma."[88]

This view is one which would be repeated in writings of the late nineteenth and early twentieth century. In 1901 Sir Arthur Evans became convinced of the idea of a single great goddess in prehistoric times when he was excavating Knossos in Crete. From this idea he subsequently chose to interpret all divine female figures at the site as a single goddess, and all male figures as a single subordinate son/consort god. This idea was expanded by the French archaeologist Joseph Dechelette, who suggested that the cult of the Great Goddess had originated in the Neolithic period in Asia Minor and the Balkans and expanded across the Mediterranean to the whole of Western Europe.[89]

Occultists would also incorporate these ideas into their world-views and hence their writings. The author George Russell (AE) in his classic work *The Candle of Vision*, published in 1918, espoused the original divinity being divided into the Great Mother and Great Father, from whom the gods and goddesses derived. This idea was also subsequently seen in the occult novels of Dion Fortune in the 1930s.

In the part version of the *Charge* published by Gardner in *Witchcraft Today* in 1954 all the names following that of Aphrodite were omitted – i.e. Ceridwen, Diana, Arianrhod and Bride – giving the impression that the Celtic Goddesses were later additions. It is also interesting here to note the difference between the version of the *Charge* attributed to Doreen Valiente and published in the *Witches Bible* where the goddess Diana is changed into *Dana* and the name of the Greco-Roman Egyptian goddess *Isis* is added before that of Bride.

---

88 The Survival of the Pagan Gods, Seznec, 1953
89 Manual d'archeologie prehistorique Celtique et Gallo-Romaine, Dechelette, 1908

Reference to Melusine occurred in Crowley's *Law of Liberty*, and some discussion of her is called for here to put her inclusion into perspective. Melusine was described in the late fourteenth century tale of *Mélusine de Lusignan*.[90] Melusine can be seen as the archetypal fairy wife. In different versions of the tale she is half fish, serpent or dragon. The gist of the story is that she married Remond, who became the Conte de Poitiers. She made Remond swear that on Saturdays he would allow her privacy, but after his brother made him wild with jealousy, Remond burst in on Melusine and realised her true nature. She then left him, in the manner of the fairy wife whose true nature has been discovered. The inclusion of such a figure may seem strange, but Melusine was a tremendously popular figure, like Morgan Le Fay, whose roots hint at earlier divine origins. Her inclusion does however provide a further clear illustration that this piece of prose does not have Roman origins as Gardner suggested.

We may also conclude that it is possible that the person who compiled the earliest versions of the *Charge* had read Crowley's *Law of Liberty* – material from which can be found in both the earlier *Lift up the Veil* and the later *Charge of the Goddess*. Crowley mentioned Melusine in the *Law of Liberty* when he wrote: *"Do not embrace mere Marian or Melusine; she is Nuit Herself, specially concentrated and incarnated in a human form to give you infinite love, to bid you taste even on earth the Elixir of Immortality"*. We can see here the equation of Nuit as the universal goddess, and the idea of the High Priestess as being the representative of this goddess in ceremonies.

This introductory line to the *Charge* is generally thought to be the original material of the author(s) thereof, as no known precedent exists in the works which otherwise influenced it.

This part of the *Charge* corresponds directly to that used in the *Lift Up the Veil* charge dated to 1949, which could then be said to be the earliest known source, presumably written by either Gerald Gardner

---

90 Mélusine de Lusignan, Jean d'Arras, 1393

himself (as this was pre-Valiente) or it could possibly be part of an original piece of prose currently lost to us today.

As an aside, for those who love life's little coincidences, we thought we would include something similar which we found in a book published in 1920 on the subject of the Native American tribe of the Iroquois, which reads *"My Children, listen to the words of the Great Mother. You are burdened and troubled; your little ones are silent and fearful..."*[91] There is nothing of course to suggest that this is directly related to the compilation of the *Charge*, but it is a fascinating parallel usage which we thought worthy of inclusion.

"High Priestess: At mine Altars the youth of Lacedaemon in Sparta made due sacrifice."

Interestingly here, we find that Gardner wrote in *Witchcraft Today* *"At mine altars the youth in Lacedaemon made due sacrifice"*. However, it is noteworthy that in Gardner's rendition of it there, he at least omitted a rather obtuse error in this first line of this version of the *Charge*, but of course we don't know whether this was an accidental mistake or a deliberate omission in an effort to not reveal too much of the prose.

So what is wrong with this statement? Put simply the geography is all wrong. Sparta was a city in Lacedaemon, not the other way around, this statement is like saying England is in London or America is in New York! Then there is an apparent contradiction with the line *"Nor do I demand aught in sacrifice...."* which is found later in the same version of this *Charge*. So, whilst the goddess seems to be saying that sacrifice was made, she is also saying that she demands no sacrifice now! This is probably a side effect of the use of literature from a number of sources and the conflation of the myths of a variety of goddesses to represent

---

91 The Hero of the Longhouse, Mary Elisabeth Laing, 1920

the words spoken by one, or it could indicate a change of position on the part of the goddess, or her worshippers!

The reference to the *'youth of Sparta,'* is to the ritual flogging which took place at the altars of the goddess *Artemis Orthia* (*"Artemis of the steep"*) during the Roman period. As part of the rites, young boys would be scourged on Artemis' altar until it was smeared with their blood, being both their ritual purification and their sacrifice to this virgin huntress.

The origins of this rather grim ceremony are believed to have come from the discovery of an image of Artemis Orthia which had been lost from a temple for some time before being rediscovered. Two Spartan warriors, Astrabakos and Alopekos, discovered it and upon doing so immediately went completely insane. Following this a temple was erected around the rediscovered statue in honour of Artemis and through doing so the goddess was temporarily propitiated. However, during a sacrifice taking place on the altar, rival groups of Limnatians, Kynosourians and Mesoans got themselves into a brawl and as a result many of them were killed on and around the altar. Artemis, not known for forgiveness, decided to kill the rest of those involved through disease as a punishment for defiling her temple.

The Spartan people made desperate appeals to an oracle for advice on what to do and were told that the only way to stop the disease was to stain the altar with human blood as an offering to Artemis. For many years they offered human sacrifices at the altar (the sacrifice being chosen by lot) until this practice was eventually substituted with that of the whipping of young prepubescent boys. The boys were scourged until enough blood had been produced to stain the altar anew and thus ensured another period of peace with the goddess. During the scourging a priestess would hold a light wooden image of the goddess with which she would be able to tell if the men who were doing the scourging were slacking on the amount or the severity of the blows given to the boys based on beauty or rank. If the statue grew heavy it was due to the men

147

slacking and the priestess would chastise those doing the whipping to ensure that Artemis' offerings were made correctly and appropriately.

As an interesting aside, flogging is a theme which recurs in the worship of the goddess Artemis. It also played a part in the cheese-stealing rituals recorded by Xenophon in *Lakedaimonion Politeia* in the fifth/fourth century BCE. Here two groups of young men would contest a piece of cheese which was placed on the altar of Artemis. The first group defended the cheese with whips, whilst the other group had to try and steal it. Though there is no direct connection here with sacrifice, which is clearly indicated in the example of Artemis Orthia, it may be that this was another variation of a similar rite as those being scourged would undoubtedly bleed onto the altar, making a blood sacrifice as part of the ceremonial goings on.

The use of the scourge in an ancient ceremony was well exemplified by the frequently quoted Roman festival of Lupercalia, where young men clad in skins would rush around beating people with strips of goatskin, which was believed to promote fertility and easy childbirth. However this does not really bear much resemblance to the use of the scourge in the Wiccan tradition. In medieval times the scourge was described as being used frequently for punishment of witches. One such example is seen in Murray's *The God of the Witches*:

> *"The accused escaped with her life, but her sentence was, 'To be scourged from the end of said town to the other. And thereafter to be banished from the country'."*

Another common suggestion is the claim that the Knights Templar used scourging, a reference Gardner himself makes in his works. Whether they did or not, there is certainly a well-documented history of self-flagellation within the Christian church as a means of *'purification'*, so this is a much more likely source of the magickal beginnings of using the scourge to be *"properly prepared"*.

"Whenever ye have need of anything, once in the month, and better it be when the Moon is full. Then ye shall assemble in some secret place and adore the spirit of Me who am Queen of all Witcheries. There ye shall assemble, ye who are fain to learn all sorcery, yet who have not won its deepest secrets. To these will I teach things that are yet unknown. And ye shall be free from slavery, and as a sign that ye be really free, ye shall be naked in your rites..."

Gardner omits *"Whenever ye have need of anything"* in *Witchcraft Today*. He also writes *"meet in some secret place, and adore me who am Queen of all the magics... for I am a gracious Goddess, I give joy on Earth, certainty not faith, while in life; and upon death unutterable, rest and the ecstasy of the Goddess. Nor do I aught in sacrifice..."* At this point Gardner tells us that he is forbidden to reveal any further part of the charge.

This piece is clearly derived with only minor changes from chapter one of the *Aradia*, which reads:

"Whenever ye have need of anything, once in the month, and when the Moon is full, ye shall assemble in some desert place, or in a forest all together join to adore the potent spirit of your queen, My mother, great Diana. She who fain would learn all sorcery yet has not won its deepest secrets, them my mother will teach her, in truth all things as yet unknown. And ye shall all be freed from slavery, and so ye shall be free in everything; and as the sign that ye are truly free, ye shall be naked in your rites, both men and women also."

Here it is necessary to look at the difference in use of the text. In the *Aradia*, it is the goddess Diana who addresses her daughter, Aradia, giving her instruction on how to teach witchcraft to humanity. In the context of use within the Wiccan tradition, the priestess is said to channel a goddess and speak these words to the witches. This may seem like a small inconsistency, but one which has quite a huge magickal implication, as well as of course a spiritual one, both of which are worthy of some consideration.

"...and ye shall dance, sing, feast, make music, and love, all in my praise."

Another piece from *Aradia*, this time chapter two, shortened and rewritten, finishes this part of the *Charge*: *"... and, the feast over, they shall dance, sing, make music, and then love in the darkness, with all the lights extinguished: for it is the Spirit of Diana who extinguishes them, and so they will dance and make music in her praise."* Dancing, singing, making music and love are all classic ingredients in the *'imagined'* witches Sabbath as described in the major works of the height of the persecutions by such infamous figures as Peter Binsfeld (*Tractatus de confessionibus maleficorum et sagarum*, 1591), Nicolas Rémy (*Daemonolatria*, 1595), Martín del Río (*Disquisitionum magicarum libri sex*, 1599), Francesco Guazzo (*Compendium Maleficarum*, 1609), and Pierre de Lancre (*Tableau de l'inconstance des mauvais anges et demons*, 1612, and *L'incredulité et mescréance du sortilege plainement convaincue*, 1622).

"For mine is the ecstasy of the Spirit, and mine is also joy on earth. For my Law is Love unto all beings."

The latter part of this line comes from Crowley's *Law of Liberty*, quoting *"ecstasy be thine and joy of earth"* (AL I.53) and *"love is the law"* (AL I.57). Although these pieces are pulled out of context and put together, it is worth noting that the beginnings of the two relevant verses are *"This shall regenerate the world"* (AL I.53) and *"Invoke me under my stars!"* (AL I.57), both concepts of great relevance to the Wiccan tradition, and also hinting at their union in the Orphic Oath of *"I am a child of earth and starry heaven."* So although seemingly out of context, this line retains a great deal of relevant symbolism, even if quite concealed.

This phrase is an inspirational one, as can be seen by the following quote from the nineteenth century English poet and literary critic John Addington Symonds, *"The mania of Plato was a permanent ecstasy of the spirit, in which love led the way to heaven, and raised a man above himself."*[92]

We may also note the occurrence of the phrase *'ecstasy of the spirit'* in the writings of the late fifteenth century poet John Skelton, when he wrote in a way which strongly resembles the reincarnation theme found in the Charge, *"Is it possible that in some such passionate ecstasy of the spirit we pass through death into the life beyond death?"*[93] Skelton also mentioned the triplicity of Diana, Luna and Persephone in his work *Garland of Laurels* in 1523 when he wrote *"Diana in the leaves green, Luna that so bright doth sheen, Persephone in hell"*.

"Keep pure your highest ideal. Strive ever towards it. Let naught stop you or turn you aside. "

Again this line draws straight from the *Law of Liberty*, where Crowley wrote: *"Keep pure your highest ideal; strive ever toward it, without allowing aught to stop you or turn you aside."* This key line refers to the concept of the true will, and doing only what is right to achieve your full potential.

---

92 An Introduction to the Study of Dante, Symonds, 1890
93 Essays in Romance and Studies from Life, Skelton, 1878

"For mine is the secret door which opens upon the land of youth;"

This is somewhat rewritten from the earlier version of the *Charge* (*Lift Up the Veil*), which draws more directly from Liber Al, *"There is a secret door that I shall make to establish thy way in all the quarters"* (AL III.38). The reference to the quarters is one which is not used in the *Charge*, but interesting from the point of view of Wiccan terminology, where the four directions are sometimes referred to as *quarters*. It also hints at the grimoires where the magick circle was often divided into quarters, as seen in the *Heptameron* and subsequent grimoires. The *'land of youth'* is a translation of the name of the Irish otherworldly realm of Tir-na-Nog, home of the Irish pantheon of the Tuatha de Danaan. As the nineteenth century author Thomas Croker observed in *Fairy Legends and Traditions of the South of Ireland* (1828), *"It is called the Land of Youth, because time has no power there, no one becomes old."* The presence in the Charge of this Celtic otherworld clearly indicates the relevance of the Celtic goddesses in the initial list of names.

"and mine is the cup of the Wine of Life: "

This line seems to derive from the Catholic Liturgy, as part of the reading drawn from the Byzantine Matins, in the Table Blessing for Holy Thursday, which goes, *"Instructing his friends into the divine mysteries, Jesus, the wisdom of God, prepares a table that gives food to the soul, and mingles for the faithful the cup of the wine of life eternal. Let us all, therefore, draw near the mysterious table, with pure souls let us receive the Bread of Life"* The real question here, which we can neither prove or disprove at this point, is whether this was a deliberate use or whether it was a phrase merely imbedded in the psyche of the person who compiled the *Charge*, who consequently used it without realising the source of their inspiration?

"and the Cauldron of Ceridwen, which is the Holy Grail of Immortality."

This seems to be original material. The reference to the *"Cauldron of Ceridwen"* brings in another of the goddesses mentioned at the start of the charge. The equation of the cauldron to the Holy Grail, a very Christian symbol, is somewhat puzzling and inappropriate, but it has a nice poetic ring and flows on naturally from the previous line which as we have shown was likely borrowed from Christian liturgy. It is of course also a popular theme in the Arthurian and Grail Mysteries, which might have influenced the person(s)who compiled this piece, due to its inherently *'Celtic'* overtones.

Years later, in *An ABC of Witchcraft* (originally published in 1973), Valiente quoted from Hargrave Jennings' *The Rosicrucians, Their Rites and Mysteries* in her entry for the *Cauldron*. In this, if indeed she was the author of these lines, she may have revealed her inspiration for their inclusion, but this is purely speculation on our part, and certainly is not an adaptation of words / phrases as found throughout the *Charge*. *"We claim the cauldron of the witches as, in the original, the vase or urn of fiery transmigration, in which all things of the world change"*[94]

The idea of immortality is raised in relation to the incarnation of the Goddess on Earth in *Law of Liberty*, as we have seen in regards to the inclusion of Melusine earlier with the phrase *"Elixir of Immortality"*

"I am the Gracious Goddess who gives the gift of Joy unto the heart of Man.
Upon Earth I give the knowledge of the Spirit Eternal,
and beyond death I give peace and freedom,

---

94 An ABC of Witchcraft, Doreen Valiente, 1984

and reunion with those who have gone before.
Nor do I demand aught in sacrifice, "

This is another extract from the *Law of Liberty*, derived from Liber AL 1.58 adapted and expanded on from Crowley's original: *"For hear, how gracious is the Goddess; ``I give unimaginable joys on earth: certainty, not faith, while in life, upon death; peace unutterable, rest, ecstasy; nor do I demand aught in sacrifice."*

"...for behold, I am the Mother of all things,
and my love is poured out upon the earth."

In *The Golden Ass*, Isis says of herself, *"I am she that is the natural mother of all things,"* giving a likely source for the use of this phrase. In this context it could also possibly be derived from the Qabalistic title of the Sephira of Malkuth, *"Mother of all living things"*. Other than this these lines seem to be the original writings of the person(s) who compiled the *Charge*. The phrase *"Mother of all things"* is also found in Milton's *Paradise Lost*, in Book XI where he wrote, *"Eve rightly called, mother of all mankind, mother of all things living, since by thee Man is to live."* This may be significant as a subsequent line in the Charge also seems to originate with this same work by Milton.

"HP: Hear ye the words of the Star Goddess, "

Once again the text returns to Crowley's *Law of Liberty*, *"We have heard the voice of the Star Goddess"*, emphasising the Egyptian stellar goddess Nuit, who represents the entire universe in the cosmology of Thelema.

"She in the dust of whose feet are the hosts of Heaven, whose body encircleth the universe."

This line appears to be more original material which is most likely a continuation of the reference to Nuit, who in Egyptian mythology is perceived as encircling the universe. The phrase *"Hosts of Heaven"* is very widely used, but it is worth noting here that it may refer to the company of Angels in heaven in popular Christian use as it occurs several times in the Bible, or indeed to the Moon and Stars in the Occidental traditions, which again supports the idea that this line refers to the goddess Nuit.

"HPS: I who am the beauty of the green earth;
and the White Moon amongst the Stars; and the mystery of the
Waters; and the desire of the heart of man,"

This is largely original material, though it is possible the line *"desire of the heart of man,"* may have been inspired by Crowley's book *The Vision and the Voice* (1909) where we find *"I am the blind ache within the heart of man"*. We may note however that the phrase *"beauty of the green earth"* used in conjunction with stellar references was a common occurrence in Christian writings of the nineteenth and early twentieth century, so this is a well documented analogy. Illustrating this point with two examples, in *The British Preacher* (1831) we read *"How good must that light be which reveals to us the grandeur of the starry heavens, and the beauty of the green earth,"* and in *Evangelical Christendom* (1893) we see, *"if the glories of the starry heavens, if the beauty of the green earth never taught man of God"*.

"call unto thy soul: arise and come unto me. "

This line is clearly again derived from Crowley's work, as *"arouse the coiled splendour within you: come unto me!"* is found in both the *Law of Liberty* and its inspiration Liber AL I.61.

"For I am the Soul of nature who giveth life to the Universe; From me all things proceed; and unto me, all things must return."

Uniquely this part of the *Charge* appears to come from the *Ritual for Transformation* of the Hermetic Order of the Golden Dawn, in which we find *"O Soul of Nature giving life and energy to the Universe. From thee all things do proceed. Unto Thee all must return."* Alternatively it is possible that the author of the *Charge* took the line, *"From me all things proceed; and unto me, all things must return"*, directly from Milton's *Paradise Lost*, which was the probable source of inspiration for the Golden Dawn.

"and before my face, Beloved of the Gods and men,"

This is again probably original material. Although almost certainly just coincidental, we thought it amusing to mention that this line is also found in a novel published in 1908 which has a character called Doreen in![95] In Norse myths, Baldur, the son of Odin is often referred to as *"beloved of Gods and men"* which might have provided some inspiration for the use of the term; however this seems strange and unlikely considering he is male. With these being words of the goddess this would be an inappropriate usage. However, the Greek goddess of

---

95 Mary Ware: The Little Colonel's Chum, Johnston, 1908

love, Aphrodite, was also sometimes referred to by the same title, and it is hopefully more likely that the author(s) of the *Charge*, may have taken their inspiration from this goddess rather than using the title of a male god.

"let thine inmost divine self shall be enfolded in the raptures of the infinite."

Again this seems to be derived from two more quotes merged from the *Law of Liberty*: *"He is then your inmost divine self"* and *"in the constant rapture of the embraces of Infinite Beauty"*. These quotes are in reference to words spoken by Hadit, the masculine divine in the cosmology of Thelema. Thus it is being used completely inappropriately as words spoken by the Goddess, as in fact it originates in relation to the God. This may indicate that the person compiling this version of the *Charge* was not familiar with Crowley's work or philosophy, but thought of the words themselves as mere poetry to be used, as it would seem from this that the material used to compile the *Charge* was used regardless of its original context and symbolism, instead being purely utilised for its poetic and emotive effects. This recalls Valiente's remark in *An ABC of Witchcraft* that Gardner told her he *"had supplied words which seemed to him to convey the right atmosphere, to strike the right chords in one's mind."* If this is the case, then it could also support the idea that Gardner was the author, or one of the authors, of the original, as it seems to have been rewritten from the *Lift Up the Veil* charge.

"Let my worship be within the heart that rejoiceth, for behold:"

The line *"heart that rejoiceth"* could be taken from Crowley's *Vision and the Voice*, though it is not a unique phrase so this may be coincidence.

"all acts of love and pleasure are my rituals; "

More from the *Law of Liberty*, here emphasising the sexual and sensual components of magickal ceremony in a very Crowleyan manner, *"Remember that all acts of love and pleasure are rituals"*

*"and therefore let there be Beauty and Strength,
Power and Compassion,
Honour and Humility, Mirth and reverence within you."*

The reference to *"beauty and strength"* could be from Liber Al (AL II.20) or may be coincidence. The rest all seems to be original, though it may have been inspired by *"let there be Harmony and Beauty in your mystic loves, that in us may be health and wealth and strength and divine pleasure according to the Law of Liberty";* words spoken by the Deacon during the *Gnostic Mass*, another of Crowley's works.

"And thou who thinkest to seek me, know that thy seeking and yearning shall avail thee not unless thou know the mystery, that if that which thou seekest thou findest not within thee, thou wilt never find it without thee, for behold; I have been with thee from the beginning, and I am that which is attained at the end of desire."

The inspiration here comes from Crowley's Liber LXV, lines 59-60, *"But I have called unto Thee, and I have journeyed unto Thee, and it availed me not. I waited patiently, and Thou wast with me from the beginning."*

Lift Up the Veil

The earlier *Lift Up the Veil* charge, dated to roughly 1949, draws more directly on material written by Aleister Crowley, especially in the second part of the charge spoken by the High Priestess. The material in this instance is drawn directly from Liber Al (*The Book of the Law*) and Liber XV (*The Gnostic Mass*), but in most instances the material found in *Lift Up the Veil* is also found in *Law of Liberty* which as we have already seen played an important role in the inspiration for the later rewrite of the *Charge*.

In the *Gnostic Mass* the priestess declares what is known as the Nuit speech saying: *"I love you! I yearn to you! Pale or purple, veiled or voluptuous, I who am all pleasure and purple, and drunkenness of the innermost sense, desire you. Put on the wings, and arouse the coiled splendour within you: come unto me!"* (AL I.61) which is the inspiration for the first part of the second half of the *Lift Up the Veil* charge. Interestingly, this also appears in *The Law of Liberty* where the Nuit speech is broken into two parts as a result of Crowley's commentary.

This is then strangely followed by the words spoken by the priest, who is the manifestation of the male principle Hadit in the Gnostic Mass saying: *"I am the flame that burns in every heart of man, and in the core of every star..."* (AL II.6). Furthermore, Crowley also utilises this piece of prose in *Law of Liberty*. In both instances it is the words of Hadit, the masculine divine speaking and once again inexplicably puts words originally intended for the god into the mouth of the High Priestess who is representing the feminine divine! This recalls the earlier remark about Gardner's possible involvement in creating the charges.

The next line that follows this in the *Lift Up the Veil* charge again draws from Crowley's *Law of Liberty* for its inspiration. Here the Priestess says: *"Let it be your inmost divine self who art lost in the constant rapture of infinite joy"* which is clearly influenced by*" He is then your own inmost divine self; it is you, and not another, who are lost in the constant rapture of the embraces of Infinite Beauty."*

Lift Up the Veil ends with a paragraph which is composed of a further amalgamation of Crowley's material. Firstly, we find *"Let the rituals be rightly performed with joy & beauty!"* originally from Liber Al (AL II.35), which is also used by Crowley in Liber XV and is used verbatim in *Lift Up the Veil*. This is then followed by another line which draws inspiration from *Law of Liberty* being *"Remember that all acts of love and pleasure are rituals"* which does not appear in Liber Al or Liber XV at all. Next is a line which takes its inspiration from Liber Al *"Beauty and strength, leaping laughter and delicious languor, force and fire, are of us"* (AL II.20) a line which once again also appears in *Law of Liberty*. *Lift Up the Veil* ends in a similar way to the later rewritten *Charge* taking inspiration from Liber LXV, lines 59-60, *"But I have called unto Thee, and I have journeyed unto Thee, and it availed me not. I waited patiently, and Thou wast with me from the beginning"* blended with what seems to be original material.

There are many idiosyncrasies in *Lift Up the Veil* as there are indeed in the later *Charge of the Goddess*. Most curiously it is the use of material blended from Crowley's writings which were meant at times for the Priestess and at times for the Priest. This shows a clear lack of understanding on the part of the person(s) who wrote this prose for the symbolism of the material they were using and may indicate that the person(s) were relatively unfamiliar with Crowley's material – either that or perhaps they liked the sound of the words. What is interesting is that almost all the material can be found in the *Law of Liberty* which would also imply its nature as a source as we have already shown. Though there has been some suggestion over the years that the author(s) of this piece of prose drew their inspiration from the Gnostic Mass or from the Book of the Law, it would seem from the evidence that this is only in as much as that the material from both the *Book of the Law* and *Gnostic Mass* also appears in the *Law of Liberty*.

We also find that in the later *Charge of the Goddess* that some of the material from Crowley's work is indeed removed, though by no means a significant part of it. What is even stranger is that some of the

Crowley material which is removed is then replaced with further material which seems to be clearly influenced by texts written by Crowley! This once again seems to imply that if Doreen Valiente indeed was responsible for the later rewrite of the Charge as she claimed, she only changed the phraseology in places, and though she may have added some original words – inspired either by material written by Crowley, The Hermetic Order of the Golden Dawn or by Church of England liturgy, she clearly only contributed a small part to the mystery of these pieces of prose which have become such an important part of both the esoteric and exoteric traditions of Wicca today.

What is clear is that the Charge of the Goddess, whilst drawing on a range of earlier sources, has developed a huge significance in the Wiccan tradition which cannot be ignored, irrespective of its provenance.

CHAPTER 12

CAKES AND WINE

The ceremony of Cakes and Wine forms an important part of all Wiccan ceremonies; through the actions of the High Priestess and High Priest and the words which are spoken, the symbolic union of the divine feminine and masculine is enacted. It is usual for the High Priestess to first bless the wine, which is held in the cup by the High Priest, by inserting her athame into it. Likewise the High Priestess uses her athame to bless the cakes which are placed on the platter on top of the pentacle and held by the High Priest. Following the blessing of both the cakes and wine, they are passed around the circle and all members of the coven partake thereof.

The act of partaking of the cakes and wine in the magick circle is often confusingly and incorrectly referred to as grounding. Grounding is the act of regaining a normal balanced state of energy after a ceremony in which energies have been raised which affect those present. With this in mind, it is clear that the consecration of, and sharing of cakes and wine during a Wiccan ceremony does not fulfil this function. So what is the function of this part of the ceremony and where does it originate from?

The cakes and wine are shared communally in a Eucharistic act, through which all participants partake of the divine essence with the aim of strengthening their own being towards spiritual and magickal evolution. This becomes more apparent when it is taken into consideration that the ceremony is performed by the High Priestess as the avatar of the divine feminine and the High Priest as the representation of the divine masculine. As such every part of the ceremony has a deep and evolving symbolic meaning and impact on all those who participate.

A fourteenth century Sufi reference quoted in part by Crowley at the beginning of his work on sex magick, *Liber Agapé*, emphasised the Eucharistic nature of the cup of wine in magickal ceremonies, equating the two to the Moon and Sun. It says:

> *"The Sun is the wine and the Moon is the cup.*
> *Pour the Sun into the Moon if you want to be filled."*[96]

Writing in his book *Magick* about the use of food and drink as a Eucharist, Crowley observed:

> *"The magician becomes filled with God, fed upon God, intoxicated with God. Little by little his body will become purified by the internal lustration of God; day by day his mortal frame, shedding its earthly elements, will become in very truth the Temple of the Holy Ghost. Day by day matter is replaced by Spirit, the human by the divine; ultimately the change will be complete; God manifest in flesh will be his name."*

This is not a new concept, and it may find its magickal beginnings in the ancient Egyptian process known as the *"reversion of offerings"*. This was the process where food and drink were offered to the gods, who were believed to partake of the essence of them, and subsequently the food would then revert to the priests for consumption. A variant of this more akin to Wiccan practice is the *Grace before a Meal* spell recorded at Edfu. Here the table was equated to the creator god Atum, so all the

---

96 The Moon of Love, Hafiz, circa 14th century

food and drink, though offered to the gods, was also blessed by the creator before its reversion to the priesthood for consumption.[97]

Although the Eucharist is central to much of Christianity, it has sometimes been vilified when used as a practice by rivals. Writing in the second century CE, St Irenaeus accused the Gnostic teacher Marcus of perverting the Mass by faking consecration of cups of wine, so that his followers would believe they were imbued with the divine presence of Charis ('*Grace*'), a name given to Divine Thought. What is significant here is that the Gnostics should be consecrating the wine with the divine presence, whether the Church chose to slander it or not.

> "*Pretending to consecrate cups mixed with wine, and protracting to great length the word of invocation, he contrives to give them a purple and reddish colour, so that Charis, who is one of those that are superior to all things, should be thought to drop her own blood into that cup through means of his invocation, and that thus those who are present should be led to rejoice to taste of that cup, in order that, by so doing, the Charis, who is set forth by this magician, may also flow into them.*"[98]

Of course the Catholic practice of the Mass has the Eucharist as the centre of its mystery, but as was often the case with Christianity, this was a practice they adopted from earlier cultures, rather than an original component. So even if the Christian Mass is viewed as the obvious source of Cakes & Wine in the Wiccan tradition, it comes from earlier pagan roots.

The *Key of Solomon* contains a reference to what we now call Cakes & Wine, though it is in the context of offerings rather than the previously discussed Eucharistic form.

---

97 Practical Egyptian Magickal Spells, Ritner, 1998
98 Against Heresies, Irenaeus, 2nd century CE

"But when we make sacrifices of food and drink, everything necessary should be prepared without the Circle, and the meats should be covered with some fine clean cloth, and also have a clean white cloth spread beneath them; with new bread and sparkling wine."

The idea of the Cakes & Wine as offerings is also as valid as that of the Eucharist. As already stated, the Egyptians offered food and wine to their gods, and also to their ancestors. This has been a common practice in many cultures around the world throughout history.

In the Adeptus Minor ritual of the Golden Dawn, the dagger is dipped into the chalice of wine, before the aspirant is consecrated. The symbolism of this act within the Golden Dawn system does however not equate to that of the consecration of the wine in the Wiccan tradition, and as such cannot be seen as a precedent in its form beyond the symbolic actions, although it is sometimes claimed as such.

This symbolism of the dagger being placed in the chalice of wine is one that is central to the Wiccan tradition as representing the union of the Goddess and the God. The chalice represents the divine feminine and the athame the divine masculine, the symbolic union of the two when the athame enters the cup brings forth blessedness through their union. There is a significant issue of polarity being balanced and exchanged with the blessing of the wine, which should be symbolically obvious to anyone who has partaken of the ceremony.

"O Queen most secret, bless this food unto our bodies, bestowing health, wealth, strength, joy, and peace, and that fulfilment of Will, and Love under Will, which is perpetual happiness."

These words come straight from Crowley's *Gnostic Mass*, and emphasise the Eucharistic nature of the sacrament. That they are used in a slightly adapted form in Wicca clearly indicates that the emphasis is on the Eucharistic nature of Cakes & Wine, particularly when they are consecrated after the Great Rite.

Feasting is a significant communal part of ritual, and the importance of feasting at the gatherings is stressed by Murray in *The God of the Witches,* where she described a number of feasts, referring to *"wine to drink and wheat bread to eat",* which is a combination that will be very familiar to Wiccans. This may be where the change in emphasis from Eucharist to feast comes from.

The cup is not a tool with much magickal history outside of Christianity. The use of cups in the *Greek Magickal Papyri* is exclusively for love, passion or death spells. The other main use of the cup is as a skrying aid. The Eucharistic cup of communion is a focus in some branches of Christianity. This use is clearly paralleled in Wicca, although both sides would probably prefer to ignore this. The Bible gave a clear indication of this use when St Paul wrote in *1 Corinthians* 10:16,

> *"The chalice of benediction, which we bless, is it not the communion of the blood of Christ?"*

Again pointing to a possible influence of the *Key of Solomon* in Wiccan practice, it is interesting to note that during the presentation of the tools in the first degree initiation ceremony, the chalice is often omitted, whilst the eight other tools are given precedence. The cup plays a lesser role in Solomonic rites, which is the reason sometimes given for it being omitted.

In *Witchcraft Today* Gardner mused about the exclusion of the chalice during initiations, which all those working within the tradition will know is an important tool as it is used in all ceremonies, including initiations. Gardner wrote *"At first I was puzzled by the absence of the Cup from the witches' working tools and the inclusion of the unimportant pentacle, said to be used to command spirits..."*; going on to say that he was told that the exclusion of the chalice was a remnant of the *Burning Times* as any mention of the cup would have led to an *"Orgy of torture"* due to a perceived parody of the Christian Mass. However, this is a ridiculous justification as the chalice, regardless of its omission in the traditional initiation rites, is still a tool which is, as previously stated, used in every single ceremony – so it is unlikely that anyone who saw a Wiccan ceremony being performed, or who chanced upon a Book of Shadows, and who was looking for evidence of a Christian parody would not notice the inclusion of the chalice! Even on a very simple level, though it may not be presented in the First Degree Initiation, it is still used for the Cakes & Wine component of the ceremony which forms a part of it. Gardner's comment that the pentacle is unimportant is a puzzling one. As all consecrations are performed on the pentacle, it is an extremely significant tool.

The cakes are placed on a wooden platter which is then put on top of the pentacle. The use of an offering plate for food is one that dates back thousands of years. The Greeks and Romans used a patera (offering plate), and many of the depictions seen as carvings, statues and on gems of Romano-Celtic deities found in Britain show both goddesses and gods bearing a patera. These include an unnamed horned goddess, four figures of the genius (spirit) standing next to an altar with flame on top,[99] and figures and gems of such deities as the goddesses Fortuna, Juno and Minerva and the gods Mercury and Jupiter, as well as many others.

The significance of Cakes & Wine as a magickal act has been emphasised, and its use as a part of all Wiccan ceremonies reinforces its nature as a Eucharistic act to further the development of the practitioners. The Christian Eucharist is the most likely source of this practice, although it derives from earlier pagan religions.

---

99 A Corpus of Roman Engraved Gemstones from the British Isles, Henig, 1974

CHAPTER 13

THE GREAT RITE

The Great Rite is performed as part of the Third Degree initiation ceremony, as well as at some of the Sabbats and other important rites. The ceremony of Cakes and Wine is sometimes referred to as the *'symbolic Great Rite'* as it, like the Great Rite, represents the union of the divine feminine with the divine masculine. By its very nature the Great Rite is one of the most private ceremonies of the Wiccan Tradition, and it is usual for all members of the coven to turn their backs or leave the circle when it is being performed in *'actuality'*, that is as a sexual consummation, rather than in *'token'*, that is its symbolic form without sexual consummation. The Great Rite is performed by a High Priestess and High Priest who have both attained Third Degree within the tradition and is, of course, only performed between consenting adults.

When considering the origins of the Great Rite we need to examine both the words and actions found in this Wiccan ceremony, as well as its purpose and symbolism as a magickal act.

At the start of the ceremony the High Priest declares the body of the High Priestess as being the altar:

> *"Assist me to erect the ancient altar, at which in days past all worshipped, the great altar of all things. For in old times woman was the altar. Thus was the altar made and placed;"*

The idea of a woman being the altar in magickal ceremonies dates back many hundreds of years and it is not unreasonable to believe that it may have entered the Wiccan Tradition by virtue of inspiration from one of the earlier sources. This idea is also found prominently in the writings of Dion Fortune's novel *The Sea Priestess* where the hero Wilfred Maxwell has a soliloquy about his fiancé Molly saying:

> *"When the body of a woman is made an altar for the worship of the Goddess who is all beauty and magnetic life, and the man pours himself out in worship and sacrifice, keeping back no part of the price but giving his very self for love, seeing in his mate the priestess serving with him in the worship - then the Goddess enters the temple."*

Fortune was likely to have been inspired by earlier esoteric works in her writing. One such influential text was written in the nineteenth century by the French historian Jules Michelet (1798–1874) in 1862, *La Sorcière*, in which he argued that witchcraft had been the original religion of Europe. Michelet, on describing the preparations undertaken by the witch, declared,

> *"with equal solemnity she purifies her person. Henceforth she is the living altar of the shrine."*

Michelet presented a model of a nature and fertility cult, which was led by priestesses and had managed to survive and flourish underground during the Middle Ages as a sanctuary for oppressed women. His labours laid the groundwork for later writers and anthropologists such as Leland and Murray, and thus arguably for the emergence of the Wiccan Tradition. In addition to emphasising the witch as a positive figure, Michelet also cited the idea of the naked body of the witch as the altar.

> *"At the Witches' Sabbath woman fulfils every office. She is priest, and altar, and consecrated host."*

In doing so Michelet may have been drawing on accounts from the witch trials and the famous case of La Voisin, a major French scandal of the seventeenth century. In 1679 one of king Louis XIV's mistresses, Madame de Mountespan, enlisted the aid of Catherine La Voisin, an infamous sorceress and poisoner. Both the women played the part of altar for black masses performed by Abbé Guiborg, a renegade Catholic priest. Noteworthy in the descriptions of these events are that *"as often as the priest was to kiss the altar, he kissed the body,"*[100] and *"at the end of the Mass, the priest went into the woman"*.[101]

For those familiar with the Great Rite it is also worth commenting here that the women were described as holding black candles in their hands during the ceremony and that the chalice would be placed upon their naked bellies. Though of course not performed for the same reasons, nor with the same intentions, it is interesting to note the similarities here between a Black Mass and the Wiccan ceremony of the Great Rite.

If we consider the difference between the symbolic and actual Great Rite, the symbolic version ends with the blessing of the wine, and does not contain sexual union. The actual Great Rite may have its magickal roots in several distinct areas which need to be considered in turn, such as the ancient hieros gamos (*"holy union"*). In his work *Occultism, Witchcraft & Cultural Fashions*, the noted anthropologist Mircea Eliade observed that:

> *"The importance of ceremonial nudity and ritual intercourse must not be interpreted as merely lustful inclinations. The recent sexual revolution has made obsolete such types of pretence and masquerade. Rather, the purpose of ritual nudity and orgiastic practices is to recapture the sacramental value of sexuality."*

---

100 The Satanic Mass, Rhodes, 1955
101 The Satanic Mass, Rhodes, 1955

Returning to the writings of Dion Fortune, she seemed to be hinting at the ultimate purpose of such a union of the divine female and male through sexual union in *The Sea Priestess* when she wrote:

> *"Do you not know the Mystery saying that all the gods are one god, and all the goddesses are one goddess, and there is one initiator? Do you not know that at the dawn of manifestation the gods wove the web of creation between the poles of the pairs of opposites, active and passive, positive and negative, and that all things are these two things in different ways and upon different levels, even priests and priestesses"*

It should be observed that although an act of sexual magick might have seemed socially shocking, on an esoteric level there were several magickal orders which performed sex magick by the 1930s, including the O.T.O., the G.B.G. (Great Brotherhood of God) and the Fraternitas Saturni (Brotherhood of Saturn).

Looking back in time, the earliest root of the hieros gamos can be seen in ancient Sumeria, with the public ritual union of the king and the priestess of the goddess Inanna as an act of fertility, empowerment and prosperity. The king took the part of the shepherd god Dumuzi and the priestess of Inanna, the great goddess who loved him, and the two enacted a graphic and beautifully poetic dialogue prior to their union. There was even a blessing of the food by the divinely inspired king after the hieros gamos which parallels the blessings after the Great Rite:

> *"The king reaches out his hand for food and drink.*
> *Dumuzi reaches out his hand for food and drink.*
> *The palace is festive."*[102]

---

102 Inanna: Queen of Heaven and Earth, Wolkstein & Kramer, 1984

This is quite clearly one of the earliest sources of the ideas expressed by the Great Rite, both in symbolic form and actuality, in an act which is pure Hieros Gamos, as opposed to the act of Sacred Sex.

The Celts also had their own version of the hieros gamos in their myths and tales. The Celts viewed the land as being female, and the sovereign responsibility of the goddess in one of her guises, which is reflected in the Bestower of Sovereignty tales. The ancient idea of the *'king and the land are one'* is clearly expressed through the testing of the hero. If the king (or knight) accepts the goddess and sees past the hideous physical appearance she assumes, to recognise her sovereignty of the land, which he holds through her grace, she transforms into the beautiful young goddess and consecrates him as the rightful king (or rewards him with a beautiful and faithful magickal wife). This theme occurs in Irish myths, such as *Niall of the Nine Hostages*, and *The Adventure of Daire's Sons*.

This theme of the sovereignty bestowing hag who transforms into a beautiful maiden during the hieros gamos continued as a very popular one into British literature throughout the fourteenth century and into the fifteenth century. We see it in *The Wedding of Sir Gawain and Dame Ragnell, The Marriage of Sir Gawain, The Ballad of King Henry, The Ballad of Kemp Owyne The Ballad of the Knight and the Shepherd's Daughter, Tale of Florent* and Chaucer's *The Wife of Bath's Tale*. The Scottish tale *Nighean Righ fo Thuinn ("The Daughter of the King under the Waves")*, and the Icelandic *Saga of King Hrolf Kraki,* also demonstrate the popularity of this theme.

The goddess in alchemy is often shown with either a lunar crescent on her head, or a crescent or full moon for her face, and indeed is often referred to as Diana, harking back to ancient Rome (and also witchcraft). Likewise the god is often referred to as Apollo, and shown with a Sun on his head or a rayed solar face. Whilst all the classical planets were depicted and significant in alchemy (especially Mercury as Hermes), it was the interaction of female and male, Diana and Apollo, that embodied the alchemical process of transformation. From here the model of the solar male and lunar female united in the hieros gamos became an iconic image found in many texts.

If we look particularly at the alchemical imagery from the sixteenth and seventeenth century of the union of the king and queen, we can see a strong case for a precursor of the Great Rite. In these images the empowered man and woman (i.e. king and queen) are united sexually in a sacred vessel, such as a sepulchre (*The Rosary of the Philosophers, La Bugia*) or flask (*Anatomia Auri*), which can be seen as representing the otherworldly space of the magick circle as a place of divine union.

Returning to the Great Rite, we will continue to consider the wording of the invocations and incantations used by the High Priest as he consecrates the High Priestess for this ceremony. As with many of the most beautiful texts found in the Wiccan Book of Shadows, it draws heavily from the writings of Aleister Crowley, in particular his channelled text, the *Book of the Law* and also *Liber XV*, better known as the *Gnostic Mass*.

> *"and the sacred point was the point within the centre of the circle. As we have of old been taught that the point within the centre is the origin of all things, therefore should we adore it."*

The point within the centre of the circle is a classic image, which is seen in astrology as the image of the sun. In alchemy this image symbolises perfection and the universal quintessence as part of the *Golden Chain of Homer*.[103] This symbol also represents the union of the goddess Nuit (the circle) with the god Hadit (point) in the cosmology of Thelema.

The first part of the invocation is clearly derived from the following extracts from Chapter I in the *Book of the Law* addressing the Egyptian stellar goddess Nuit:

---

103 Aurea Catena, Homer, 1723

"O Nuit, continuous one of heaven, let it be ever thus, that men speak not of Thee as one but as none; and let them not speak of Thee at all, since Thou art continuous!"[104]

This is then followed with the words of Hadit, from Chapter II in the *Book of the Law*. Hadit is the masculine principle from the perspective of this text,

"I am the flame that burns in every heart of man, and in the core of every star. I am life and the giver of life, yet therefore is the knowledge of me the knowledge of death."[105]

"I am alone: there is no god where I am."[106]

The *Gnostic Mass* also contains a number of Crowley quotes which are used in the Great Rite and which are not from *The Book of the Law*. These are:

"Thee therefore whom we adore we also invoke, by the power of the lifted lance."

"O circle of stars whereof our Father is but the younger brother, marvel beyond imagination, soul of infinite space, before whom Time is ashamed, the mind bewildered, and the understanding dark, not unto Thee may we attain, unless Thine image be Love."

"O secret of secrets that art hidden in the being of all that lives, not Thee do we adore, for that which adoreth is also Thou. Thou art That, and That am I."

---

104 Liber Al, Aleister Crowley, 1904
105 Liber Al, Aleister Crowley, 1904
106 Liber Al, Aleister Crowley, 1904

"Make open the path of creation and of intelligence between us and our minds. Enlighten our understanding. Encourage our hearts. Let Thy light crystallize itself in our blood, fulfilling us of Resurrection."

This latter quote is interesting, as according to Janet and Stewart Farrar writing in *The Witches Bible* this piece was written by Doreen Valiente. Again there has either been a misunderstanding or Valiente seems to have claimed credit for another piece of Crowley's writing.

There is a Qabalistic reference in the Great Rite which was probably drawn from the writings of the Golden Dawn. This is the reference to the twin black and white pillars, Boaz and Jachim. These two pillars are the Black Pillar of Severity (Goddess) and White Pillar of Mercy (God) of the Tree of Life. As you look at the image of the Tree of Life, the Black Pillar is on the left, and the white Pillar is on the right. This symbolism is clearly expressed (significantly) in the High Priestess tarot card in the Rider Waite deck. This deck was first published in 1910 and illustrated by the magickal artist Pamela Colman-Smith. In the trump, the High Priestess is seated on an altar between the two pillars, with the black pillar on the viewer's left and the white pillar on the viewer's right. The pillars are marked with the letters B and J respectively, representing Boaz and Jachim. This symbolism is also why in some traditions the Goddess candle is placed on the left on the altar, and the God candle on the right on the altar.

The eighteenth century Masonic tract *The Grand Mystery Lodge Laid Open* (1726) described the *"five points of fellowship"* where bodies should touch during the ritual embrace, as *"foot to foot, knee to knee, breast to breast, hand to back, cheek to cheek"*. This is clearly the origin of the use of this term in the Great Rite ceremony, though it is not identical. Here we should however clarify that the five points of fellowship from a Masonic viewpoint are defined as part of the work undertaken by a mason.

These five key principles can be summed up as:

- Morality
- Assiduity
- Sobriety
- Obedience
- Nobility

In Masonry, as in Wicca, the *"five-points of fellowship"* are represented by the symbol of the pentagram. For the mason, this may also represent the five wounds of Christ when he was crucified at Golgotha.

In the Great Rite, the changing of one of these phrases to *"lance to grail"* is undoubtedly a reference to the Arthurian Grail legends, perhaps to imply Celtic mysteries and myths. In doing so the emphasis is then superficially moved to the sexual symbolism, and in reality is referring to the blood of Christ, as the Grail legends are focused on the grail being used by Joseph of Arimathea to collect Christ's blood after his side was pierced by the lance when he was hanging on the cross. So it is the literal blood of life of the man-god, not the symbolic blood/wine of the Eucharist, which is actually implied here.

Although there are many earlier precedents of the hieros gamos and sacred sex, the Great Rite in Wicca is most likely to draw its practice from the Thelemic magickal orders of the early twentieth century, like the Ordo Templi Orientis, Great Brotherhood of God and Fraternitas Saturni, which all used sex magick as part of their practices.

When considering the origins of the Great Rite, possibly the most controversial and easily misunderstood aspect of the Wiccan tradition, we felt we should end this chapter with a quote from the nineteenth century American sex magician Pascal Randolph, whose work undoubtedly influenced many who would follow, including the magickal orders we have just mentioned, even though he is rarely credited. In writing on sexual magick Randolph said:

176

"The union of the man with the woman must be innocent. Lust for pleasure must not be the main purpose. Transcending carnal pleasure, aim at the union of the spirits, if you want your prayer to be exhausted in ecstasy. If you conform to these principles, the sexual act will become a source of spiritual and material force for you and a fountainhead of wisdom, happiness and peace. In magic, you search for that which is called the fortune of spirit."[107]

---

107 Magia Sexualis, Randolph, 1876

CHAPTER 14

OF CHANTS

Words have always been thought to hold an inherent magickal power since the creation of language, and Wiccans, like the practitioners of many other magickal traditions, make good use of them in their ceremonies in chants and spells.

The best known chant associated with Wicca today is the *Witches Rune*. This chant appears in different forms in Books of Shadows originating from different time periods, and may be familiar to readers as starting with:

"Darksome night and Shining Moon, East, then South, then West, then North, Hearken to the Witches Rune: Here I come to call thee forth..."

In some versions of the *Witches Rune* it is combined with the refrain of *"Eko, eko, azerak, eko eko, zamilak..."* and in others not.

In 1948 a poem called *Lundy Cave* by Lawry Hawkey was published in the book *A Cornish Chorus*, a collection of Cornish poetry. This poem, which may or may not have been a nominal source of inspiration, contained the phrase *"The Witch's Rune"*. For the curious reader we include an excerpt of this poem to demonstrate the essence it expressed:

"Out of the black dark
Under the moon
That is the way

Of the witches' rune.
Shriek and scrabble
Scream and shout,
Over and under,
In and out,
The wave comes up
And the witch goes in,
Back to the cauldron
Black as sin!"

A very commonly used chant in Wicca comes from the writings of Rudyard Kipling. The chant *Oak and Ash and Thorn,* which is one of the six verses of the poem *A Tree Song,* was taken from the collection of stories *Puck of Pook's Hill* (1906) and used in a number of the Sabbat rituals in a very slightly modified form.

"Oh, do not tell the priest of our plight,
Or he would call it a sin;
But - we have been out in the woods all night,
A-conjuring Summer in!
And we bring you news by word of mouth
Good news for cattle and corn,
Now is the Sun come up from the South
With Oak, and Ash, and Thorn!"

It is interesting to note that in the same book Kipling also referred to the smith god Weland (*The Runes on Weland's Sword*) and to Mithras (*A Song to Mithras*), and included a poem called *A Pict Song* which may well have influenced Gardner's view of the Picts as the original fairy folk as portrayed in his later books.

Another popular chant used in some Wiccan traditions is found in Valiente's work *Witchcraft for Tomorrow.* The chant begins *"Black spirits and white, red spirits and grey."* We may note the inspiration for these

179

words, i.e. their magickal beginning, in Thomas Middleton's 1613 play *The Witch,* where the chief witch Hecate says these exact same words.

Another significant chant in the Wiccan tradition is the *Healing Rune.* The *Charm of the Sprain* (No. 130) in *Carmina Gadelica* may be the origin of the *Healing Rune,* which is found in some of the traditions derived from the teachings of Gardner. It reads:

> *"Bride went out*
> *In the morning early*
> *With a pair of horses;*
> *One broke his leg,*
> *With much ado,*
> *That was apart,*
> *She put bone to bone,*
> *She put flesh to flesh,*
> *She put sinew to sinew,*
> *She put vein to vein,*
> *As she healed that*
> *May I heal this."*

However a likely candidate for being the origin of both the *Healing Rune* and the *Charm of the Sprain* is an old Norse incantation which has been shortened to:

> *"Baldur rade. The foal slade.*
> *Set bone to bone,*
> *Sinew to sinew,*
> *Heal, in Odin's name!"*

This Norse version is an abbreviated form of the Second Merseberg Charm, written in Old High German in the tenth century CE. This short version was given in *Witches Still Live* in 1929, with a fascinating bit of contextual material, where the author reported that *"the incantation used by this modern witch, to such very good effect, was a variation of (this)"*. As this is far closer to the Healing Rune, the fact that the witch was using a variant of the Norse charm in 1929 (possibly the Healing Rune?) does give some strong hints again of at least some pre-Gardnerian goings on.

Words which do not fit into the common language, with strange sounds, are known as barbarous words, and have a long history of magickal use. In his classic work *Magick*, Crowley observed of barbarous words that:

> *"The long strings of formidable words which roar and moan through so many conjurations have a real effect in exalting the consciousness of the magician to the proper pitch."*

The Greek playwright Euripides first mentioned the phenomenon of witches using barbarous words of power in his play *Iphigenia among the Taurians*, written around 414-412 BCE, when he had Iphigenia preparing the sacrifice of Orestes, as she *"shouted barbarous words, as a true witch"*. The use of barbarous words also played a significant role in the *Greek Magickal Papyri*, where they were used as a major component of the vox magica of the spells. Interestingly barbarous words also continued into Christian magick, as seen in Coptic magickal papyri dating from the first through to the twelfth century CE.

So why do Wiccans use barbarous words and names in ritual? The Greek philosopher Iamblichus, in response to a question by Porphyrii, gave what we think is a good explanation of the benefits and purpose of barbarous words in his book *On the Mysteries* when he wrote around the end of the third century CE:

> *"But you ask, 'Why, of significant names, we prefer such as are Barbaric to our own?' Of this, also, there is a mystic reason. For because the Gods have shown that the whole dialect of sacred nations, such as those of the Egyptians and Assyrians, is adapted to sacred*

concerns; on this account we ought to think it necessary that our conference with the Gods should be in a language allied to them. Because likewise, such a mode of speech is the first and most ancient. And especially because those who first learned the names of the Gods, having mingled them with their own proper tongue, delivered them to us, that we might always preserve immoveable the sacred law of tradition, in a language peculiar and adapted to them. For if any other thing pertains to the Gods, it is evident that the eternal and immutable must be allied to them."

As well as barbarous words, words from a foreign language, particularly one with an associated magick, have also been perceived as having power. This is referred to in the *Chaldean Oracles of Zoroaster,* translated and published by Wynn Westcott of the Golden Dawn in 1895, with a strict imprecation:

"When you see the lunar spirit approaching, offer the stone called Mnizouris, while you pray. Do not alter the foreign names!"

The Enochian words received by Dr John Dee in the late sixteenth century are another good example of a language that sounded like barbarous words, and is often used with great effect and potency by modern magickians. Enochian has its own language and linguistic structure, and has the coherence one would expect from any language. Whilst the true meaning and origins of this language remain a mystery, the pronunciation of the words has been believed since the time of Dee to be a powerful magickal act. Gerald Gardner was certainly both impressed and familiar with Enochian, mentioning its use in *The Meaning of Witchcraft*:

"Words in an unknown tongue, especially 'Enochian', as used by Dr Dee and Edward Kelley (and later Aleister Crowley), or a string of words of unknown meaning, 'the barbarous names of evocation', have

the best effect; though to use them effectively you must learn them by heart"

The Wiccan tradition makes use of barbarous words, and there has been much debate about the chant first seen in this context in *High Magic's Aid* and subsequently reproduced in the Book of Shadows and elsewhere. This chant is commonly referred to simply as the *Bagabi* or the *Bagabi Rune*:

> *"Bagabi laca bachabe*
> *Lamac cahhi achababe*
> *Karrelyos*
> *Lamac lamac Bachalyas*
> *Cabahagy sabalyos*
> *Baryolos*
> *Lagoz atha cabyolas*
> *Samahac et famyolas Harrahya."*

Over the years there has been much debate about the origin and nature of the *Bagabi*. It can be traced to a thirteenth century play called *Le Miracle de Théophile* written by a French troubadour called Ruteboeuf. The chant was given as a barbarous invocation used by the magician of the story to invoke the devil (the story of Theophilus is discussed further in the next chapter *The Sabbats*). The use of it was recounted in subsequent books during the nineteenth century, including *Histoire des Francais des divers etats* published in 1853:

> *"Par exemple, dans le miracle de Theophile, qui ne tremble quand le*
> *sorcier Salatin appelle le Diable par cette terrible incantation:*
> *Bagahi, laca, bachahe!*
> *Lamac, cahi, achabahe!*
> *Karrelyos!*
> *Lamac, Lamec, Bahalyos!"*

And as illustrated here by its use in the novel *The Day He Died* in 1947, the chant was not at all obscure at the time that Gardner emerged with his witch cult in the early 1950's:

> *"Karrelyos - Lamac lamec Bachalyas," he chanted his voice rising and falling rhythmically. "Cahagy sabalyos, Baryolas, Lagoz atha Cabyolas..."*

The author Michael Harrison attempted to equate this chant to the Basque language in his *The Roots of Witchcraft* in 1973, giving a possible translation for this chant which results in a rather entertaining English rendition. His translation of the whole chant, rather than the initial part quoted above which is used more widely, goes something like:

> *"Kill (for the Feast) in November, kill! I shall transport thee there myself, and without the aid of a sieve, to scour the plates and dishes with sand: work (which must be done) with those plates and dishes. (We shall meet our friends) ready for the drinking-cup if they shall go (to the Feast), their bellies full with quaffing from the drinking-cup. O Sons (of the Master) with your Families, (shout His praises with the cry:) 'HURRAHYA'!"*

If this indeed is a correct translation, it would make it a rather ridiculous and bizarre chant to be using in the context of raising power in a Wiccan ceremony, yet when used the *Bagabi* does definitely seem to have an inherent power of its own. One can also easily see why it is appealing to try and link the *Bagabi* to the Basque region of Spain, considering the history of witchcraft persecutions this area suffered.

No linguistic equivalent in any language, or barbarous version in grimoires or old magickal papyri seems to exist for this particular chant. However, considering the villain in the original tale of Theophilus is a Jewish magician, it is possible that the Bagabi is in fact a corrupted Hebrew chant. Alternatively, we suggest it could equally likely just have been made up in an attempt to appear mystical, and decided for the purposes of this volume to demonstrate how easily this can be done and how easily it can be given meaning.

For the purposes of this exercise, completely in the name of curiosity and fun, we decided to analyse *"Eko, eko, azerak, eko eko, zamilak"* as this is significantly more important in Wicca today, forming part of the popular *Witches Rune* chant as well as being used in some instances with the *Bagabi* in the Books of Shadows of some traditions. We decided to apply the logic which might have been used to create such a chant during the first part of the twentieth century, around the first time this particular part of the chant appears to surface. This is what we came up with:

Chant Words	Our "Logic"	Meaning
Eko, Eko	If you reverse "eko" you get "oke" which is an old spelling for "oak". Of course the Oak tree has much symbolism in British and European Magick.	Oak, Oak
Azerak	If you reverse this word you get "kareza" a tantric technique for sustained sex without orgasm.	Sex
Eko, Eko	See Above	Oak, Oak
Zamilak	This sounds like "semiiak", an Ancient Greek word of power associated with the Sun. Again the Sun is a powerful symbol in magick and associated with the God in Wicca.	Sun

This would then give *"Eko, eko, azerak, eko eko, zamilak "*a meaning of *"oak, oak, sex, oak, oak, Sun"*, which though we are not claiming it as the real meaning, is as valid an argument as any other! Another plausible explanation for the use of *eko* in this chant is that it might originate with the word *eke*, as in eke-name, the old version of 'nick-name'.

The barbarous phrase *"Eko, eko, azerak, eko eko, zamilak"* can be traced back to 1921 when it was published by J.F.C. Fuller, one of

Crowley's disciples who went on to become a top general and the inventor of blitzkrieg, in the magazine *Form,* and was subsequently reproduced in the *Occult Review* in 1923. *Form* magazine was edited by a magician who claimed a connection to traditional witchcraft, the artist Austin Osman Spare, who would later meet Gardner as already mentioned. The chant as written by Fuller goes:

> *"Eko! Eko! Azarak! Eko! Eko! Zomelak!*
> *Zod-ru-kod e Zod-ru-koo*
> *Zon-ru-koz e Goo-ru-mu!*
> *Eo! Eo! Oo...Oo...Oo!"*[108]

Interestingly, in a footnote in *Eight Sabbats for Witches* the Farrars quote Doreen Valiente as saying that she believed that the *eko eko* was part of an old chant. She then went on to say that they (presumably a reference to her work with Gardner) used it as part of the *Bagabi* but that she believed it to be *"part of another chant"* which she then went on to quote, as being, apart from a few phonetics, exactly the same as the one given by Fuller! Doreen also suggested that the words *Zomelak and Azerak* are the names of Gods, an idea we shall return to very shortly. Whilst Doreen's account on this is interesting, it is clear that she was either given access to the version published by Fuller, through Gardner or someone else, or that she as a well read lady may have been familiar with the article written by Fuller herself.

Where Fuller got the chant from, or whether he made it up, is the next question when considering this significant short phrase. Considering the words we came up with the following possibilities. The word *eko,* if taken as a written form of how a word sounds, would equate to the Italian *ecco,* meaning *'here'.* So this would then equate to *"here, here,"* which would fit with a calling to the gods. A word which

---

108 The Black Arts, 1921 in Form magazine, Fuller, reprinted in 1923 in The Occult Review.

could be a prototype for *azerak* appeared in the fourth century CE Gnostic Baptism of Fire. This word is *azarakaza*, which is one of the imperishable names of God.[109] We were unable to find any word which is close to Zomelak, the nearest being the aforementioned Semiiak. So, hypothetically, *"eko, eko, azerak"* might be *"here, here, imperishable god."* It is tempting to imagine this is the case as Valiente suggested, and that *zomelak* is an as yet undiscovered goddess name.

Words have power through repetition and use – thus chants, songs and prayers which have been used for a long period of time by many people for the same purpose will have a power inherent in them. This point is well made in the *Chaldean Oracles*:

> *"Never change barbarous Names;*
> *For there are Names in every Nation given from God,*
> *Which have an unspeakable power in Rites."*

As can be seen a long history for the use of such words of power exists. Examples can be found back throughout history and in nearly every culture and magickal tradition, in different guises, but always with the belief that such words have their own special power. In many instances certain words of power are only shared amongst initiates of a particular tradition.

The words of power in Wicca will continue to gain more power from use. Both the English and barbarous words are effective as part of the process of raising energy for magickal results, and clearly continue an ancient tradition of vox magicae.

---

109 Ancient Christian Magic, Meyer, 1999

CHAPTER 15

THE SABBATS

The celebration of the Sabbats forms the axis around which the Wiccan year revolves. The eight Sabbats are celebrated roughly every six to seven weeks, marking the seasonal changes experienced through the year. Unlike the Esbats, which are focused on magickal work, the Sabbats are focused on devotion and celebration. This is not to say that magickal work may not occur at Sabbats, but the flavour is very different between the two types of Wiccan ceremony.

Murray's descriptions of the meetings held by witches may be the template from which the Wiccan tradition has drawn inspiration. However it should be noted that Murray used the term *'Sabbath'* rather than *'Sabbat'*, a small but significant difference.

But what is the origin of the word *Sabbat* and when was it first used? It is clearly derived from Sabbath, and the term Sabbath first occurs in relation to witchcraft in the inquisitorial records of trials in the Carcassonne and Toulouse regions of France between 1330 and 1340.[110] In these records it was used to describe the regular witches' meetings, occurring on Friday nights and particular festivals:

> *"Frequently on Friday nights they have attended the Sabbath which is held sometimes in one place, sometimes in another … the he-goat in return taught her all kinds of secret spells; he explained poisonous plants to her and she learned from him words for incantations and*

---

110 A History of the Inquisition of the Middle Ages, Lea, 1887

how to cast spells during the night of the vigil of St John's day, Christmas Eve, and the first Friday in every month."[111]

There has been a lot of debate as to the source of the word Sabbath, but considering the medieval tendency to also refer to gatherings of witches as a *'synagogue'*,[112] probably because of the persecution and suspicion directed towards Jews in medieval Europe, then it seems likely, as the Spanish Basque anthropologist Baroja states in his *The World of the Witches,* that it was simply a borrowing of the Jewish word. This linking of Jews to witchcraft probably had its roots in the sixth century tale of Theophilus, a frustrated cleric who on the advice of a Jewish magician sold his soul to the devil for power, and repented at the time of delivery, appealing to the Virgin Mary, who descended into hell, took the contract and delivered Theophilus to heaven. This story would be translated into many languages and held up in medieval times as an example of the evil of Jews, the devil and by extension demonic pacts (associated with witchcraft). The story is significant in that it was the prototype drawn on for the medieval *Le Miracle de Théophile* (source of the *Bagabi* chant) and also the legend of Faust.

This then also fits in with the use of Friday night as the time for the Sabbaths, as sundown on Friday is the beginning of the Jewish Sabbath (until sundown on Saturday). That this was a well-known idea can be seen in instances such as the artwork of the fifteenth century German artist Conrad Witz. He named one of his paintings that formed part of an altar triptych *The Synagogue* (1435), which depicted a witch with a broken staff and two tablets covered in gibberish, defeated by the power of the church.

Sabbat is simply an alternative transliteration of Sabbath, from the Hebrew word *Shabat,* (ShBT) meaning *"to cease, rest",* and used in the

---

111 Les jardins de l'Histoire, Gebhardt, 1911
112 Zauberwahn, Hansen, 1900

book of *Genesis* to refer to Saturday as the seventh day of the week. The Hebrew word *Shabbatai* comes from the same root, and means *'Saturn'*, so the connection to Saturday is clear to see. Sabbat is also the French and Old English word, probably derived from Shabat or the Latin *Sabbatum* or Greek *Sabbaton* which also all have the same meaning.

Another possible meaning postulated by Robert Graves and others is that Sabbat was derived from the Moorish term *az zabat* meaning *'the powerful occasion'*. As already discussed the evidence for the Moorish connection is lacking, so although this is an appealing idea, and also sounds similar to the word *azerak*, it is probably coincidental. We may note however that the heretical medieval Christian sect of the Waldenses were known in Spain as *inzabatos*, derived from the word *zabat* signifying a *'shoe'*.[113]

One other possible meaning of Sabbat which we should consider is as a derivative of the term *Sabazia*, the festival of the Thracian god Sabazius, who has been linked to the Greek god Dionysus. Michelet suggested this connection in his 1862 work *La Sorcière* as part of his argument for the survival of ancient pagan worship into the witch cult. Again, whilst an interesting idea, this seems far less likely than the use of the word Sabbath in its Jewish connection, which as we have shown has a great deal of supporting evidence.

In *The God of the Witches* Murray gave the dates of the four Sabbaths, shifting the emphasis from a weekly gathering associated incorrectly with the devil by the medieval Christian church to a quarterly festival connected with the natural cycle:

> *"The Sabbaths were held quarterly, on the second of February (Candlemas day), the Eve of May, the first of August (Lammas), and the Eve of November (All Hallow E'en)."*

---

113 History of the Waldenses, Blair, 1832

Although Murray attributed these Sabbaths to witches' celebrations, in fact they were originally linked to druids. Robert and William Chambers recorded an early occurrence of the celebration of the four great festivals in their 1842 work, *Chambers Information for the People:*

> *"Cormac, bishop of Cashel in the tenth century, records that in his time four great fires were lighted up on the four great festivals of the druids - namely in February, May, August, and November: probably Beltane and Lammas were two of these."*

This is an extremely significant reference which seems to have been largely overlooked. The text the Chambers are referring to is in fact the late ninth century Irish *Psalter of Cashel*, which contained reference to the four great Sabbats being celebrated by the druids as a cycle. This then gives us a clear precedent for celebration of the cycle of the four great Sabbats more than one thousand years ago by the Irish druids.

In *The Witch Cult in Western Europe*, Murray actually mentioned all eight of the modern Sabbats, though she stated the Equinoxes were not celebrated in England. Nevertheless it does give a precedent for the model of the Wheel of the Year found in the evolution of the Wiccan tradition.

> *"The chief festivals were: in the spring, May Eve (April 30), called Roodmas or Rood Day in Britain and Walpurgis-Nacht in Germany; in the autumn, November Eve (October 31), called in Britain Allhallow Eve. Between these two came: in the winter, Candlemas (February 2); and in the summer, the Gule of August (August 1) called Lammas in Britain. To these were added the festivals of the solstitial invaders, Beltane at midsummer and Yule at midwinter; the moveable festival of Easter was also added, but the equinoxes were never observed in Britain."*

These festivals were dates kept by the peasantry, not celebrated as part of witchcraft. Although the witchcraft trial records must be viewed as questionable, what is consistent is the timing of the Sabbats to Fridays and specific Christian feasts, not a cycle of eight seasonal celebrations.

A significant source of material regarding the idea of the Sabbats is *The Golden Bough*. Frazer devoted a chapter of the book to it, discussing the prevalence and importance of the fire festivals in ancient Europe, thus giving an appealing provenance of ancestry to these rites. Frazer himself may well have been influenced by Michelet, who suggested in *La Sorcière* that the Sabbat was part of the celebration of the witches' fertility cult for ensuring abundant crops.

> *"All over Europe the peasants have been accustomed from time immemorial to kindle bonfires on certain days of the year, and to dance round or leap over them."*

These opening words of the chapter *"The Fire Festivals of Europe"* in *The Golden Bough* may well have inspired Gardner in his justification of Wicca as the survival of ancient rites, giving provenance to the antiquity of Wicca. Frazer also made the point of connecting witches to many of the fire-festival celebrations, a point which Gardner or his possible predecessors are unlikely to have ignored. Frazer, as one would expect from a folklorist, detailed many customs associated with the fire festivals, which have subsequently been included in the Wiccan tradition and more modern pagan ceremonies. From jumping the Beltane fires to the burning of the Yule log, Frazer was a prime source of information for anyone looking to discover more about old customs to use and apply in their ceremonies. That such luminaries as Frazer and Murray were folklorists may well have inspired Gardner to become a member of the Folklore Society himself, and avail himself of their not inconsiderable library, though of course he already had a life-long interest in local customs.

"English witchcraft, therefore, was neither a religion nor an organisation. Of course, there were many pagan survivals - magic wells, calendar customs, fertility rites - just as there were many types of magickal activity."[114]

It should by now be clear that the Witches Sabbats were not seasonal celebrations. This idea seems to originate in the writings of Murray, and then be mingled with Frazer's *Golden Bough* and records of ancient Druid practices. Here we should also remember the friendship between Gerald Gardner and Ross Nichols, founder of the Order of Bards, Ovates and Druids and the driving force behind the modern Druidic revival. Nichols also edited Gardner's book *The Meaning of Witchcraft*, and was the deputy editor of the magazine *The Occult Observer*. This friendship may well have provided some of the ideas regarding the Sabbats which would expand the material Gardner already possessed.

Another possible source for the idea of seasonal rites is Dion Fortune in her novel *The Winged Bull* (1935). In this story the hero and heroine perform a Spring Equinox ritual that bears a strong resemblance in concept to the Wiccan perspective of the Sabbat.

"Ursula represents the earth in spring. You are the Sun-god gradually gathering strength as the days lengthen."

"He knew they danced together to slow rhythms. He knew they came up to the altar and drank together from the cup of dark, resinous-tasting wine, and ate together of the broken bread dipped in the coarse salt."

Whilst it has been suggested that early Wiccans only celebrated the four Greater Sabbats, this is not strictly true, as the celebration of

---

114 Religion and the Decline of Magic, Thomas, 1980

Yule is also referred to in early writings by Gardner. He refers in some detail to the Yule rite in chapter 1 of *Witchcraft Today* in 1954. Some of the early Books of Shadows also include a Yule rite, giving five Sabbat celebrations - perhaps there was still a desire to have a party around the time of Christmas!

The term *'Wheel of the Year'* is now commonly understood to correspond to the cycle of eight Sabbats celebrated at intervals of roughly six to seven weeks throughout the year. However, although it may not have been knowingly directly borrowed from there, it is interesting to note that the term Wheel of the Year is first found in the classic ancient Indian text, *The Mahabharata*, describing the god Krishna:

> *"He it is that constitutes the wheel of the year, having three naves and seven horses to drag it. It is in this way that He supports the triple mansion (of the seasons)."*

The Wheel of the Year was a common term from the mid-nineteenth century onwards in written and other published materials. We find it in the book *What the Moon Saw by* Hans Christian Andersen which was published in 1866, the American *Talisman of Battle: And Other Poems* published in 1864, and in popular Welsh poetry such as that found in *Gweithiau: Wedi eu trefnu a'u golygu gan* in 1891 and even in English translations of *The Mahabharata*. The first appearance of this term in a way that blatantly connects it to a cycle of festivals seems to have been in Herman Wouk's work *This Is My God* in 1959, contemporary to Gardner's writings. Chapter 5 of the book is called *The Nature Festivals*, with the first subsection being called *The Wheel of the Year*. Shortly after this the term would start to occur in more occult works, such as Juan Cirlot's *A Dictionary of Symbols* in 1962. The term does not seem to occur in published modern Witchcraft or Wiccan works until the late 1970s.

Considering the medieval persecution of witches, the idea of Wicca borrowing from Christianity may seem rather peculiar. However there are aspects of Wicca that have been clearly derived from Christian sources, just as Christianity drew heavily from earlier pagan religions. A prayer from *Carmina Gadelica*, entitled *God of the Moon* (197), was adapted by Doreen Valiente for the 1953 Yule ritual, which became a standard part of the Book of Shadows ever after. According to Valiente, Gardner challenged her on the day of the ritual to come up with an invocation, so she drew from the *Carmina Gadelica*.[115] Was this simply a challenge, or because Gardner was not good at spontaneous ritual? The original goes:

> *"God of the Moon, God of the Sun,*
> *God of the globe, God of the stars,*
> *God of the waters, the land, and the skies,*
> *Who ordained to us the King of promise.*
> *It was Mary fair who went upon her knee,*
> *It was the King of life who went upon her lap,*
> *Darkness and tears were set behind,*
> *And the star of guidance went up early.*
> *Illumed the land, illumed the world,*
> *Illumed doldrum and current,*
> *Grief was laid and joy was raised,*
> *Music was set up with harp and pedal-harp."*

It is ironic that the provenance of such pieces should have been hidden by Gardner under the pretence of ancient roots, when there were far more genuine ancient roots in the material he had to hand. He published a version of this invocation in his book *Witchcraft Today* in 1954, without any credit to Valiente.

> *"Queen of the Moon, Queen of the Sun,*
> *Queen of the Heaven, Queen of the Stars,*

---

115 Triumph of the Moon, Ronald Hutton, 1999

Queen of the Waters, Queen of the Earth,
Bring to us the Child of Promise.

It is the great mother who giveth birth to him,
It is the Lord of Life who is born again.
Darkness and tears are set aside
When the Sun shall come up early..."

Instead he claimed that he had seen it as part of an interesting ceremony *"the Cauldron of Regeneration and the Dance of the Wheel, or Yule"* for which he stated the above chant was used as part of the ceremony of Drawing Down the Moon, with the members of the coven chanting and dancing in a sunwise direction. Was Gardner referring to the ceremony he did with his own Coven here, or did he indeed hear the chant previously and was Doreen Valiente mistaken when she claims to have written the invocation herself for Yule 1953?

Regardless, it seems that the *Carmina Gadelica* was a popular source of inspiration for Sabbat rituals. Another piece from the same work, the charm, *The Guardian Angel* (18), contains lines in one of its verses that were incorporated into the Spring Equinox ceremony. The verse goes:

"Be thou a bright flame before me,
Be thou a guiding star above me,
Be thou a smooth path below me,
And be a kindly shepherd behind me,
Today, tonight, and forever."

The origins of the Sabbats are one of the most debated issues in the Wiccan tradition. Based on the evidence, we feel the cycle of the four Greater Sabbats of Imbolc, Beltane, Lammas and Samhain, are derived from the precedent of the practices of the Irish druids as mentioned in the tenth century *Psalter of Cashel*. The later inclusion of the solar cycle of the equinoxes and solstices may be derived from more contemporary sources such as the writings of Frazer or Murray, but we have no conclusive evidence for this.

The Sabbats are, as stated in the beginning of this chapter, the central axis of Wicca, providing the basis for the celebrations in a natural, mythical and magickal manner. It is the Sabbats which differentiate Wicca from other contemporary magickal traditions by linking it into the seasonal cycle. By so doing they emphasise the interconnectedness of the Wiccan with nature, a fact that is all too easy to forget in the modern world.

CHAPTER 16

THE PENTAGRAM

The pentagram has become a symbol which is used to represent the Wiccan tradition, as well as a number of other modern Pagan traditions in more recent times. In the tradition of Wicca it is taken to represents the four elements - Air, Fire, Water & Earth - in perfect balance thereby creating the fifth element, that of Spirit. These elemental attributions can be traced back to at least ancient Greece.

However in the past the association of the pentagram with witchcraft was basically a negative one, serving in an apotropaic manner to protect from the devil and witches. Thus in Germany in the 1820s we find its use described in an amuletic manner:

> *"on these mountains on the night of the thirtieth of April, the witches, with the fallen spirits, held a great festival, a witch demoniac carousal ... on that night they make a pentagram on the threshold of their doors, to prevent his satanic majesty, or any of his imps, from entering their houses."*[116]

This theme is mirrored in Goethe's *Faust*, where the pentagram is a protection from demons and devils, which Mephistopheles complains to Faust about.

---

116 Travels in the North of Germany: In the Years 1825 and 1826, Dwight, 1829

"Mephistopheles: Remove that parchment, and the path is plain.
Faust: Oh, 'tis the pentagram that gives you pain."

This idea was not restricted to Germany, as can be seen by the following example, taken from a story reproduced in two different women's magazines of the late 1830s in England:

"The dog, or rather the devil, could not escape through the door, on account of a pentagram described upon the threshold; this figure, "the Druid's foot," "sive salutis signum," being a bound which spirits cannot pass without permission."[117]

Indeed the pentagram was being used as a Christian symbol long before it was associated with witchcraft. It was linked to the wounds of Christ, and also referred to in the third century Jewish proto-grimoire, the *Testament of Solomon*.

"The above mark [pentagram] was heretofore used as the signe of the + is now, that is, at the beginning of letters or bookes, for good luckes sake: and the women among the Jews did make this mark on the childrens chrysome cloathes. – Aubrey MS [1686] – This figure (observes Bishop Kennett, in the margin of the same MS.) of three triangles intersected and made of five lines, is called the Pentangle of Solomon; and when it is delineated on the body of a man, it is pretended to touch and point out the five places wherein our Saviour was wounded. And, therefore, there was an old superstitious conceit, that this figure was a fuga demonum: - the devils were afraid of it."[118]

---

117 The New Monthly Belle Assemblée, Rogerson, 1838 and The Ladies' Cabinet of Fashion, Music & Romance, Henderson, 1839
118 Time's Telescope for 1826, 1826

The Sumerians were already using the pentagram by 3000 BCE. They called it *Ub*, meaning *'region'*, *'direction'* or *'heavenly quarter'*. Interestingly the Sumerians often drew their pentagrams inverted. The Sumerians used a five direction system of East, South, West, North and Above, with Above corresponding to the goddess Inanna, so it has been speculated that these directions were attributed by them to the pentagram.

In ancient Greece, the Pythagoreans called the pentagram Ugieia, meaning *'soundness'*. They wrote the letters around the points of the pentagram, but as there were six in the word they combined the epsilon (e) and second iota (i) to make a theta (th) which looks the same as the two vowels combined. They thus labelled the points of the pentagram with the letters upsilon (U), gamma (G), iota (I), theta (Th), and alpha (A). These are also the first letters of words corresponding to the elements. Thus we have *Hudor* (Water),[119] *Gaia* (Earth), *Hierion* (divine or holy thing, i.e. Spirit),[120] *Therma* (Heat i.e. Fire) and *Aer* (Air) corresponding to the points of the pentagram.

These attributions started at the top and went anticlockwise around the pentagram, giving this set of attributions:

Point	Greek	GD/Wicca
Top	Water	Spirit
Upper left	Earth	Air
Lower left	Spirit	Earth
Lower right	Fire	Fire
Upper right	Air	Water

119 The H is added to the beginning of the word in transliteration from the Greek, so it actually starts with the letter U (upsilon).
120 Again the H is added in transliteration, so the word starts with the letter I (iota).

(Contemporary Wiccan attributions of the elements to the pentagram)

The Greek letters can be seen drawn around an inverse pentagram in Agrippa's *Three Books of Occult Philosophy,* showing that this idea was recognised and used in the sixteenth century.

When did the attributions change from the ancient Greek ones to those used in modern magick? The answer may well lie with the Elizabethan magus Dr John Dee. The Great Table of Dee's Enochian system is comprised of the Four Elemental Tablets (or Watchtowers) combined. The sequence of their combination is relevant for the elemental attributions, as we can see the elemental attributions applied to the pentagram were clearly derived from here.

When creating the Great Table, the top half (or row) is formed by placing the Tablet of Air on the left and the Tablet of Water on the right, as you look at it. Likewise the bottom half (or row) is formed by placing the Tablet of Earth on the left and the Tablet of Fire on the right. If you then read anticlockwise from Air in the top left, the sequence is alphabetical, proceeding to Earth in the bottom left, Fire in the bottom right and Water in the top right, exactly as is seen with the elemental attributions on the points of the pentagram (with Spirit at the top).

The wearing of a pentagram ring, popular amongst Wiccans and pagans today, has a precedent in the third century CE *Testament of Solomon.* In this work King Solomon was given a ring bearing the pentalpha (pentagram) by the archangel Michael to compel the obedience of demons who he summoned to build the temple in Jerusalem. Descriptions of the ring also refer to it having four gems representing the elemental archangels embedded in it.

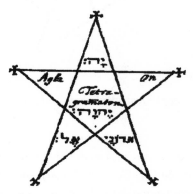

(The engravings of the pentagram ring used in the grimoire tradition, this example from Sloane MS 2731 – Lemegeton)

The inverse pentagram, associated in the Wiccan tradition today with the second degree as a symbol of the face of the horned god can be found in Crowley's writings, drawing from *The Key of the Mysteries* by Eliphas Levi (1861):

> *"The flaming star, which, when turned upside down, is the hieroglyphic sign of the goat of Black Magic, whose head may then be drawn in the star, the two horns at the top, the ears to the right and left, the beard at the bottom."*

In the ritual of the *"Mark of the Beast"*, Crowley made reference to the inverse pentagram with respect to the goat-headed god Baphomet, inspired by Levi's Goat of Mendes, when he wrote, *"About me flames my father's face, the star of force and fire."*[121] It is also interesting to observe the use of the inverse pentagram for second degree elevation when considering the Sumerian link, with the single point being associated with the goddess Inanna, whose descent to the underworld also inspired part of a mystery play which traditionally forms part of the second degree initiation ceremony.

Much has been said about the use of the pentagram in Christianity and in Freemasonry and how that may have contributed to its use and popularity within modern Wicca. However, here it is necessary to mention that the five-pointed star as the endless knot can be found in use all over the world, throughout history at one time or another and as such it is not important here in this context beyond what has already been discussed. The pentagram has always been a powerful symbol, and is likely to continue to be so.

---

121 Magick, Aleister Crowley, 1929

PERIPHERAL VISIONS

CHAPTER 17

CERNUNNOS

In Wicca the dynamic polarity and interplay of the goddess and the horned god through the seasons is at the heart of the celebrations. The Gallic Celtic horned god Cernunnos quickly became accepted as the horned god of Wicca. The meaning of his name is commonly taken as *'horned one'*, though some older texts give variants of this such as *'horned spear'* which may have been superseded as our knowledge of the ancient languages increases.

Cernunnos as a possible candidate for the position of god of the witches was made popular by Margaret Murray in her book *The God of the Witches* (1933). The inclusion of Cernunnos, a Celtic-Gallic god, as the male companion and partner to Aradia, has been criticised as being an inappropriate mixture of pantheons and as a highly unlikely match by some. Regardless of how implausible this appears to be, it is not so when we take into consideration that the tribes we now collectively refer to as the Celts, moved around a great deal. The idea became even less far fetched when we discovered that an inscription to Cernunnos was found at Polenza in Northern Italy and what could be considered a very early depiction of him was found in Val Camonica, also in Northern Italy. The depiction at Val Camonica was described by Anne Ross in *Pagan Celtic Britain:*

> *"Here the stag-god, Cernunnos, is portrayed in a standing posture, wearing a long garment, and having his feet turned in. He wears a torc the magico-religious significance of which is well known, over*

both his right and left arm, while some attribute, no doubt the horned serpent, can be distinguished beside his left elbow. From his head spring tall antlers."

This image which dates from around the fourth century BCE, does not depict the god as being phallic, as he is often shown in modern depictions, rather it shows the worshipper as being so in an exaggerated manner.

Cernunnos is a horned god associated with nature and animals, and he is also known as *'Lord of all Wild Things'*. His name is usually taken as being derived from a piece of altar found in Notre Dame (Paris) dating to 17 CE which reads *ERNUNNO*, and depicts a bull-horned god, not the stag-horned god of the Gundestrup Cauldron.

> *"'Tis no Rarity to meet with horned Gods in Paganism : such was Jupiter Ammon, Pan the Fauns, the Satyrs, &c. But this Gallic God is known under the Name of Cernunnos, only since the Discovery of the Bas-relief of Notre-Dame Church. Thus we need not be surprised if the Learned, both in France and Germany, who have attempted to explain these Monuments, differ so much from one another with respect to this God; the two most probable sentiments upon this Subject, are that of the Author of the History of the Religion of the Gauls, and that of M.Eccart. The former takes Cernunnos to have been a rural God, who among our ancient Gauls presided over Hunter, as Alces, or Alics, according to Tacitus, was the God of the same exercise in the Province of ancient Germany, which was possessed by Nabarvali. The strongest Argument which he brings in Support of his Opinion is that the Horns of Cernunnos, the Diadem which he wears upon one of his Figures, and the Animals which holds in his Hand upon that of M.de Chazelles, are all Characters of a God of Hunting, as justified by several figures of Diana, the Goddess of the same exercise among the Greeks and Romans, where we find all these Symbols. M. Eccart thinks this God represents Bacchus, or*

Dionysius, an Opinion which wants not Probability; but after all, can he flatter himself that he has discovered what was the fettled Opinion the Gauls had concerning a God who is so little known even at present.

To conclude, the Name of Cernunnos, is composed of two Celtic Words, whereof the first Cern, imports a Horn, and the second Yna, or Ona, a Spear."[122]

That *Ernunno* is an abbreviation of the name Cernunnos has been confirmed from inscriptions and finds from other parts of Europe through the variants discovered. An inscription with the name *Cernunnos* was found at Polenza in Italy, and a variant, *Cernenus* at Verespatak in Rumania where he was equated with Jupiter. Other European inscriptions include one to *Deo Cernunico* at Seinsel-Rëlent in Germany and a Greek inscription at Montagnac in France to *Karnonos*. When the Romans encountered Cernunnos first in Gaul, they associated him with their god Mercury, although Julius Caesar likened him to *Dis Pater* (*'the wealthy father'*) as the major god.

The classic image on which most of the modern perception of Cernunnos is based comes from the Gundestrup cauldron, a beautiful piece of silverware found in Denmark dating between the fourth to first century BCE. The image shows a seated horned figure and a female figure, with various animals around them. Evidence on the style, dating and construction of the cauldron has confirmed it originally came from the Indus Valley, and depicted a god called Pashupati, whose name means *'Lord of the Animals'*, and who has been viewed as the earliest form of the Hindu god, Shiva.

Other seals found in the Indus Valley from around 3,000 BCE also depict Pashupati in the same posture, with deer hooves instead of feet, surrounded by animals, and significantly, with bull horns. That this transition from bull horns to stag horns is seen in both Pashupati and

---

122 The Mythology and Fables of the Ancients, Antoine Banier, 1739

Cernunnos is suggestive of a trend, perhaps from an image of the virility of the bull to the wildness of the stag. Stags cannot be tamed like bulls, and may be seen to symbolise more clearly the wild nature of the lord of the beasts. When Gardner wrote in *Witchcraft Today* that the God in the *Myth of the Goddess* was Shiva, he was probably nearer to the truth than he realised:

> *"Again you can say it is simply Siva, the God of Death and Resurrection; but here again the story is different."*

Pashupati as the root of the horned god in the Wiccan tradition actually fits perfectly when you consider that the Harappan culture in the Indus Valley from which he came also worshipped a mother goddess. So the Harappans actually provide us with an example of a culture five thousand years ago, who worshipped a mother goddess and a horned god! The pre-eminent mother goddess was worshipped for thousands of years in India, gaining a variety of names, in a manner similar to that later seen in the Wiccan theology.

As an aside, we would also point out that though he may not be directly related to Wicca, the biggest temple complex in the ancient world is the temple of the goat horned god, Amun-Ra at Karnak in Egypt, which means the world's biggest temple is to a horned god!

The Horned God as viewed in Wicca today does leave us with an interesting problem. None of the known historical horned gods had any associations with witchcraft, whereas the goddesses whom we have considered here, did in some instances have strong associations with witchcraft practices throughout their history. The question that we may need to ask ourselves here, regardless of the ancient providence of horned gods, is why exactly did a horned god become associated with the practices of the Wiccan tradition?

The possible answer to this question takes us down the route of medieval Christianity and its propaganda against witchcraft, in which the devil was often a Christianised version of earlier Pagan Gods. It may be through the images which surfaced through Christian scaremongering that the inspiration for a horned God in Wicca manifested.

> *"The first is a figure of Robin Goodfellow, which forms the illustration to a very popular ballad of the earlier part of the seventeenth century, entitled 'The mad merry Pranks of Robin Goodfellow;' he is represented party-coloured, and with the priapic attribute. The next is a second illustration of the same ballad, in which Robin Goodfellow is represented as Priapus, goat-shaped, with his attributes still more strongly pronounced, and surrounded by a circle of his worshippers dancing about him. He appears here in the character assumed by the demon at the sabbath of the witches."*[123]

The popular image of the Goat of Mendes, or Baphometic Goat, is taken from the writings of Eliphas Levi, from 1855-56. The Golden Dawn magician and scholar Arthur Edward Waite translated Levi's works *Dogma de la haute Magie* (1855) and *Ritual de la haute Magie* (1856) and compiled them in English as *Transcendental Magic* in 1896.

Levi's image of the hermaphroditic goat, with the torch between its horns, and hands in the *'solve et coagula'* position seems to sit halfway between the alchemical and classical worlds. The link to Mendes is interesting, as this connects it back to ancient Egypt, and the many horned gods worshipped there. Ironically Mendes was the cult centre of worship for Banedjet, who was a ram-horned god, not goat-horned. Banedjet was seen in the late period as representing the *ba* (spirit or soul) of the four gods Re, Osiris, Shu and Geb. This is symbolically appropriate from a Wiccan perspective as these gods embodied the sun (Re), the underworld (Osiris), the air (Shu) and the earth (Geb), thus actually combining the most common attributes of the Wiccan horned god.

---

123 The Worship of the Generative Powers, Wright, 1865

Returning to Levi's image of the Goat of Mendes, it was also referred to as Baphomet, the name given to the idol said to be worshipped by the Knights Templar. Levi made this link, which subsequent magickians picked up on. Levi's goat also showed features like the torch between the horns in common with other contemporary witchcraft images he may have drawn from, such as the image of the devil in *The Sabbat* frontispiece for Collin de Plancey's 1818 classic work *Dictionnaire Infernal*.

The popularity of horned gods in English and French writings of the nineteenth century, together with striking imagery, could have contributed to the adoption of the horned god in Wicca. The attention brought to the horned god as the centre of the witch cult by the writings of Margaret Murray also provide a possible source for his entry into the Wiccan tradition. Although medieval Christianity undoubtedly demonised any of the old gods with horns, the horned god of the wilds is an ancient figure and one which fits in with the life-positive polarity and philosophy of the Wiccan tradition. Though he may be called by many names, the horned god is clearly here to stay.

CHAPTER 18

ELEMENTAL ORIGINS

As a core concept in Wicca, the four elements need to be quantified and qualified to make their path into the Wiccan tradition clear. The four elements are perceived as being part of and making up everything. They are not merely Earth, Air, Fire, and Water - but are concepts, energy states, states of being, and philosophical concepts. The philosophy of the four elements originates with the ancient Greek philosopher Empedocles, who came up with the idea in the fifth century BCE and elaborated it in his work *Tetrasomia* (*"Doctrine of the Four Elements"*). Empedocles expressed the idea that the four elements were not only the physical building blocks of the material universe, but also spiritual essences.

In fact Empedocles equated the sources of the elements to deities, with Zeus as Air, Hera as Earth, Hades as Fire and Nestis (Persephone) as Water. From this you can also see the origins of the attributions of Air and Fire as masculine elements and Earth and Water as feminine elements. Interestingly the goddess name Hera means *'Lady'*, recalling the use of this term sometimes found in modern Wiccan traditions.

> *"Now hear the fourfold Roots of everything:*
> *Life-bringing Hera, Hades, shining Zeus,*
> *And Nestis, moistening mortal springs with tears."*

We should observe that Empedocles did not call his four principles *'elements'* (*stoikheia*), but used the terms *'roots'* (*rhizai*) and 'root-clumps' (rhizômata). Empedocles was an herbal magician or root cutter (rhizotomoi) and applied his theory to developing a doctrine of occult sympathies in plants. Aristotle in the fourth century BCE expounded further on the elements as spiritual essences, concentrating on their qualities in his *De Generatione et Corruptione*. In his work *Timaeus*, Plato postulated a different view of the elements, suggesting that the elements were changeable as qualities of the primary matter.

The Stoics held a different view of the elements, attributing only one quality each to them rather than the two suggested by Empedocles, Aristotle and Plato. They declared *"Fire is the hot element, water the moist, air the cold, earth the dry."*[124] These two somewhat different views would influence the early Christian theologians like Athenagoras, Aristides and Eusebius and Jewish philosophers like Philo and Josephus. Even though both views were influential, and permeated the views of the time, they did not go off on the tangent seen in Gnosticism, where the elements were divided into good and evil. The Christian view of the body was that it was made up of the four elements with the fifth (ether) being the animating soul. This view is very much the one which would continue through the centuries into the western esoteric traditions and the various schools of magick working within it.

Returning to the Greek views of the elements, in the third century BCE the Ptolemaic Egyptian high priest and historian Manetho recorded deity attributions which seem to almost sit as a bridge between the ideas of Empedocles and those of the Wiccan Tradition.

> *"The Egyptians say that Isis and Osiris are the Moon and the Sun; that Zeus is the name which they give to the all-pervading Spirit, Hephaestus to Fire, and Demeter to Earth. Among the Egyptians the moist element is named Oceanus and their own river Nile; and to him*

---

124 Vitae, Diogenes Laertius

they ascribed the origin of the Gods. To Air, again, they give, it is said, the name of Athena."[125]

In the fifth century C.E. Proclus developed the ideas introduced by Iamblichus in the fourth century CE in his classic Theurgic work further. He also divided the daimons (spirits) into five classes of being:

- Rulers of Fire
- Rulers of Air
- Rulers of Water
- Rulers of Earth
- Rulers of the Underworld

Not only were the elements attributed to the pentagram in ancient Greece, but also to the directions. Philolaos, a Pythagorean philosopher of the fifth century BCE wrote of the fourfold ordering of the elements to the four segments of the zodiacal circle, giving the quarters and the elements. Following on from him some centuries later, the famous Greek spiritual alchemist Zosimos of Panopolis wrote in the fourth century CE of the attribution of the elements to the four cardinal points (and to the four letters of the name of the first man, ADAM) in his classic work *Upon the Letter Omega.*

There is an intriguing comment in the section of *Gypsy Sorcery* headed *The Vilas-Sylvana Elementary Spirits*, where Leland draws a link to be often found in the roots of Wicca, between Renaissance magick and witchcraft. Might this have inspired Gardner to look into the grimoire magick of the Renaissance for material, and led him to the *Key of Solomon*?

"Among the Slavonic and gypsy races all witchcraft, fairy- and Folk-lore rests mainly upon a belief in certain spirits of wood and wold, of

---

125 Manetho, Fragment 83, Waddell (trans).

earth and water, which has much more in common with that of the Rosicrucians and Paracelsus"[126]

The sequence of elements was based on the qualities of the elements until the Golden Dawn. This point needs further expansion to explain how the elements were perceived as interacting prior to the changes introduced by the Golden Dawn.

Element	Qualities	Function	Concepts
Earth	Dry & Cool	Passive & Descending	Ground, Land, Soil
Fire	Warm & Dry	Active & Ascending	Flame, Lightning, Sun
Air	Moist & Warm	Active & Ascending	Cloud, Heaven, Sky
Water	Cool & Moist	Passive & Descending	Moisture, Rain, Sea

For each element it was seen as having two qualities, the first of which given is the dominant quality for that element. Thus the dominant quality for Earth was dryness, for Fire warmth, for Air moistness and Water coolness. Air and Fire are the active elements, which are seen as ascending, and this is why they are both later represented by the upward pointing triangle (with the horizontal bar for Air). Conversely Earth and Water are the passive elements, which are seen as descending, and this is why they are both subsequently represented by the downward pointing triangle (with the horizontal bar for Earth).

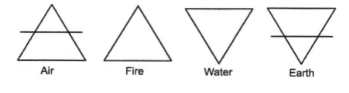

Air   Fire   Water   Earth

---

126 Gypsy Sorcery, Charles G Leland, 1889

The sequence of elements in the original ancient Greek model sees each element share a quality with the elements on either side of it when placed on a square. Thus Earth is followed by Fire, then Air, then Water, and back to Earth. This differs from the Golden Dawn model, which has Air and Fire transposed. The Golden Dawn also created the sequence of elemental attributions to the point of the pentagram used in Wicca. This draws once more from the magick of John Dee, as the elemental attributions to the points of the pentagram can be seen to be drawn from the four Enochian Tablets, or Watchtowers as the Golden Dawn called them.

The Greek influence on early Kabbalah was significant, and one part of this was the transmission of concepts such as the elements into Kabbalistic[127] philosophy. This can be seen in the first great Kabbalistic text, the *Sepher Yetzirah* (*Book of Formation*), written sometime in the late first or second century CE. The third of the six chapters refers to the elements, though the emphasis is more on Air, Fire and Water, with Earth being secondary. Thus we see in *Sepher Yetzirah* 3:4 -

> *"Heaven was created from Fire*
> *Earth was created from Water*
> *And Air from Breath decides between them."*

The influence of the elements was not a dominant theme in the grimoires, which tended to be more planetary in nature. However the four elements as manifestations of the three alchemical principles (salt, mercury and sulphur) were a constant theme through the magickal and mystical writings of the medieval and renaissance alchemists. The transformation of the three into the four was also an expression of the astrological aspect of alchemy. The three (cardinal, fixed and mutable) principles are manifested through the four elements, giving the twelve (zodiacal signs) steps of the alchemical process. This relationship

---

127 This spelling is used to indicate the Jewish branch of Kabbalah.

between the four elements and the alchemical process is clearly illustrated in Simon Forman's sixteenth century work *Of the Division of Chaos:*

> *"Then out of this Chaos, the four elements were made:*
> *Heat and cold, moist and dry, in like wise,*
> *Which are the beginning of all creatures wide,*
> *That under the globe of Luna do abide."*

The qualities of the four elements were well known in the Renaissance world, as can be illustrated by an example from Shakespeare's *Sonnet 65*, written in 1609, where he equates Air to thought and Fire to desire:

> *"The other two, slight air and purging fire,*
> *Are both with thee, wherever I abide;*
> *The first my thought, the other my desire,*
> *These present-absent with swift motion slide.*
> *For when these quicker elements are gone*
> *In tender embassy of love to thee,*
> *My life, being made of four, with two alone*
> *Sinks down to death, oppressed with melancholy"*

Apart from the alchemists, the other significant medieval magickal reference is the discussion by Agrippa in his *Three Books of Occult Philosophy* (1533), which is reproduced in Barrett's *The Magus*. However it is in the writings of the French occultist Eliphas Levi that the elements really start to gain more noticeable prominence, particularly in works such as his *The Magickal Ritual of the Sanctum Regnum* (1896), with exorcisms of the four elements and prayers to the elementals of the four elements.

As the Golden Dawn synthesised material from the Qabalah, Levi, alchemy and the classics, it is no surprise that the elements should become a more dominant theme in their ceremonies and teachings. A consequence of this is that the elements also feature in the work of Aleister Crowley. From these two major sources, Wiccan practices continued to emphasise the four elements in the symbolism and ceremonies within the circle. However we should emphasise that the idea of magick circles is a fairly universal concept, as seen in this speech by the Ogala Sioux, Black Elk (1863-1950):

> *"You have noticed that everything an Indian does is in a circle, and that is because the Power of the World always works in circles, and everything tries to be round. In the old days when we were a strong and happy people, all our power came to us from the sacred hoop of the nation, and so long as the hoop was unbroken, the hoop flourished. The flowering tree was the living center of the hoop, and the circle of the four quarters nourished it. The East gave peace and light, the South gave warmth, the West gave rain, and the North with its cold and mighty wind gave strength and endurance. This knowledge came to us from the outer world with our religion. Everything the power of the World does is done in a circle."*

This clearly shows that the idea of the four directions being attributed to the four elements, within a circle, is not unique to the Western Mystery Tradition. In fact, upon closer examination the attributions given indirectly by Black Elk here correspond quite well with those used in Wicca.

Direction	Attributions	Element
East	Peace, Light	Air
South	Warmth	Fire
West	Rain	Water
North	Cold, Strength, Endurance	Earth

So even though some modern traditions of Wicca, especially those originating in North America have been criticized for including a number of chants, practices and ideas from the various indigenous first nation tribes, there is a striking similarity which cannot be ignored, though it is highly unlikely that there is any direct link with the development of modern Wicca. This example comes from a Sioux holy man, but the idea of the four directions being important in the indigenous cultures of the first people of the Americas can be found in many different tribes. In an Arapaho legend telling about the *'Sun Dance Wheel'* we find the tale of why eagle feathers are used on the cardinal points of the wheel and how they represent the four old men of the four directions, an idea, when you think about it, which is not too far from what the Kings of the Elements may be seen to represent!

The four elements were not significant in the grimoires, and became significant in Victorian ceremonial magick through the influence of writers like Eliphas Levi. Thus the origins of the use of the four elements in Wicca are probably fairly recent, dating back to the influence of perhaps the Hermetic Order of the Golden Dawn or Levi.

CHAPTER 19

THEBAN SCRIPT

The Theban script, which is found in the texts of many of the Wiccan traditions today and is sometimes referred to as the 'Witches Alphabet' is used for carving, writing names and sometimes entire books of shadows with. Its inclusion in the Wiccan tradition was probably drawn from Francis Barrett's *The Magus* published in 1801. Barrett in turn drew his information from Cornelius Agrippa's *Three Books of Occult Philosophy* which were published in 1531 and is often considered to be the first written source in which the Theban script was recorded. This is not actually true, as the Theban script was first published in 1518 in the less well known *Polygraphia*, the book of magickal alphabets compiled by Trithemius (published posthumously).

(Theban script from Francis Barrett's The Magus, 1801)

However Agrippa does note in his *Three Books of Occult Philosophy* that the Theban script is *"those which Peter Apponus notes, as delivered by Honorius of Thebes."* This is clearly a reference to Peter de Abano, author of the *Heptameron*, and to the *Sworn Book of Honorius*, which declares in its introduction that it was delivered by Honorius of Thebes. Neither of these texts contains the Theban script or anything resembling it, so this seems more a case of attempting to give provenance to lend authenticity to it at the time, although it is quite possible that it might be recorded in a now lost manuscript copy of one of these works.

In an interesting parallel to its use by some Wiccans today, Francis Barrett also copied entire magickal grimoires into Theban script at the turn of the nineteenth century for his personal use. According to Prof. Ronald Hutton writing in his book *Triumph of the Moon*, Valiente described Gardner wearing his silver ring with his OTO name engraved on it in Theban script.

The term *'Theban Script'* presents us with another interesting hypothesis which may indicate that its use in Wicca today could be down to a possible misunderstanding. At this point we have already established that the Wiccan tradition drew some teachings and inspiration from the Hermetic Order of the Golden Dawn, but what is less known is that the Enochian alphabet which is used in that system is also sometimes referred to as the *'Theban alphabet'*.[128] Taking this into consideration it leaves a question as to whether there might have been a misunderstanding somewhere which may have led to the adoption of Theban as *'the Witches Alphabet'* rather than the Enochian alphabet.

---

128 The Golden Dawn, Israel Regardie, 1937

CHAPTER 20

GRIMOIRES OF MAGICK

Throughout this work reference has been made to a number of grimoires and their relevance to the Wiccan tradition. To give a clearer picture of the timescale involved we felt it was appropriate to show the line of descent of the relevant grimoires themselves, and also the level of earlier pagan input into the grimoire tradition.

The grimoires themselves really started from the thirteenth century and ran through to the eighteenth century. Prior to this the style of conjurations and practices found in them can be seen in an earlier form in the *Greek Magickal Papyri* and the *Coptic Magickal Papyri*. As the former of these contains practices from the second century BCE to the fifth century CE, and the latter from the first to twelfth century CE, we can see that there is a continuous chain of written magickal manuscripts extending more than two thousand years from late antiquity through to the Industrial Revolution and beyond.

The influence of works like the *Greek Magickal Papyri* can be seen in the level of classical material found within the grimoire tradition. Although the popular perception of the grimoire tradition is of a heavily Judeo-Christian framework, in fact there are also many elements which point to the influence of the classical religions and folk practices. The clearest of these are the number of deities from old religions who occur in the grimoires, sometimes by their own names and at other times in bastardised forms. Amongst these we see Roman and Greek deities like Apollo, Diana, Hades, Pluto, Python and Serapis, as well as other ancient deities like Astarte (Ashtoreth), Baal (Bael) and Horus (Hauros), and classical mythical creatures like Cerberus and the Phoenix (Phenex).

The grimoires also contain frequent references to working magick with fairies and elementals as well as angels and demons. Angels of course have pre-Christian roots, from the Sumerian winged guardian spirits through to the Intelligences of Aristotle and the writings of neo-Platonists like Porphyry and the theurgic writings of Iamblichus, to the angels of the *Chaldean Oracles of Zoroaster*. It was only in the sixth century that pseudo-Dionysus the Areopagite wrote the work *Celestial Hierarchies* which established the angelic hierarchy of nine orders of angels under the archangels that was to influence both the grimoires and Christian doctrine.

The first of the grimoires is *Liber Juratus*, or *The Sworn Book of Honorius*, which can be dated by references to it in the thirteenth century under its other name of *Liber Sacer* or *Liber Sacratus*. Existing manuscripts of this grimoire can be dated to the fourteenth century (e.g. Sloane MS 3854), and it is known that John Dee had a copy of this grimoire (Sloane MS 313, with Dee's marginal notes). *Liber Juratus* contains the original Sigillum Dei Aemeth (*'Seal of God's Truth'*) used by Dee and others, the oath at the beginning, long lists of appropriate angels for planetary and zodiacal work, and a whole host of material results to perform rituals for.

Next is the *Heptameron* (*'Seven Days'*) of Peter de Abano, a manual of planetary magick with the planetary archangels. This book was first published in 1496, and then also published with Agrippa's *Fourth Book of Occult Philosophy* as an appendix in 1554, and in Latin in 1600, being subsequently translated into English by Robert Turner in his 1655 edition of the *Fourth Book*. The disparity between the publication date and the earlier lifetime of Peter de Abano has been held up as a reason for it not being his work, and it has been suggested he was not a magician. However, not only were magickal books often published posthumously, but de Abano was twice tried by the Inquisition as a magician (unsuccessfully) and also mentioned grimoires in his 1310

222

work *Lucidator*. There is also good evidence to support the attribution of the Italian scholar Peter de Abano (1250-1316) as the author of the *Heptameron*.[129] The conjurations in this book are extremely important, having influenced the *Key of Solomon* and the *Lemegeton*. Included in its contents are the creation of the magick circle, the consecrations of salt, water and incense, and planetary hours. This is all material which would be repeated and adapted throughout the subsequent grimoires.

The works of the German Abbot Johannes Trithemius (1462-1516) have also played a significant part in influencing both the subsequent magick of the grimoires and also the Wiccan tradition. Trithemius wrote the *Steganographia*, which contributed directly to the *Lemegeton* as the sub-books of the *Theurgia-Goetia* and the *Ars Paulina*. Dee also used a copy of the *Steganographia* as part of the inspiration for the Enochian system. Trithemius' work *The art of drawing spirits into crystals* contains the magick circle used by Alex Sanders, and also has reference to the use of the wand in conjuring the magick circle, and words spoken during this conjuration. One of his other books, *Polygraphia*, seems to be the origin of the Theban Script.

Trithemius was thus not only a significant magickal scholar, whose influence can be seen not only in the work he produced, but also in his students whose work would find its way into later magickal traditions, namely Henry Cornelius Agrippa (1486-1533) and Paracelsus (1493-1541). Although Trithemius himself was very anti-witchcraft, as can be seen by his statement in *Liber Octo Quaestionem*, this did not prevent the use of his works subsequently in witchcraft. His antipathy towards witches and support of the church line was clear when he declared:

"Witches are very pernicious; they make pacts with demons and by solemn profession of faith, become vassals of the demons, whom they

---

129 See The Goetia of Dr Rudd, Skinner & Rankine, 2007

worship everlastingly. They must not be tolerated, but rather terminated wherever found."[130]

Henry Cornelius Agrippa (1486-1535) was a student of Trithemius whose work was a foundation stone of modern magick. His three volume *Three Books of Occult Philosophy* were distributed privately as manuscripts around 1510, and then printed in 1531. This work is a huge collection of material from natural magick to Qabalah and sigilisation. The other classic work of Agrippa's is his *Fourth Book of Occult Philosophy*. This book, of six parts, was only partially written by Agrippa, who wrote the first two sections, *Of Geomancy*, and *Of Occult Philosophy, or Magickal Ceremonies*. The latter contains significant material on creating the magick circle, the Liber Spirituum, consecrations and invocations. The remainder of the book includes the *Heptameron* of Peter de Abano (discussed previously), and the *Arbatel of Magick* (covering Olympic Spirits). Agrippa also wrote one of the first books which could be considered feminist and was ahead of its time, in his 1529 work, *Female Pre-eminence: or the Dignity and Excellency of that sex, above the Male.*

Johann Weyer (1515-1588) was a student of Agrippa's, whose contribution is more through transmission of material and attitude. Weyer's book *Praestigiis Daemonum*, published in 1563, contained a harsh rebuttal of the hideous *Malleus Maleficarum* which had been used so cruelly by the church. Sigmund Freud rated this book as one of the ten most significant books of all time, possibly because Weyer was the first person to adopt a psychological approach to the issues of both the witches and the witch-hunts. The 1583 edition of this book contained an appendix called *Pseudomonarchia Daemonum*, of sixty-nine demons, (almost identical to the list of seventy-two demons in the *Goetia*), which was reproduced by Scot in his *Discoverie of Witchcraft*.

---

130 Liber Octo Quaestionem, Trithemius, 1515

Reginald Scot (1538-1599) produced a grimoire in spite of himself! Scot wrote the book *The Discoverie of Witchcraft* in 1584 to diminish fear and belief in witches. However, as we have already shown, this work became a standard manual for those seeking to learn more of the practices of magick and witchcraft, drawing as it did from a wide range of sources. Thus, for example, we see the recipe given by Scot for flying ointment being copied and spoken by the chief witch (called) Hecate in Thomas Middleton's 1613 play *The Witch*.

Scot found himself in direct opposition to King James I of England (who was also known as King James VI of Scotland), who ordered the book to be burned and wrote his own extreme anti-witchcraft work of 1597, *Daemonologie*.

It is amusing to note that later versions of the book included even more grimoire material, adding further to the sources available to its readers. The third edition in 1665 gained a second book to the *Discourse of Devils and Spirits* and nine extra chapters on conjurations. Scot listed many of the grimoires, as can be seen in the list below (our notes in square brackets), perhaps unintentionally providing a reading list for his readers:

> *"these conjurors carrie about at this daie, bookes intituled under the names of Adam, Abel, Tobie, & Enoch...Abraham, Aaron and Salomon [Key of Solomon]...Zacharie, Paule [Ars Paulina], Honorius [Book of Honorius], Cyprian [probably Clavis Inferni], Jerome, Jeremie, Albert [Albertus Magnus], and Thomas: also of the angels, Riziel, Razael [Sepher Razael], and Raphael...Ars Almadell [Almadel], ars Notoria [Notory Art], ars Bulaphiae, ars Arthephi, ars Pomena, ars Revelationis, &c."*

Dr John Dee (1527-1608), the astronomer and mathematician to Queen Elizabeth I, produced a range of magickal work. From the perspective of his legacy, the most important work is that from the 1580s which generated the Enochian system (with its watchtowers) such as

Tabula bonorum angelorum invocationes (Sloane MS 3191). Dee used wax disks with the Sigillum Dei Aemeth on, under the feet of his skrying table and also under the crystal ball (as a pentacle). This may be where the idea of the wax pentacle mentioned by Gardner in his writings originates from. Dee's many other works, of those which survived, have not had any tangible influence on the Wiccan tradition.

The *Lemegeton*, comprises five parts known respectively as the *Goetia, Theurgia-Goetia, Ars Pauline, Ars Almadel*, and *Ars Notoria*. The earliest known manuscript of the *Lemegeton* is in English and dates to around 1640 (Sloane MS 3825), and the latest to 1712 (Harley MS 6483). Nevertheless the sources for the *Lemegeton* date back earlier, to the early fourteenth century with de Abano, and to the fifteenth century through sources such as the French *Livre des Esperitz*[131] and the *Steganographia* of Trithemius. A version of the first part (*Goetia*) was produced by Aleister Crowley in 1904 from a transcription stolen from MacGregor Mathers. The influence of the *Goetia* is seen in Gardner's work *High Magic's Aid*, but beyond the occasional use of the triangle of the art is not really felt very much in the Wiccan tradition per se.

The *Key of Solomon* or *Clavicula Salomonis* has been a major influence on the Wiccan tradition. Of the several dozen we have examined, they cover the period from 1572 to 1825 and are in a variety of languages. The predominant language is French, followed at some distance by English, Italian and Latin. Of all the grimoires, the *Key of Solomon* has experienced the strongest hostility from Christianity, particularly the Catholic Church. This is probably because the *Key of Solomon* was involved in the attempted magickal murder of Pope Urban VIII in 1633. Cardinal d'Ascoli, the nephew of Cardinal Giacomo Centini, liked the idea of being the Pope's nephew and enlisted the aid of a hermit and a man referred to as Frater Cherubino. This trio, with the aid of a Frater Domenico supplied by Giacomo set about trying to

---

131 Trinity MS 0.8.29., circa 15th century

kill the Pope through magic. They failed and met unpleasant ends at the hands of the Inquisition.[132]

Following these events the Roman Catholic Church in Italy was quick to focus attention on grimoires generally and the *Key of Solomon* specifically, as can be seen by the treatment of the Viennese witch Laura Malapiero discussed in chapter 1 *Emergence*. The Church also resented continued interest in the *Key of Solomon* from within their own ranks, as shown by a 695 page manuscript dealing entirely with accusations against monks for using the *Key of Solomon*.[133]

Of the material within the *Key of Solomon*, there are significant components borrowed into Wicca. These include the words for the salt and water consecrations, the consecration of the magick sword/athame, the magick circle, and the markings on the hilt of the athame. Considering its occurrence all across Europe, the influence of the *Key of Solomon* into witchcraft practices is no surprise.

The other grimoire we need to consider is the *Grimoire of Pope Honorius*, which should not be confused with the *Sworn Book of Honorius*. Copies of this black magick grimoire, usually in French, can be found dating from 1670 to 1800. The magick circle, calling of spiritual creatures at the cardinal points, and double-edged black-handled knife are all components it has in common with the subsequent Wiccan tradition.

The period of five hundred years or so which comprises the main corpus of the grimoire tradition from the thirteenth to eighteenth century also coincides with the witch trials and changes in attitude to magick from occasional tolerance to hostility to ridicule. The survival relatively unscathed of practitioners of grimoire magick may be due to their social position, as the surviving manuscripts have usually been passed through the hands of the educated social elite, such as royalty and aristocracy, clerics, doctors and lawyers. Nor can we ignore the

---

132 Renaissance in Italy. Symonds, 2001

133 MSS Busta 102

scope of this tradition as a transmitter of magickal practice when we consider the high number of manuscripts that have survived. Research for another book has unearthed more than fifty different manuscripts of the *Key of Solomon,* for example. Allowing for the destruction of a high percentage of the manuscripts, this clearly shows that the grimoire tradition thrived for many centuries.

In the nineteenth century the tradition continued through the reproduction of the material in both books and by hand. This can be seen with the publication of Francis Barrett's his classic work *The Magus* in 1801, which compiled large amounts of grimoire material with Qabalah and natural magick. Likewise in the early nineteenth century the occult book dealer John Denley, based in Covent Garden, London, employed Frederick Hockley to copy manuscripts for resale at a handsome profit. Hockley would later leave much of his material to the Freemason Kenneth Mackenzie, and some was also bought by Wynn Westcott, indicating the transmission of grimoire material into the Golden Dawn.[134]

That the two currents of the grimoires and witchcraft are interlinked has been demonstrated numerous times in this work, and the grimoires remain a useful source of information for Wiccans and other magickal practitioners.

---

134 The Goetia of Dr Rudd, Skinner & Rankine, 2007

CONCLUSIONS

Having presented the wealth of information in this book, we feel that several different conclusions can be drawn as to the possible magickal beginnings of Wicca. These are:

1. that the Wiccan tradition is a continuation of the grimoire tradition;

2. that the Wiccan tradition is the continuation of a Victorian ceremonial magick system;

3. that the Wiccan tradition was the creation of Gerald Gardner and his associates;

4. that the Wiccan tradition is the survival of a British folk magick system; or

5. that the Wiccan tradition is the final form of a tradition of European witchcraft with its roots in classical Greece and Rome.

We will present each of these possible conclusions in turn, together with our evidence for them and with our opinion as to the relative likelihood of each possibility.

1. Wicca is a continuation of the grimoire tradition

The amount of material found in the Wiccan tradition drawn from the grimoires, including the *Key of Solomon, Heptameron* and *Grimoire of Honorius,* is such that this must be considered a serious possibility. As we have already demonstrated, grimoires were highly derivative, drawing on earlier works that had a proven track record for being effective. The derivative nature of Wicca from earlier material is in keeping with the way information evolved through grimoires over the centuries, as is the copying of the material between magicians from master to trainee.

The grimoire tradition appeared to be fading out by the mid-nineteenth century, with the last derivative copies of manuscripts being made, and the publication in 1801 of Barrett's work *The Magus* increasing the availability of much of the grimoire material in a published form to a wider audience, as Scot's *Discoverie of Witchcraft* had done some centuries earlier in 1584. However based on the evidence we cannot say that interest in the grimoires was waning, and if new grimoires were not created this may well have been due to the magickal work being conducted with those proven texts already in existence.

We have already shown that there was a higher level of pagan input into the grimoires than is commonly acknowledged, which also supports the possible conclusion that this tradition could have continued into Wicca, and makes it clear why all the works which have sought to gather together grimoire material, including Agrippa's *Three Books of Occult Philosophy,* Scot's *Discoverie of Witchcraft* and Barrett's *The Magus,* have done so side-by-side with folk magick concerning fairies, elementals and the like.

As Barrett reproduced much of Agrippa's earlier work, together with that of Trithemius, and juxtaposed grimoire material with Qabalah and folk magick, it is possible that his work was used as the basis for what would become the Wiccan tradition. We have demonstrated that the influence of Trithemius was greater than has previously been acknowledged, so this needs to be given due consideration. Furthermore, in *The Magus* Barrett offered to teach magick, and we know he had students, as one produced a work entitled *Directions for the Invocation of Spirits by a student of Francis Barrett* in 1802. Therefore we must accept the possibility that a synthesis of earlier grimoire material was created during the nineteenth century by Barrett or one or more of his students. Considering the increased availability of published material and the higher levels of literacy in society, it seems a reasonable suggestion that people should continue refining and practising the magick of the grimoires as they had for many centuries previously.

Another significant point we must consider is that the grimoire tradition was also referred to as *'the Craft'*, as seen in grimoires such as the *Key of Solomon*. This could then have been encountered by Gardner, who understandably mislabelled it and subsequently added additional contemporary material to this system in a manner consistent with the grimoire tradition itself. Were this actually the case, then Wicca would be the end product of a tradition which can be shown to originate in the thirteenth century or possibly much earlier. If we summarise the evidence then this conclusion has to be viewed as a serious possibility:

- There is a high level of material drawn directly from the grimoires in the Wiccan tradition, including the process of casting the magick circle, the use of tools including the black-handled knife, the Book of Shadows, Cakes and Wine, and Theban Script;
- Both the Wiccan and grimoire traditions are referred to as *'the Craft'*;
- The publication of syntheses of grimoire material such as *Discoverie of Witchcraft* and *The Magus* made it available to a wide audience, alongside other types of material like folk magick and Qabalah;
- The nineteenth century saw an increase in interest in the grimoires, as seen by the publication of books and the trade in copies of grimoires, and the work of people such as Frederick Hockley and students of Francis Barrett, and later MacGregor Mathers.

231

2. Wicca is the continuation of a Victorian ceremonial magick system

The second possibility is that Wicca began as a Victorian ceremonial magick tradition. The quantity of material derived from the works of Aleister Crowley; together with material from the Golden Dawn make this a possible conclusion. Here we must first consider that the Golden Dawn itself was the product of a synthesis of a wide range of earlier magickal practices based around the translation of an alleged cipher manuscript. Accordingly the Golden Dawn combined Qabalah, Enochian magick based on Dee's work, Egyptian magick, alchemy, grimoire material and other diverse sources to create a working system of ceremonial magick.

Crowley was initiated into the Golden Dawn, and subsequently drew much of his inspiration from this melting-pot of magick. That one of its founders, Mathers, should be so involved with the translation of key grimoires like the *Key of Solomon* and the *Goetia*, further adds to the level of material available which was subsequently found in the Wiccan tradition. We may also observe that the writings of the Golden Dawn scholar J.W. Brodie-Innes on witchcraft around 1917 show a level of knowledge which heavily hints at the content of the Wiccan tradition.

The Golden Dawn was created in 1887, giving us the earliest likely date for the creation of a tradition based on its work. Crowley's book *The Blue Equinox* (Vol 3 No 1) was published in 1919, and this is the most significant Crowley work drawn on in the Wiccan tradition for material. This would give us a second date of 1919 onwards for the creation of the tradition, or for a revision of what could have already existed from some point after 1887. The number of magickians within the Golden Dawn and its derivative orders (including those of Crowley) during this time period would number in the hundreds. Thus we have to consider that there was a large body of magickally trained people (of differing standards, undoubtedly) with access to a wide range of magickal material, many of whom could have created the Wiccan tradition within the time period of 1887-1939 (the date Gardner claimed to have been initiated).

We can assert that if this was the case, then Crowley was not directly involved in the creation of Wicca. Although his material is used, particularly for the *Charge of the Goddess* and Great Rite, the way quotes from the *Book of the Law* are taken out of context would have been anathema to Crowley, for whom this was his most holy text. This misuse implies a person or persons who were unfamiliar with the philosophy of Crowley's work, and thus suggests it would have been more likely to have been someone from a Golden Dawn derived order, or Gardner himself, rather than one of Crowley's orders where the philosophy was taught.

Summarising the evidence for this conclusion, again we must consider this a serious possibility:

- The Golden Dawn began as a synthesis of practices from different magickal traditions, in a similar manner to Wicca;
- The Golden Dawn has clear links to the grimoire tradition;
- A large amount of the material found in the Wiccan tradition is drawn in part or whole from the writings of Aleister Crowley, a Golden Dawn initiate, including the *Charge of the Goddess*, the Great Rite, and the blessing of the cakes;
- Material in the Wiccan tradition is also drawn from the writings of the Golden Dawn, including the use of the Watchtowers, parts of the first degree initiation oath, and the elemental and colour attributions;
- The Golden Dawn with its derivative orders, and those of Crowley, trained many people who would have had the skills and access to the material necessary to produce the Wiccan tradition; including people whose work may have been influential on the Wiccan tradition like Israel Regardie, Dion Fortune and Jack Parsons.

3. Wicca is the creation of Gerald Gardner and his associates

This conclusion is a view popularised by a number of modern authors and researchers, based on Gardner's publication of the material in his books and his work to promote Wicca in the media to ensure its survival as a tradition. Gardner himself insisted that he was initiated into an existing tradition, and that he gained permission from his elders in the tradition to make material public to prevent its demise. A number of claims made by Gardner in his writings have subsequently been shown to be misinformed or false, and so it has been suggested that this throws all of his claims into question, though we would argue that this does not invalidate the practices of the tradition itself. However what has usually been ignored by people seeking to disprove Gardner's claims is that if he was telling the truth about his initiation, then the elements of falsehood in his writings could be deliberate blinds, to ensure he did not break his initiatory vows in what he publicised.

Another frequent claim made by people seeking to disprove the pre-Gardnerian origins of Wicca is that Gardner drew heavily on the works of Margaret Murray to create the tradition. Whilst it is true that Gardner knew Murray, and that she wrote the short foreword to his book *Witchcraft Today*, study of the practices within the tradition shows scant evidence to support the claim that they were derived from Murray's work.

Much has been made of the amount of plagiarised material found in the Wiccan tradition, though this can be explained by Gardner's claim that he expanded on fragmentary rituals. Gardner's exposure to a wide range of magickal groups and practising magickians in the years from his return to England in 1936 through to the publication of his three relevant books (*High Magic's Aid* (1949), *Witchcraft Today* (1954) and *The Meaning of Witchcraft* (1959)) gives a time period from 1936 to 1954 which could have been used to synthesise a tradition, either from nothing or by expanding on existing fragments. This would explain the use of contemporary work such as Crowley's material and components borrowed from Freemasonry. Gardner's membership of the Folklore Society and acquaintance with people steeped in the grimoire tradition could also be seen as possible contributory channels of information into such a synthesis.

The naive nature of Gardner's comments in his books on how magick works does not suggest a man who would create such an effective magickal system, which though simple, has many layers of complexity contained within it. Therefore we believe that Gardner's claims were genuine insofar as he was initiated into an existing tradition, and that he did as he claimed and added material to the fragments he received that were in keeping with its essence. So although Gardner did not create the tradition, he did add to it.

This conclusion of his addition to the existing material is a strong possibility, based on the evidence:

- Gardner became involved in any magickal groups that he could, so this could well have included the coven which he claimed initiated him;
- Gardner's acquaintance with so many major magickians and folklorists of the time;
- Gardner's opinions on magick do not fit with the practical nature of the Wiccan tradition;
- If Gardner was initiated he would have been oathbound to keep certain material secret, thus explaining the presence of obviously false or incorrect statements in some of his work.

4. Wicca is the survival of a British folk magick system

As we have shown, there are areas of Wiccan practice which have precedents in folk magick, particularly from nineteenth century Ireland. These practices include some of the most significant components of the Wiccan tradition, such as the use of the magick circle and the black-handled knife. However when we consider that these are usually individual practices found in isolation, i.e. not as a single coherent body of material, this seems highly unlikely as a possible origin for the Wiccan tradition.

At this point we will reiterate that the grimoires were influential on the practices of cunning folk, who were still practising their eclectic forms of magick in the nineteenth century, merging such material with folk practices and whatever else they could access that worked. This would then seem to be an option, however the solitary nature of cunning practices, together with the fact that they were effectively part of an anti-witchcraft tradition, and the lack of reliable evidence does not support this conclusion.

It could be argued that the Wiccan tradition grew from a transformation of cunning practices, i.e. that the cunning magick became its antithesis. This switch from being opposed to witchcraft to becoming amalgamated with witchcraft has historical precedents, such as can be seen with the Benandanti of Italy.

This conclusion is very unlikely based on the evidence:

- Although there are individual practices seen in folk magick which parallel those subsequently found in Wicca, these tend to be isolated and not a coherent whole;
- The claims that Wicca grew from the Cunning tradition cannot be substantiated and consequently the lack of reliable evidence means this claim is disregarded.

5. Wicca is the final form of a tradition of European witchcraft with its roots in classical Greece and Rome

The last of our possible conclusions is that Wicca was the final form of a tradition of European witchcraft, with its roots in the Greco-Roman witchcraft found referred to in numerous classical texts. Some practices found in the Wiccan tradition have parallels in medieval witchcraft and some in the witchcraft of ancient Greece and Rome. This idea is supported by the Christian church, which propagated ideas such as the survival of an ancient cult of the witch goddess Diana through to the Middle Ages. It is also supported by the writings of Michelet in mid-nineteenth century France, which would influence writers such as Leland, Frazer and Murray.

The idea of a pre-Christian witch cult that survived underground for thousands of years, whilst appealing, cannot be considered a realistic option when we explore the low level of influence seen in the Wiccan tradition from earlier witch practices. To be a realistic option this proportion would need to be far higher. Also the level of corruption of names, practices, beliefs, etc in an oral tradition spanning so many centuries would probably be highly significant, and this is not seen in the Wiccan tradition.

Another consideration is that the perception of witchcraft in ancient Greece and Rome, through to the Middle Ages, was distinctly that of a malefic tradition. This is in direct contrast to the essence of Wicca as a tradition. So although ideas and terms may have been borrowed from earlier witchcraft traditions, such as the phrase *'Drawing Down the Moon'*, these were often used out of context, possibly to hint at an ancient provenance which did not exist as a direct line of descent, though the essence found in some practices did continue into later traditions and emerge in Wicca.

So this final conclusion, popularised by writers such as Michelet and Murray, cannot be considered a realistic possibility, and again we must disregard it as a possible origin for the Wiccan tradition:

- There is a low level of influence from ancient and medieval witchcraft on the Wiccan tradition;
- It is unlikely that such a tradition would have survived for so long without a high level of corruption of practices and beliefs;
- These ancient and medieval witchcraft practices were malefic and in direct opposition to the essence of the Wiccan tradition.

Our Personal Conclusions

Of these five options, we conclude the first is the most likely. This then suggests that Wicca is a continuation of the grimoire tradition which was later supplemented with material from Victorian ceremonial magick systems such as the Golden Dawn and the Ordo Templi Orientis, either by persons unknown in the years preceding Gerald Gardner's initiation, or later by Gerald Gardner and his associates. If the Crowley and Golden Dawn material is stripped away from the Wiccan practices as being a later addition by Gardner or persons unknown, what is left is a bedrock of grimoire material with fragments of folk practices, which would fit with the idea of a continuation of the grimoire tradition as postulated in our first possible conclusion above, and which we feel is the most likely conclusion. Based on this conclusion we can suggest that at some point in the nineteenth century or early twentieth century, the core practices of what would become known as the Wiccan tradition, which are grimoire-based, coalesced as an evolved manifestation of the grimoire tradition. However, as traditions usually coalesce over a period of time and do not miraculously spring into being overnight, we draw no specific conclusion as to when the tradition started and leave that conclusion to you.

One point we must make is that the further back in time we go, the less evidence there is for direct lines of descent for practices and beliefs. Nevertheless, as we have demonstrated, there are techniques and references from the ancient world which parallel some of the practices found in Wicca. This includes practices from ancient Sumeria, with hints from ancient Egypt and some references from the literature and records of ancient Greece and Rome. So although these practices may in some instances date back up to five thousand years, their presence in Wicca perhaps best demonstrates the idea that there are magickal truths which will always seek expression.

One issue which must be emphasised is that much of the material used in Wicca seems to have been taken out of its original context, which can lead to a great deal of confusion. Whether this was done deliberately or through ignorance or simply because it was added onto an existing system is not a major issue, compared to the use of the material, and the provenance it then enables us to establish when looking at the magickal beginnings of the techniques used in the Wiccan tradition. Whatever conclusions you may draw from this material we have gathered, we feel that the magickal beginnings of Wicca add to the effectiveness and beauty of the tradition, and hope they will inspire you to always explore and look for mystery in unexpected places.

APPENDIX

APPENDIX A

MAGIC OR MAGICK?

Aleister Crowley is often credited with inventing the use of the term *magick* (with a k) as opposed to *magic*. The addition of the *k* increases the magickal potency of the word as *k* is the eleventh letter of the alphabet and eleven is a number considered to contain a lot of inherent magickal power within the western magickal system (being the one beyond ten). Crowley himself also emphasised that he used the spelling of *magick* in order to differentiate the term from the variety of *magic* practiced by stage performers. It is however also interesting to note that the use of both *'magick'* and *'magic'* occurs in medieval and renaissance grimoires, as well as other documents of the time, as there was no standardisation of spelling. For example, in the book *History of Magick* published in 1657 we find:

> *"From these four different wayes, we infer four kinds of Magick: Divine, relating to the first, Theurgick, to the second, Goetick, to the third, and Naturall, to the last..."*

Richard Boulton's two volume work of 1715-16, *A Compleat History of Magick, Sorcery and Witchcraft* continued this use with a *'k'*. Likewise in a completely non-esoteric context, we find it used in a scientific document published in 1811: *"To describe the construction of the Magick Lantern"*[135]

Throughout the nineteenth century both spellings continued to be used frequently, and as Crowley was a well read man he would certainly have been familiar with the alternative spelling. So one could say that Crowley did popularise the *Magick* spelling, but also that he revived the use of this manner of spelling for the word (which was still after all widely in use a few decades earlier), whichever way - he certainly did not invent it. On a personal basis, we use this spelling to differentiate and emphasise, like Crowley, the difference between stage conjuring and the work done within the Western Mystery Traditions, which includes that of Wicca.

---

135 Institutes of Natural Philosophy, William Enfield, Alexander Ewing, Samuel Webber, 1811

APPENDIX B

MAGICKAL PHILOSOPHY

The use of magick is an integral part of the Wiccan tradition: the ceremonies, the spells, healing, and divination all form part of the corpus of magick practiced in one form or another by all its practitioners. Although some may focus their attention more on the devotional and spiritual aspects of the tradition, there is no getting away from the fact that the very act of casting a circle or asking for the blessings of a deity or other spirit is an act of magick, or that Wicca is a magickal system. So what is meant by the term '*magick*'?

A popular definition, often quoted by modern day practitioners of magick, is that put forward by Aleister Crowley in his book *Magick* when he wrote that magick is *"the science and art of causing change to occur in conformity with the will"*. It is necessary here to understand Crowley's point of view when you use this as a definition, so that you can view it in the context of its original meaning. For Crowley, acting in accordance with '*will*' was an act of magick, whether ceremonial or not, as it represented alignment to the cosmic tendency towards perfection. Crowley called such acting in accordance with will '*performing your true will*', as only such positively intended acts embodied truth as their vessel and content. The performance of the true will is also another name for the pursuit of the Great Work, the magickal realisation of personal divinity and expression of that divinity through every deed and action.

Crowley expressed a universal notion in a very concise way, that will is the driving force of magick, providing the mental power which is

244

focused into intent as the lens to produce a magickal result. Actions, words, tools and symbols can all contribute to a magickal act as fuel to power the intent, but it is the intent which is the engine for the will. The training of the mind required to focus it for effective direction of the will was central to Crowley's work to achieve change in conformity with will, as he expressed it, *"the method of science, the aim of religion."* In other words, to follow your true will you must apply the discipline and rigour of science to training your mind to expand its horizons to unite with the infinite, the aim of religion. The idea of magick being a science is not a new one, being the norm until recent centuries. The often ignored American occultist and sex magician Pascal B Randolph (1825-1875), whose writings would influence Crowley and many others, wrote lucidly and significantly in his book *Magia Sexualis* that:

> *"Magick is a science. It is the only science which occupies itself, theoretically and practically, with the highest forces of nature, which are occult."*

Gerald Gardner described magick rather curiously writing in his book *Witchcraft Today:*

> *"My view is that it is simply the use of some abnormal faculty. It is a recognised fact that such faculties exist. So-called calculating boys are famous, and very many people have the faculty under hypnotic control to calculate time most accurately."*

A few years later in his subsequent book *Meaning of Witchcraft* Gardner defined magick as *"Attempting to cause the physically unusual."* These definitions are very much what one would expect from someone with an interest in the esoteric, but certainly not from an experienced practitioner of the magickal arts as they represent a very naive view of the practices and results associated with magick as practiced within the Wiccan Tradition.

In an essay written in 1946 and reproduced in a collection of essays by Jack Parsons, entitled *Freedom is a Two-edged sword* he wrote:

"Magick is a system of philosophy and a way of life which, as a common denominator of all cultures, is universal to mankind"

This sums up the philosophy of the magick practiced in modern Wicca very well, the idea that it is a *"way of life"* is one shared in both the esoteric and exoteric traditions and one which describes the inherent necessity to live magick, rather than to consider it something which is only done at feast days. Furthermore, the idea that it is a common denominator spanning all cultures is one which is particularly appropriate for Wicca, because as we have seen throughout this volume the roots of this tradition are firmly rooted in a number of traditions and practices originating in different parts of the world. Indeed, Wicca when taken back to basics, and stripped bare, can be said to be a tradition of magick which has truly global potential.

APPENDIX C

PERFECT LOVE AND PERFECT TRUST

The phrase *'Perfect Love and Perfect Trust'* is an important concept for those undertaking an initiatory path in the Wiccan tradition. It has been suggested that it is drawn from the phrase *"Perfect love, perfect faith, perfect trust, and you are unassailable."* from Crowley's *The Revival of Magick*, published in 1917. Gardner (or indeed Crowley) could have drawn from a number of sources however, both contemporary and centuries older. The phrase occurred in books both fictional and factual from the mid-nineteenth century onwards. For example, in 1914 Oliver Huckel wrote in a study of Wagner that, *"Perfect love and perfect trust are the essence of religion, and the only source of heavenly joy."*[136]

A famous example of the combination of these words, in a Christian context, is the church reformer Martin Luther's comment *"The words, 'Thou shalt love the Lord, thy God,' require perfect obedience, perfect fear, perfect trust, and perfect love"* in 1535.[137]

---

136 Richard Wagner, the Man and His Work, Huckel, 1914
137 Commentary on the Epistle to the Galatians, Luther, 1535

APPENDIX D

ALEX'S CIRCLES

The photographs from the late 1960s and 1970's of the late Alex Sanders and members of his coven working in a double circle[138] have often been attributed to the *Key of Solomon*. However as we have already seen, the magick circle instructions given in the *Key of Solomon* calls for the circle to be marked thrice, not twice. Additionally the markings are completely different in the circles Sanders is shown in from those associated with the *Key of Solomon*.

So it is interesting to note this difference and look at other possible source for the use of this form of the magick circle by Sanders. Clues can be found in the *Grimoire of Pope Honorius III* where circles are provided for each day of the week, in double form. Likewise, in the *Goetia* (Crowley/Mathers edition) a double circle is given for use, illustrated with a serpent inscribed with Hebrew divine names. However, the divine names and symbols marked in the double circle used by Sanders does not equate to either of these sources and are clearly derived from a circle published in *The Magus* of Francis Barrett in 1801. This circle is described as *"The Magic Circle of Simple Construction in which the operator must stand or sit when he uses the Chrystal"*. Francis Barrett, the author of *The Magus*, took the image directly from *The Art of Drawing Spirits into Crystals* written by Johannes Trithemius. The sigil used by Trithemius in this particular circle construction was taken from

---

138 King of the Witches, June Johns (1969) and Maxine The Witch Queen (1976), Maxine Sanders.

the even earlier *Heptameron* which was penned by Peter de Abano in the fourteenth century.

The Magus is one of the first books to be published which draws together strands from different magickal grimoires and traditions into one volume. Very few copies exchanged hands during the early part of the nineteenth century; most known copies were in collections owned by urban middle and upper class occultists.

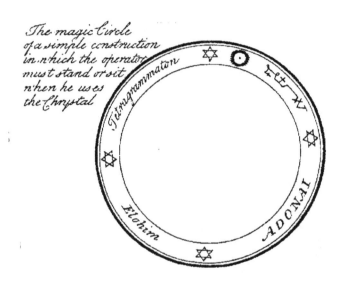

(The Magick Circle of Simple Construction from Trithemius, reproduced in Francis Barrett's The Magus, 1801)

We do however need to give consideration here to key differences between the way in which the circle is marked by Sanders in comparison to Gardner, as it does bring with it interesting questions about his reasons for doing so. Sanders was often accused of having stolen a Book of Shadows from one of Gardner's High Priestesses, a story which some still continue to perpetuate even today, though evidence is completely lacking. However, if this was the case then surely with something as important and central to the practices of Wicca as the magick circle is, it is unlikely that Sanders' source for it would be so dramatically different from that used by Gardner. Especially as it is well documented that the *Key of Solomon* was hugely influential on Sanders' work and there is no doubt that he would have easily been able to create a circle casting procedure based thereon, but he did not. Could this be because the roots, or at least parts thereof, for the Alexandrian tradition might indeed come from elsewhere, as have long been claimed by some?

It would further interest readers familiar with Sanders' work that the sigil used in this circle is that of the archangel Michael, a name which was of particular importance to Sanders. Furthermore, if it was a conscious decision on the part of Sanders to use this circle it shows clearly that he had a solid understanding of magickal practice in regards to the type of work he did as this circle is probably the most appropriate for Wiccan type magick as it is focused for techniques such as skrying and divination. The association with the Archangel Michael further indicates Solar associations as demonstrated by the Sun sigil found next to the Michael sigil. The Archangel Michael is of course associated with the powers of achieving goals and destinies, protection, justice, marriage and music – all corresponding to types of magick which might be wrought in a Wiccan ceremony. Furthermore Michael is the ruler of the Order of the Angels known as the Malakhim, or *'Kings'* who are discussed in more detail in the chapter *The Mighty Ones*.

The circle used by Gardner on the other hand is more appropriately designed for use in evocation of demons, as indicated by the triangle shown next to it. As evocation does not form a traditional part of Wiccan ritual, it is a strange choice and one which can only be attributed to the influence of his novel *High Magic's Aid* in which demons are evoked several times.

Developments

Later it would become customary in many Wiccan traditions for the circle to be of singular construction, sometimes thrice cast, but only marked once. And in time the circle would not be marked out on the ground at all by some, simply visualised and demarcated on the astral. Likewise the Qabalistic divine names which are often found written in and around the circles found in the grimoires, and used by both Gardner and Sanders, would fall out of fashion within some esoteric traditions, whilst it doesn't seem to be used in any of the exoteric traditions at all.

These changes may have been the result of a desire for simplicity, or possibly a conscious move away from the perceived Christian influence of the magick of the grimoires. So just in the few decades since Wicca came to the public attention, the circle, arguably one of the key parts of the practices of the tradition, has seemingly evolved from being marked thrice, to twice, once and nowadays not marked at all, but only visualised.

APPENDIX E

SO MOTE IT BE!

The phrase *So Mote it Be* is one which is heard recurrently at the end of statements of importance in Wiccan ceremonies. It is used to emphasise and reiterate the statements, giving greater importance to them within the context of what is being done. The phrase was popular with Aleister Crowley, who used it in many of his ceremonies, notably *The Gnostic Mass,* which as we have shown inspired many other rituals of importance in the Wiccan tradition.

The possible influence of Freemasonry may also be found here, as this is a exclamation which is found as far back as 1390 CE in *The Regius Poem* which lays out the guidelines for Freemasonry and contains the phrase *"so mot hyt be!"* which in contemporary English is *"so mote it be!"* The phrase continued in popular use throughout the centuries, both in Freemasonry and in prose inspired by Freemasonry. It is known that both Crowley and Gardner had some level of involvement with Freemasonry at some time in their lives and as such we have to conclude that this is the likely source for the use of this term in Wicca today.

BIBLIOGRAPHY

Abano, Peter, *Anulorum Experimenta*, 1303, Codex lat. 7337, Bibliotheque Nationale, Paris

Adler, Margot, *Drawing Down the Moon*, 1986, Beacon Press, Massachusetts

Adlington, William (trans), *The Golden Ass of Apuleius*, 1913, Grant Richards Ltd, London

AE (George William Russell), *The Candle of Vision*, 1918, MacMillan & Co., London

Agrippa, Henry Cornelius, *Three Book of Occult Philosophy*, 2005 (first published in 1531), Llewellyn, Minnesota

----------, *The Fourth Book of Occult Philosophy*, 1978 (first published in 1655), Askin Press, London

Ainsworth Magazine, *Hereward of Brunne*, 1854, Chapman and Hall, London

Allman, George Johnston, *Greek Geometry From Thales to Euclid*, 1889, Hodges, Figgis & Co., Dublin

Ankarloo, Bengt & Clark, Stuart (eds), *Witchcraft and Magic in Europe: Volume 2 Ancient Greece and Rome*, 1999, Athlone Press, London

---------- & ---------- (eds), *Witchcraft and Magic in Europe: Volume 4 The Period of the Witch Trials*, 2002, Athlone Press, London

Anon, *Oriental MSS 6360*, 1700, British Library, London

Anon, *Sloane MSS 3847*, 1572, British Library, London

Anon, *The Testament of Solomon*, 3rd century CE

Athanassakis, Apostolos N. (trans), *Hesiod: Theogony, Works and Days, Shield*, 1983, John Hopkins University Press, Maryland

Athanassiadi, Polymnia & Frede, Michael, *Pagan Monotheism in Late Antiquity*, 1999, Oxford University Press, Oxford

Bailey, Michael D., *From Sorcery to Witchcraft: Clerical Conceptions of Magic in the Later Middle Ages*, 2001, in *Speculum 76:4*

----------, *The Disenchantment of Magic: Spells, Charms, and Superstition in Early European Witchcraft Literature*, 2006, in *The American Historical Review 3:2*

Banier, Antoine, *Mythology and Fables of the Ancients*, 1739, A Millar, London

Barrett, C.K., *New Testament Background: Selected Documents*, 1956, SPCK, London

Barrett, Francis, *The Magus or Celestial Intelligencer*, N.D. (first published in 1801), I.G.O.S., California

Barry, Kieren, *The Greek Qabalah: Alphabetic Mysticism and Numerology in the Ancient World*, 1999, Samuel Weiser Inc., Maine

Baroja, Julio Caro, *The World of the Witches*, 1961, Weidenfeld & Nicolson, London

Bartlett, Anne Clark & Horstmann, C. (eds), *Yorkshire Writers: Richard Rolle of Hampole and his Followers: I, II*, 1999, D.S. Brewer, New York

Bellows, Henry A. (trans), *The Poetic Edda*, 1936, Princeton University Press, Princeton

Bennett, Mary, *The Jew's Daughter or The Witch of the Water-Side*, 1838, John Saunders, London

Betz, Hans Dieter (ed), *The Greek Magickal Papyri in Translation*, 1996, University of Chicago Press, Chicago

-----------, *Magic and Mystery in the Greek Magickal Papyri*, in *Magika Hiera: Ancient Greek Magic & Religion*, 1991, Oxford University Press, Oxford

Bingham, Rev Joseph, *The Works of the Reverend Joseph Bingham*, 1855, Oxford University, Oxford

Blackman, A.M., *The King of Egypt's Grace before Meat*, in *Journal of Egyptian Archaeology*, 1945, vol. 31:57-73

-----------, *The Significance of Incense and Libations*, in *Zeitscrift fur Aegyptische Sprache und Altertumskunde*, 1912, vol 50: 69-75

Blair, Adam, *History of the Waldenses*, 1832, Adam Black, Edinburgh

Bonomo, Giuseppe, *Caccia alle streghe*, 1959, Palumbo, Palermo

Boon, George C., *A Coin with the Head of the Cernunnos*, September 1982, in *Seaby Coin & Medal Bulletin*, p276-82

Borghouts, J.F., *Ancient Egyptian Magickal Texts*, 1978, Nisaba Volume 9, E J Brill, Leiden

Boulton, Richard, *A Compleat History of Magick, Sorcery and Witchcraft*, 1715, W. Taylor, London

Boyse, Samuel, *A New Pantheon*, 1753, H & J Ramsey, Waterford

Bracelin, Jack, *Gerald Gardner: Witch*, 1999 (first published 1960), I-H-O Books, Thame

Brahe, Tycho, *Calendarium*, 1620, Frankfurt

Brodie-Innes, J.W., *Witchcraft*, 1917, in *The Occult Review*, Vol 25 No 5, p264-71

-----------, *Witchcraft Rituals*, 1917, in *The Occult Review*, Vol 25 No 6, p328-36

Browning, John (trans), *The History of Tuscany, from the Earliest Era*, 1826, Young, Black and Young, London

Bruno, Giordano, *Des fureurs héroïques*, 1585, Parigi

Buckland, Raymond, *The Tree*, 1974, Weiser Books, Maine

Butler, E.M., *Ritual Magic*, 1949, Cambridge University Press, Cambridge

Carmichael, Alexander (ed), *Carmina Gadelica*, 1992 (first published in 1900), Lindisfarne Books

Carpenter, Edward, *Pagan & Christian Creeds: Their Origin and Meaning*, 1920, Harcourt Brace & Co., New York

Causabon, Meric, *A True & Faithful Relation of what Passed for Many Years between Dr John Dee and Some Spirits*, 1973 (first published in 1659), Askin Press, London

Cavendish, Richard, *The Black Arts*, 1967, Routledge & Kegan Paul Ltd, London

----------, *The Powers of Evil in Western Religion, Magic and Folk Belief*, 1975, Routledge & Kegan Paul Ltd, London

----------, *A History of Magic*, 1987, Arkana, London

Chambers, Robert & William, *Chambers Information for the People*, 1842, W. S. Orr, London

Cirlot, Juan Eduardo, *A Dictionary of Symbols*, 1962, Routledge & Kegan Paul, London

Clark, Stuart, *Thinking with Demons: the Idea of Witchcraft in Early Modern Europe*, 1997, Clarendon Press, Oxford

Cohn, Norman, *Europe's Inner Demons: The Demonization of Christians in Medieval Christendom*, 1993, University of Chicago Press, Chicago

Couliano, Ioan P., *Eros and Magic in the Renaissance*, 1987, University of Chicago Press, Chicago

Coulton, G.G., *Life in the Middle Ages*, 1928, Cambridge University Press, Cambridge

Cox, John D., *The Devil and the Sacred in English Drama 1350-1642*, 2000, Cambridge University Press, Cambridge

Croker, Thomas Crofton, *Fairy Legends and Traditions of the South of Ireland*, 1828, John Murray, London

Crowley, Aleister, *777 & Other Qabalistic Writings of Aleister Crowley*, 1983 (first published in 1909), Samuel Weiser Inc., Maine

----------, *Moonchild*, 1929, The Mandrake Press, London

----------, *Crowley on Christ* (first published in 1916 as *The Gospel According to Saint Bernard Shaw*), 1974, C.W. Daniel, London

----------, *The Book of the Goetia of Solomon the King*, 1996 (first published in 1904), Red Wheel/Weiser, Maine

----------, *Liber AL vel Legis* (The Book of the Law), 1938 (first received in 1904), O.T.O., London

----------, *Magick in Theory and Practice*, 1929, Lecram, Paris

----------, *The Revival of Magic & other Essays*, 1998 (first published in 1917), New Falcon, Arizona

----------, *Rodin in Rime*, 1907, privately printed, London

----------, *The Equinox Volume 3 No. 1* (The Blue Equinox), 1971 (first published in 1919), Samuel Weiser, Maine

----------, *Liber Agapé & De Arte Magica*, 1986 (first published in 1914), Kadath Press, Keighley

----------, *The Vision and the Voice*, 1972 (first published in 1909 in *The Equinox* Vol 1 No 5), Sangreal Foundation, Texas

Crowley, Vivianne, *Wicca: The Old Religion in the New Millennium*, 1996, Thorsons, London

Crowther, Patricia, *Witch Blood!*, 1974, House of Collectibles, New York

----------, *Lid Off The Cauldron*, 1981, Frederick Muller, London

----------, *High Priestess: The Life & Times of Patricia Crowther*, 1998, Phoenix Publishing Inc., Arizona

Cunningham, Scott, *Wicca: A Guide for the Solitary Practitioner*, 1988, Llewellyn, Minnesota

D'Arras, Jean de, *Melusine de Lusignan*, 1393

Davies, Owen, *Urbanization and the Decline of Witchcraft*, 2002, in *The Witchcraft Reader*, Routledge, London

----------, *Cunning-Folk: Popular Magic in English History*, 2003, Hambledon & London, London

Dechelette, Joseph, *Manual d'archeologie prehistorique Celtique et Gallo-Romaine*, 1908, Paris

Dehn, Georg & Guth, Steve (ed), *The Book of Abramelin*, 2006, Ibis Publishing, Florida

Dennis, Geoffrey, *The Encyclopaedia of Jewish Myth, Magic and Mysticism*, 2007, Llewellyn, Minnesota

De Plancy, Jacques Auguste Simon Collin, *Dictionnaire Infernal*, 1818, Paris

D'Este, Sorita (ed), *Hekate: Keys to the Crossroads*, 2006, Avalonia, London

----------, *Artemis Virgin Goddess of the Sun and Moon*, 2005, Avalonia, London

Diderot, *Encylopédie Receueil de Planches, sur les Sciences et les Arts*, 1763, Diderot & Alembert, France

Douglas-Klotz, Neil, *The Sufi Book of Life: 99 Pathways to the Heart from the Modern Dervish*, 2005, Penguin Books, London

Dolan, Terrence Patrick, *A Dictionary of Hiberno-English*, 1999, Gill & MacMillan, Dublin

Dublin University Magazine, 1849, Oxford University Collection

Duffy, Eamon, *The Stripping of the Altars: Traditional Religion in England 1400-1580*, 1992, Yale University Press, New Haven

Drury, Nevill, *The History of Magic in the Modern Age*, 2000, Constable, London

Dwight, Henry Edwin, *Travels in the North of Germany: in the Years 1825 and 1826*, 1829, G & C & H Carvill, New York

Eliade, Mircea, *Rites and Symbols of Initiation: The Mysteries of Birth and Rebirth*, 1958, Harper Torch Books, New York

----------, *The Sacred and the Profane: The Nature of Religion*, 1959, Harcourt Inc., Florida

----------, *Shamanism Archaic Techniques of Ecstacy*, 1964, Routledge & Kegan Paul, London

----------, *Occultism, Witchcraft & Cultural Fashions*, 1976, University of Chicago Press, Chicago

Empedocles, *Tetrasomia*, 5th century BCE

Enfield, Ewing, Webber, *Institutes of Natural Philosophy*, 1811

Evangelical Alliance, *Evangelical Christendom*, 1893, J.S. Phillips, London

Eymerich, Nicolas, *Directorium Inquistorum*, 1376

Fanger, Claire (ed), *Conjuring Spirits: Texts and Traditions of Medieval Ritual Magic*, 1998, Sutton Publishing Ltd, Gloucestershire

Faraone, Christopher A., & Obbink, Dirk (eds), *Magika Hiera: Ancient Greek Magic & Religion*, 1991, Oxford University Press, Oxford

Farrar, Stewart, *What Witches Do*, 1971, Peter Davies, London

Farrar, Janet & Stewart, *A Witches Bible*, 1996 (first published in 1981), Phoenix Publishing Inc, Washington

----------, *The Witches Way*, 1984, Robert Hale, London

----------, *The Life & Times of a Modern Witch*, 1987, Piatkus books, London

Fee, Christopher R., *Gods Heroes & Kings: The Battle for Mythic Britain*, 2001, Oxford University Press, Oxford

Ferguson, Ian, *The Philosophy of Witchcraft*, 1924, George G. Harrap & Co Ltd, London

Flint, Valerie I.J., *The Rise of Magic in Early Medieval Europe*, 1991, Princeton University Press, New Jersey

Flowers, Stephen, *Witchdom of the True: A Study of the Vana-Troth and the Practice of Seidr*, 1999, Runa-Raven Press, Texas

----------, *Fire & Ice: The History, Structure, and Rituals of Germany's Most Influential Modern Magickal Order: The Brotherhood of Saturn*, 1994, Llewellyn Publications, Minnesota

Flowers, Stephen, & Chisholm, James A. (trans), *A Source-Book of Seið*, 2002, Rûna-Raven, Texas

Forman, Simon, *Of the Division of Chaos*, Ashmole MSS 240, Bodleian Library, Oxford

Fortune, Dion, *The Mystical Qabalah*, 2000 (first published in 1935), Red Wheel Weiser, Maine

----------, *The Sea Priestess*, 1998 (first published in 1938), SIL Trading Ltd, London

----------, *Moon Magic*, 1995 (first published posthumously in 1956), SIL Trading Ltd, London

----------, *The Goat-Foot God*, 1989 (first published in 1936), Aquarian, Wellingborough

----------, *The Winged Bull*, 1976 (first published in 1935), Wyndham Publications Ltd, London

----------, *The Secrets of Dr Taverner*, 1989 (first published in 1926), Aquarian, Wellingborough

Frazer, James G., *The Golden Bough: A study in Magic and Religion*, 1993 (first published in 1890), Wordsworth Editions Ltd, London

Fuller, J.F.C., *The Black Arts*, 1921, in *Form* Vol. II No 2

Ganguli, Kisari Mohan (trans), *The Mahabharata*, 1894, Bharatta Press, Calcutta

Gardner, Gerald, *A Goddess Arrives*, 2000 (first published in 1939), I-H-O Books, Thame

----------, *High Magic's Aid*, 1999 (first published in 1949), I-H-O Books, Thame

----------, *The Meaning of Witchcraft*, 2000 (first published in 1959), I-H-O Books, Thame

----------, *Witchcraft Today*, 1954, Rider & Co., London

Gebhardt, Emile, *Les jardins de l'Histoire*, 1911, Paris

Geddes, Dr, *Geddes Translation of the Bible*, in *The British Critic and Quarterly Theological Review*, 1794, Volume 4, F & C Rivington, London

Gettings, Fred, *Dictionary of Occult, Hermetic & Alchemical Sigils*, 1981, Routledge & Kegan Paul, London

Gibbons, Edward, *The History of the Decline and Fall of the Roman Empire*, 1806, Vernon, Hood & Sharpe, London

Gibson, Alex, & Simpson, Derek, *Prehistoric Ritual & Religion*, 1998, Sutton Publishing Ltd, Gloucestershire

Gilbert, R.A., (ed), *The Sorcerer and His Apprentice: Unknown Hermetic Writings of S.L. MacGregor Mathers and J.W. Brodie-Innes*, 1983, The Aquarian Press, Wellingborough

Ginzburg, Carlo, *Ecstasies: Deciphering the Witches' Sabbath*, 1991, Pantheon Books, New York

----------, *Night Battles: Witchcraft & Agrarian Cults in the Sixteenth & Seventeenth Centuries*, 1985, Penguin Books, Middlesex

De Givry, Grillot, *A Pictorial Anthology of Witchcraft, Magic and Alchemy*, 1958 (first published in English in 1931), University Books, New York

Glanvill, Joseph, *Saducismus Triumphatus: Or, Full and Plain Evidence Concerning Witches and Apparitions*, 1966 (first published in 1681), Scholars Facsimilies & Reprint, New York

Glass, Justin, *Witchcraft, The Sixth Sense*, 1965, Hal Leighton Printing Company, California

von Goethe, Johann Wolfgang, *Faust*, 1950 (first published in 1808), Penguin, London

Godwin, Joscelyn, *The Pagan Dream of the Renaissance*, 2002, Thames & Hudson, London

----------- (trans), *The Chymical Wedding of Christian Rosenkreutz*, 1991, Magnum Opus Hermetic Source Works No. 18, Phanes Press, Michigan

Gollancz, Herman, *Sepher Mafteah Selomoh (Book of the Key of Solomon)*, 1903, David Nutt, London

Gordon, Walter Ralph, *Momentary Monsters: Lucan & his Heroes*, 1987, Cornell University Press, Ithaca

Graf, Fritz, *Magic in the Ancient World*, 1997, Harvard University Press, Massachusetts

Grant, Kenneth, *Nightside of Eden*, 1977, Frederick Muller Ltd, London

----------, *Remembering Aleister Crowley*, 1991, Skoob Esoterica, London

Grant, Kenneth & Steffi, *Zos Speaks! Encounters with Austin Osman Spare*, 1998, Fulgur Press, London

Graves, Robert, *The White Goddess*, 1962 (first published in 1948), Faber & Faber Ltd, London

Griffiths, Bill, *Aspects of Anglo-Saxon Magic*, 1996, Anglo-Saxon Books, Norfolk

Gummere, Francis B., *Old English Ballads*, 1894, Ginn & Co., Boston

Habicht, Christian (trans), *Pausanias' Guide to Greece*, 1998, University of California Press, California

Hansen, Joseph (ed), *Quellen und Untersuchungen zur Geschichte des Hexenwahns und der Hexenfolgung im Mittelalter*, 1901, Georgi, Bonn

----------, *Zauberwahn, Inquisition und Hexenprozesse im Mittelalter*, 1900, Oldenberg, Munich

Harrison, Jane Ellen, *Prolegomena to the Study of Greek Religion*, 1903, Cambridge University Press, Cambridge

----------, *Ancient Art & Ritual*, 1978 (first published in 1913), Moonraker Press, Wiltshire

Harrison, Michael, *The Roots of Witchcraft*, 1973, Frederick Muller Ltd, London

Hawkey, Muriel (ed), *A Cornish Chorus: A Collection of Prose and Verse*, 1948, Westaway Books Ltd, London

Heidel, Alexander, *The Babylonian Genesis*, 1942, University of Chicago Press, Chicago

Helmbold, W.C. (trans), *Plato: Gorgias*, 1952, Bobbs-Merrill, Indiana

Henderson, George (ed), *Popular Rhymes, sayings and Proverbs of the county of Berwick*, 1856, W.S. Crow, Newcastle-upon-Tyne

Henig, Martin, *A Corpus of Roman Engraved Gemstones from British Sites* (2 volumes), 1974, British Archeaological Reports 8(ii), Oxford

Herne Johannis, *Astronomical and Astrological Tracts*, 15th century, Sloane MS 636

Heselton, Philip; *Gerald Gardner and the Cauldron of Inspiration*, 2003, Capall Bann, Somerset

-----------, *Wiccan Roots*, 2000, Capall Bann, Somerset

Heydon, Thomas, *Theomagia, or The temple of wisdom in three parts, spiritual, celestial, and elemental*, 1664, Henry Brome, London

Hill, George, *A Spell against Tempest: Black Handled Knife*, 1942, in *Notes and Queries* 182:33, Oxford Journals

Hole, Christina, *Witchcraft in Britain*, 1977, Paladin, London

-----------, *A Dictionary of British Folk Customs*, 1978, Paladin, London

Holzer, Hans, *The Truth About Witchcraft*, 1969, Doubleday, USA

Homer, *Aurea Catena Homeri oder Eine Beschreibung von dem Ursprung der Natur und natürlichen Dingen*, 1723, A.J. Kirchweger

Horace, *Odes and Epodes of Horace*, 2002, University of Chicago Press, Chicago

Hornung, E., *Conceptions of God in Ancient Egypt: The One and the Many*, Cornell University Press, New York, 1982

Huckel, Oliver, *Richard Wagner, the Man and His Work*, 1914, Thomas Y Cromwell Company, New York

Hueffer, Oliver Madox, *The Book of Witches*, 1908, Eveleigh Nash, London

Huson, Paul, *Mastering Witchcraft*, 1970, Rupert Hart-Davis, London

Hutchinson, Francis, *An Historical Essay Concerning Witchcraft: With Observations Upon Matters of Fact*, 1718, R Knaplock, London

Hutton, Ronald, *The Pagan Religions of the Ancient British Isles*, 1991, Basil Blackwell Ltd, Oxford

-----------, *The Triumph of the Moon*, 1999, Oxford University Press, Oxford

-----------, *Witches, Druids and King Arthur*, 2003, Hambledon and London, London

-----------, *Shamanism: Mapping the Boundaries*, 2006 in *Magic, Ritual & Witchcraft* Volume 1 No. 2:209-213

Irenaeus, St., *Against the Heresies Vol.1*, 1992, Newman Press, Washington

Iscanus, Bartholomew, *MSS Cotton Faust A viii*, 11th century, British Library

James, Geoffrey, *The Enochian Magick of Dr John Dee*, 1994, Llewellyn, Minnesota

Jarcke, Karl Ernest, *Ein Hexenprozess*, 1828 in *Annalen der Deutschen und Auslandischen Criminal-Rechts-Pflege I*

Jastrow, Morris, *The Religion of Babylonia & Assyria*, 1893, The Athenaeum Press, Boston

Johns, June, *King of the Witches*, 1969, Pan Books Ltd, London

Johnson, Thomas Moore (trans), *Proclus' Metaphysical Elements*, 1909, Osceola, Missouri

Johnston, Sarah Iles, *Hekate Soteira*, 1990, Scholars, Press, Georgia

Jolif, Thierry, *The Cernunnos Mystery*, 2004, in *Runa* 15:2-6

Jones, Bernard E., *Freemasons' Guide and Compendium*, 1956, Harrap, London

Jones, Evan John, & Cochrane, Robert, *The Roebuck in the Thicket, An Anthology of the Robert Cochrane Witchcraft Tradition*, 2001, Capall Bann, Chievely

Kaplan, Aryeh, *Sefer Yetzirah*, 1997, Weiser Books, Maine

----------, *The Bahir Illumination*, 1979, Red Wheel/Weiser, Maine

Kapur, Sohaila, *Witchcraft in Western India*, 1983, Sangam Books, Bombay

Kelley, Aidan A., *Crafting the Art of Magic, Book I: A History of Modern Witchcraft 1939-1964*, 1991, Llewellyn Publications, Minnesota

Kenyon, Theda, *Witches Still Live*, 1929, Ives Washburn, New York

Kieckhefer, Richard, *Magic in the Middle Ages*, 1989, Cambridge University Press, Cambridge

----------, *Forbidden Rites: A Necromancer's Manual of the Fifteenth Century*, 1997, Sutton Publishing, Stroud

King, B.J.H. (trans), *The Grimoire of Pope Honorius III*, 1984, Sut Anubis Books, Northampton

King, Francis, *Ritual Magic in England, 1887 to the present day*, 1970, Neville Spearman Ltd, London

----------, *The Secret Rituals of the O.T.O*, 1973, C.W. Daniel & Co. Ltd, London

Kingsley, Peter, *Ancient Philosophy, Mystery and Magic: Empedocles and Pythagorean Tradition*, 1995, Oxford University Press, Oxford

Kipling, Rudyard, *Puck of Pook's Hill*, 1906, MacMillan, London

Knoop, D., and Jones, G.P., *A Short History of Freemasonry to 1730*, 1940, Manchester University Press, Manchester

Kovacs, David (trans), *Euripides, Volume IV. Trojan Women. Iphigenia among the Taurians*, 1999, LOEB Classical Library, London

Lady Sheba, *The Grimoire of Lady Sheba*, 1972, Llewellyn

Laertes, Diogenes, *Vitae*, 3rd century CE

Lamond, Frederic, *Fifty Years of Wicca*, 2004, Green Magic, Sutton Mallett

Lansdowne, George Granville, *The British Enchanters or No Magic Like Love*, 1732, S Powell, Dublin

Law, Rev. Robert, *Memorialls; or the Memorable Things that fell out Within this Island of Britain from 1638 to 1684*, 17th century MSS

Lawrence, Robert Means, *The Magic of the Horseshoe*, 1898, Riverside Press, Cambridge

Lazar, Moshé, *Theophilus, Servant of Two Masters: The Pre-Faustian Theme of Despair and Revolt*, 1972, in *Modern Language Notes 87*, 6:31-50

Lea, Henry Charles, *Materials Towards a History of Witchcraft*, 1957 (published posthumously), Thomas Yoseloff, New York

----------, *Superstition and force: Torture, ordeal, and trial by combat in medieval law*, 1866, Collins, Philadelphia

----------, *A History of the Inquisition of the Middle Ages*, 1887, Harper & brothers, New York

Lecouteux, Claude, *Witches Werewolves and Fairies: Shapeshifters and Astral Doubles in the Middle Ages*, 2003, Inner Traditions, Vermont

Leland, C.G., *Aradia: Gospel of the Witches*, 1899, David Nutt, London

----------, *Etruscan Roman Remains in Popular Tradition*, 1892, T. Fisher Unwin, London

----------, *Gypsy Sorcery*, 1993 (first published in 1889), Anthony Naylor & Dwina Murphy-Gibb, Thame

----------, *Legends of Florence*, 1896, David Nutt, London.

Lenormant, Francois, *Chaldean Magic*, 1877, Samuel Bagster & Sons, London

Levi, Eliphas, *Transcendental Magic*, 1979 (first published in English in 1896), Rider, London

----------, *The Magickal Ritual of the Sanctum Regnum*, 1970 (first published in English in 1896), Crispin Press, London

----------, *The Key of the Mysteries*, 1959 (first published in English in 1861), Rider & Co, London

Lewis, James R., *Magical Religion and Modern Witchcraft*, 1996, SUNY Press, New York

Linton, Lynn, *Witch Stories*, 1861, Chapman & Hall, London

Louÿs, Pierre, *The Adventures of King Pausole*, 1933 (first published in French in 1901), William Godwin, New York

Lowell, James Russell, *Among My Books*, 1870, Osgood & Co, Boston

Luck, Georg, *Arcana Mundi: Magic and the Occult in the Greek and Roman Worlds*, 1985, John Hopkins University Press

Luther, Martin, & Graebner, Theodore (trans), *Commentary on the Epistle to the Galatians*, 1965 (first published 1949), Zondervan Publishing House, Michigan

Mackey, Albert Gallatin, *An Encyclopaedia of Freemasonry and its Kindred Sciences*, 1879, L H Everts & Co, Philadelphia

Mackey, Albert Gallatin & Haywood, H.L., *Encyclopaedia of Freemasonry*, 1946, Kessinger Publishing

Magnus, Albertus, *Book of Secrets*, 1974, Oxford University Press, Oxford

Mathers, S.L. MacGregor (trans), *The Key of Solomon the King (Clavicula Salomonis)*, 1889, George Redway, London

---------- (trans), *The Sacred Magic of Abra-Melin the Mage*, 1898, John M Watkins, London

---------- (trans), *The Kabbalah Unveiled*, 1991 (first published in 1887), Arkana, London

McLean, Adam (trans), *The Magickal Calendar: A Synthesis of Magickal Symbolism from the Seventeenth Century Renaissance of Medieval Occultism*, 1994, Magnum Opus Hermetic Sourceworks No. 1, Phanes Press, Michigan

----------- (ed), *The Steganographia of Johannes Trithemius*, Book I & III, 1982, Magnum Opus Hermetic Sourceworks 12, Edinburgh

----------- (ed), *A Treatise on Angel Magic*, 1982, Magnum Opus Hermetic Sourceworks No. 15, Tysoe

Meid, W., *Gaulish Inscriptions*, 1992, Archaeolingua Alapitvány, Budapest

Meyer, Marvin W., & Smith, Richard, *Ancient Christian Magic: Coptic Texts of Ritual Power*, 1999, Princeton University Press, Princeton

Michel, Paul-Henri (ed, trans), *Bruno: Des fureurs héroïques*, 1954, Les Belles Lettres, Paris

Michelet, Jules, *La Sorcière*, 1939 (first published in French in 1862), Garner-Flammarion, Paris

Middleton, Thomas, *The Witch*, 1613

Miller, Thomas, *The History of the Anglo-Saxons*, 1856, H G Bohn, London

Milton, John, *The Paradise Lost of Milton*, 1850 (first published in 1667), Henry Washbourne, London

Mitchell, J. & Dickie, John, *The Philosophy of Witchcraft*, 1839, Paisley: Murray & Stewart, Glasgow

Mone, Franz Josef, *Uber das Hexenwasen*, 1839 in *Anzeiger fur Kunde der Teutschen Vorzeit*, p271-5, 444-5

Monteil, Amans Alexis, *Histoire des Francais des divers etats*, 1853, V. Lecou , Paris

Mookerjee, Ajit, *Kali: The Feminine Force*, 1999, Thames & Hudson Ltd, London

Mora, George (ed), *Witches, Devils, and Doctors in the Renaissance*, 1991, Medieval & Renaissance Texts & Studies, New York

Morrow, G. (trans), *Proclus: A Commentary on the First Book of Euclid's Elements*, 1992, Princeton University Press, Princeton

Murray, Margaret, *The Witch Cult in Western Europe*, 1921, Clarendon Press, Oxford

-----------, *The God of the Witches*, 1970 (first published in 1933), Oxford University Press, Oxford

Naudé, Gabriel, *Apologie pour tous les grands personages qui ont esté faussement soupçonnez de magie*, 1625, Paris

-----------, *The History of Magick*, 1657, John Streater, London

Neugebauer, O & van Hoesen, H.B. *Greek Horoscopes*, 1959, The American Philosophical Society, Philadelphia

Nichols, Ross, *The Book of Druidry*, 1990 (published posthumously), Aquarian Press, Wellingborough

Olmsted, Garret S., *The Gods of the Celts and the Indo-Europeans*, 1994, Archaeolingua, Budapest

-----------, *The Gundestrup Cauldron*, 1979, in *Collection Latomus 162*, Brussels

Padgett, Lewis, *The Day He Died*, 1947, Duell, Sloan and Pearce, New York

Page, Sophie, *Magic in Medieval Manuscripts*, 2004, British Library, London

Parsons, Jack W., *Freedom is a Two-edged Sword & other Essays*, 1990 (first published in 1946), New Falcon Publications, Arizona

-----------, *Magick, Gnosticism and the Witchcraft*, 1946, N.P., USA

Peterson, Joseph (ed), *The Lesser Key of Solomon: Lemegeton Clavicula Salomonis*, 2001, Weiser Books, Maine

----------- (ed, trans), *Grimorium Verum*, 2007, CreateSpace Publishing, California

Picton, J.A., *Hall, Wych and Salt Works*, 1874, in *Notes and Queries*, S5-11, 309-11

Pinch, Geraldine, *Magic in Ancient Egypt*, 1994, British Museum Press, London

-----------, *Egyptian Mythology*, 2002, Oxford University Press, Oxford

Pipernus, Peter, *De Nuce Maga Beneventana & De Effectibus Magicis*, 1647, Naples

Plutarch, *Plutarch's Morals*, 1870, Little, Brown & Company, Boston

Pollington, Stephen, *Leechcraft: Early English Charms Plantlore and Healing*, 2000, Anglo-Saxon Books, Norfolk

Ponce, Charles, *Kabbalah*, 1974, Garnstone Press, London

Porta, John Baptista & Giovanni Battista, *Natural Magick*, 1658, Thomas Young & Samuel Speed, London

Possekel, Ute, *Evidence of Greek Philosophical Concepts in the Writings of Ephrem the Syrian*, 1999, Peeters Publishers

Rabelais, Francois, *Gargantua and Pantagruel*, 1991 (first published in 1534), W.W. Norton & Co

Randolph, Pascal B., *Magia Sexualis*, 1987 (first published in French as *Eulis* in 1876), Ediz Mediterranee, Rome

Rankine, David & D'Este, Sorita, *The Guises of the Morrigan*, 2005, Avalonia, London

Rattenbury, John Ernest, *The Evangelical Doctrines of Charles Wesley's Hymns*, 1942, The Epworth Press

Regardie, Israel, *The Golden Dawn*, 2003 (first published in 1937), Llewellyn Publications, Minnesota

-----------, *The Middle Pillar: The Balance between Mind and Magic*, 2000 (first published in 1938), Llewellyn Publications

-----------, *Ceremonial Magic*, 1980, Aquarian, Wellingborough

Rhodes, H.T.F., *The Satanic Mass*, 1955, Citadel Press, New York

Rieu, E.V. (ed), *The Pastoral Poems: The Text of the Eclogues*, 1954, Penguin Books, London

Ritner, R.K., *Practical Egyptian Magickal Spells*, 1998, presented at the Oriental Institute Dinner

Rohrbacher-Sticker, Claudia, *A Hebrew Manuscript of Clavicula Salomonis*, 1995, in *The British Library Journal* 21.1, British Library, London

-----------, *Mafteah Shelomoh: A New Acquisition of the British Library*, 1994, in *Jewish Studies Quarterly*, vol 1

Rose, Elliot, *A Razor for a Goat: Problems in the History of Witchcraft and Diabolism*, 1962, University of Toronto Press, Toronto

Ross, Anne, *Pagan Celtic Britain*, 1967, Routledge & Kegan Paul Ltd, London

Ross, W.D., *The Works of Aristotle*, 1930, Oxford University Press, Oxford

Rudd, Thomas, *Harley MSS 6482*, 1712, British Library

Russell, Jeffrey B., *A History of Witchcraft: Sorcerers, Heretics and Pagans*, 1980, Thames and Hudson Ltd, London

-----------, *Lucifer: The Devil in the Middle Ages*, 1984, Cornell University Press

Ryan, W.F., *The Bathhouse at Midnight: An Historical Survey of Magic and Divination in Russia*, 1999, Sutton Publishing Ltd, Stroud

Sala, George Augustus, *The Strange Adventures of Captain Dangerous*, 1863, Tinsley Brothers, London

Sanders, Maxine, *Maxine The Witch Queen*, 1976, Star Books, London

Scaliger, *De aspectibus planetas ad Lunam*, 15th century

Schäfer, Peter *Mirror of His Beauty: Feminine Images of God from the Bible to the Early Kabbalah*, 2002, Princeton University Press, Princeton

Scot, Reginald, *Discoverie of Witchcraft*, 1989 (first published in 1584), Dover Publications, London

Scott, George Ryley, *Phallic Worship: A History of Sex & Sexual Rites*, 1966, Luxor Press, London

Scully, Sally, *Marriage or a career? Witchcraft as an alternative in seventeenth century Venice*, in *Journal of Social History*, Summer 1995

Seznec, Jean, *The Survival of the Pagan Gods*, 1953, Princeton University Press, Princeton

Shah, Sayed Idries, *The Secret Lore of Magic*, 1957, Frederick Muller Ltd, London

-----------, *Oriental Magic*, 1992 (first published in 1956), The Octagon Press, London

---------, *Secret Societies*, 1961, The Octagon Press, London

Shakespeare, William, *Complete Sonnets*, 1991, Dover Publications, London

Sharpe, Charles, Kirkpatrick, *Historical Account of the Belief in Witchcraft in Scotland*, 1884 Thomas D Morison, Glasgow

Sibly, Ebenezer, *A New and Complete Illustration of the Occult Sciences*, 1790, Sibly, London

Siculus Diodorus, *Library of History Books IV-VIII*, 1939, Harvard University Press, Harvard

Sikes, Wirt, *British Goblins: Welsh Folklore, Fairy Mythology, Legends and Traditions*, 1880, Sampson Low, Marston, Searle, & Rivington, London

Skelton, John, *Essays in Romance and Studies from Life*, 1878, W Blackwood and Sons, London

Skemer, Don C., *Binding Words: Textual Amulets in the Middle Ages*, 2006, Pennsylvania State University Press, Pennsylvania

Skinner, Stephen, & Rankine, David, *The Practical Angel Magic of Dr John Dee's Enochian Tables*, 2004, Golden Hoard Press, Singapore

---------- & ----------, *The Keys to the Gateway of Magic*, 2005, Golden Hoard Press, Singapore

---------- & ----------, *The Goetia of Dr Rudd*, 2007, Golden Hoard Press, Singapore

Smith, Clark Ashton, *The Master of the Crabs*, 1948, in *Weird Tales* magazine

Snell, B. (ed), *Tragicorum Graecorum Fragmenta*, 1971, Gottingen

Sommerhoff, J.C.S., *Lexicon Pharmaceutico-Chymicum*, 1701

Spence, Lewis, *An Encyclopædia of Occultism*, 1920, George Routledge & Sons, London

Stanley, Thomas (trans), *The Chaldaick Oracles of Zoroaster*, 1661, Thomas Dring, London

Stokker, Kathleen, *Narratives of Magic and Healing, Olditdens Sortbog in Norway and the New Land*, 2001, Society for the Advancement of Scandinavian Study

Storms, G., *Anglo-Saxon Magic*, 1948, Nijhoff, The Hague

Strong, Herert A, & Garstang, John, *The Syrian Goddess*, 1913, Constable & Co, London

Symonds, John, *The Great Beast: The Life of Aleister Crowley*, 1973 (first published in 1951), Mayflower, London

Symonds, John & Grant, Kenneth (eds), *The Confessions of Aleister Crowley*, 1979, Routledge & Kegan Paul plc, London

Symonds, John Addington, *An Introduction to the Study of Dante*, 1890, A & C Black, London

----------, *Renaissance in Italy. The Catholic Reaction. Part 1*, 2001, Adamant Media Corporation

Tartarotti, Girolamo, *Del Congresso Notturno Delle Lammie*, 1749, Rovereto, Italy

Taylor, Thomas, *Iamblichus On The Mysteries (translated from the Greek)*, 1821, Chiswick

Testa, Emmanuele, *Il Simbolism dei Giudeo-Christiani*, 1962, Franciscan Printing Press.

Thomas, Keith, *Religion and the Decline of Magic*, 1980, Penguin Books, London

Thompson, C.J.S., *The Mysteries and Secrets of Magic*, 1927, John Lane, London

Thompson, R. Campbell, *Semitic Magic: Its Origins and Development*, 2000 (first published in 1908), Samuel Weiser, Maine

Thornbury, Walter, *Turkish Life & Character*, 1860, Smith, Elder & Co, London

Thorndike, Lynn, *History of Magic & Experimental Science* (8 vols), 1953, Columbia University Press

Tiryakian, Edward A., *Towards the Sociology of Esoteric Culture*, in *American Journal of Sociology 78*, November 1972, p491-512

Tolkien, J.R.R., *The Lord of the Rings*, 1954, George Allen & Unwin, London

Tolkien, J.R.R. & Christopher, *The Treason of Isengard: The History of the Lord of the Rings, Part Two*, 2000, Houghton Mifflin, London

Trachtenberg, Joshua, *Jewish Magic and Superstition*, 1939, Behrman's Jewish Book House

Trinity MS 0.8.29, 15th century

Trithemius, Abbot Johannes, *The Steganographia*, 1982 (first published 1500), Magnum Opus Hermetic Sourcework No 12, Edinburgh

-----------, *Liber Octo Quaestionem*, 1515, Oppenheim

-----------, *The Art of Drawing Spirits into Crystals*, early 16th century, Oppenheim

The United States Democratic Review, Volume XIII, 1843

Valiente, Doreen, *An ABC of Witchcraft Past and Present*, 1973, Robert Hale Ltd, London

-----------, *Witchcraft Today*, 1978, Robert Hale Ltd, London

-----------, *The Rebirth of Witchcraft*, 1987, Robert Hale Ltd, London

Various, *The Westminster Review*, 1824, Baldwin, Cradock & Joy, London

Various, *Time's Telescope for 1826; or A Complete Guide to the Almanack*, 1826, Sherwood, Gilbert, and Piper, London

Various, *The British Preacher*, 1831, Frederick Westley and A.H. David, London

Various, *The New monthly belle assemblée*, 1838, Joseph Rogerson, London

Various, *The ladies' cabinet of fashion, music & romance*, 1839, G Henderson, London

Various, *The Freemason's Quarterly Magazine and Review*, 1846, London

Various, *The London Spectator*, April 22nd 1895, London

Vescovini, G. Frederici, *Pietro d'Abano, Tratatti di astronomia: Lucidator dubitalium astronomiae, De motu octavae sphaerae e alter opera*, 1992, Padoue

Virgil, *The Aeneid*

Voss, Karen-Claire, *The Hieros gamos Theme in the Images of the Rosarium Philosophorium*, 1990, in *Alchemy Revisited: Proceedings of the International Conference on the History of Alchemy at the University of Groningen*, Z.R.W.M. Martels (ed), 1990, E.J. Brill, Leiden

Waddell, W. (trans), *Manetho*, 1964, William Heinemann Ltd, London

Waite, A.E., *The Book of Black Magic and Ceremonial Magic*, 1973 (first published in 1898), Causeway Books, New York

Wallace, Lew, *Ben-Hur: A Tale of the Christ*, 1880, Harper & Brothers, New York

Walsh, Benjamin Dann (trans), *The Comedies of Aristophanes*, 1837, A H Baily and Co, London

Warden, John (ed), *The Poems of Propertius*, 1972, Bobbs Merrill Co, Indiana

Webster, Graham, *The British Celts and their Gods under Rome*, 1986, B.T. Batsford Ltd, London

West, Kate, & Williams, David, *Real Witchcraft: An Introduction*, 2003 (first published in 1996 as *Born in Albion: The Rebirth of the Craft*), I-H-O Books, Thame

Westcott, W. Wynn (ed), *The Chaldean Oracles of Zoroaster*, 1983 (first published in 1895), Aquarian Press, Northampton

Weston, Jessie L., *From Ritual to Romance*, 1997 (first published in 1919), Dover Publications, London

Whistler, Laurence; *The English Festivals*, 1947, William Heinemann Ltd, London

Wickwar, J.W., *Witchcraft and the Black Art*, 1920, Butler & Tanner London / Herbert Jenkins

Wilby, Emma, *Cunning Folk and Familiar Spirits: Shamanistic Visionary Traditions in Early Modern British Witchcraft and Magic*, 2005, Sussex Academic Press, Brighton

Wilkinson, Richard H., *The Complete Gods and Goddesses of Ancient Egypt*, 2003, Thames & Hudson, London

Williams, J.F.C. (trans), *Aristotle: De Generatione et Corruptione*, 1982, Oxford University Press, Oxford

Williams, G.S., *Defining Dominion: The Discourses of Magic and Witchcraft in Early Modern France and Germany*, 1995, University of Michigan, Michigan

Witt, R.E., *Isis in the Ancient World*, 1971, John Hopkins University Press, Maryland

Wolkstein, Diane, & Kramer, Samuel Noah, *Inanna: Queen of Heaven and Earth*, 1984, Rider & Co, London

Wouk, Herman, *This is My God*, 1959, Doubleday & Co, New York

Wright, M. R., *Empedocles: The Extant Fragments*, 1981, Yale University Press, London

Wright, Thomas, *The Worship of the Generative Powers*, 1865, J.C. Hotten, London

Xenophon, *Die Verfassung Der Spartaner, Lakedaimonion Politeia*, 1998, Wissenschaftliche Buchgesellschaft, Hesse

Zeumer (ed), *The Breviary of Eberhard of Bamberg*, in MG.LL. Sec V, Formulae, p. 650. translated in University of Pennsylvania Translations and Reprints, 1898, Vol 4:, no, 4, p7-9, University of Pennsylvania Press, Philadelphia

Index

Other Books from Avalonia

www.avaloniabooks.co.uk

HEKATE : KEYS TO THE CROSSROADS

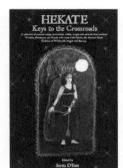

A Collection of personal essays, invocations, rituals, recipes and artwork from modern Witches, Priestesses and Priests who work with Hekate, the Ancient Greek Goddess of Witchcraft, Magick & Sorcery

Edited by Sorita D'Este

PB, £12.99, 154p, ISBN 1905297092

Hekate is one of the most fascinating Goddesses of the Ancient World. Loved, feared, hated and worshipped by people throughout history, the Witch Goddess of the Crossroads, facing three-ways, with her three faces, remains an image of power and awe in the modern world today, amongst those who understand and respect her power.

THE ISLES OF THE MANY GODS

An A-Z of the Pagan Gods & Goddesses worshipped in Ancient Britain during the first Millenium CE through to the Middle Ages

Sorita D'Este & David Rankine

PB, £17.99, 308pp, ISBN 9-781905-297108

The British Isles have long been seen as a place of mystery & magick. For many thousands of years successive waves of invaders each brought their own gods & goddesses with them, often assimilating the beliefs of the tribes they conquered.

These and many other interesting and unique titles from our growing catalogue of esoteric works can be ordered directly from:

www.avaloniabooks.co.uk

Lightning Source UK Ltd.
Milton Keynes UK
UKHW01f1824241018
331144UK00001B/85/P